Danny McDaniel

FREEDOM
Winning the Battle Within

Danny McDaniel

Freedom: Winning the Battle Within

Copyright © 2018 Danny McDaniel

ISBN: 978-1-7321740-6-1

Published by:
Danny McDaniel

Produced in the United States of America.

Scripture references are from the New King James Version, unless otherwise marked; New King James Version of the Bible, Copyright © 1979, 1980, 1982, by Thomas Nelson, Inc., Nashville, Tennessee.

CONTENTS

I Am Fully Alive Today!

Update: I am on page 70, and the book is a master's degree in the spirit with a tangible understanding of how to engage the spirit in the world and take action.

It needs a workbook alongside it. I could see it turning into a curriculum with an online program.

I'll keep going, but I wanted to update you.

Personally, a new switch went on inside of me that feels I've fully engaged all of my being with my spirit man. My personal belief and spiritual belief are united.

I am fully alive today!

—Jeremy, Texas

INTRODUCTION

"For every thousand hacking at the branches of evil, there is one striking the root." — Henry David Thoreau

I'll never forget my thoughts after experiencing spiritual freedom for the first time in December 2000. I had lived most of my life completely bound in fear. After I experienced the deliverance that Jesus so often referred to in the gospels, I asked, "Why?"

"Why am I thirty-five years old and just now hearing about this?"

"Why haven't my fellow Christians ever taught me about oppression?"

"Why hasn't anyone ever shown me how to be set free — truly free — from demonic issues in my life?"

At that point, all I knew was I wasn't going back. I could only imagine what life would be like for the next six to seven decades without all the baggage of the past attached. I was starting to envision a future of living in complete freedom!

That's what this book is about even though, quite frankly, I hadn't really planned to write a book on spiritual freedom. After all, there are many other good books out there explaining these principles. But for over twenty years, I've been on a learning journey about this subject, also called deliverance. I have had the blessing of being set free myself, and I have since helped countless people find their freedom in Jesus Christ. Yes, I am someone who believes in miracles for a good reason: I see them all the time.

For me, this book is a simple step of obedience to God. I know that God spoke clearly to me about writing this for the sake of those who would have the opportunity to read it.

Reader, I believe this book was written for you.

This isn't a book about my experience, though I share a lot of it in these pages. It's a book about what I've learned in my walk with God from His Word. You can research and verify the scriptures throughout this book, and I encourage you to do so. What may surprise you is how many of these scriptures we don't pay much attention to today. But I'll show you what God's Word clearly says about deliverance, and you'll see how you can walk out your life with new measures of freedom in Christ.

I'm passionate about freedom because finding freedom changed my life. I know it can change yours too, but that's your choice to make.

OK, time for a few disclaimers.

I know writing a book about spiritual warfare, the devil and demons, and the authority God has given us in Jesus Christ can bring critics out of the woodwork. While I do have a Master's in Education, I'm not a theologian. I'm simply a pastor and a student who has spent thousands of hours studying the

Bible and researching stacks of books on this subject. I'm also someone who has been in the trenches with men and women, boys and girls, warring with them for their personal freedom in Christ. I am well-experienced and battle-tested.

I am also not a physician or against physicians. I'm not attempting to sway you away from consulting licensed health-care professionals who can help you improve your mental and physical health. I believe in medicine. I support our medical and healthcare community. We might have lost our youngest son had it not been for the rapid intervention of a medical doctor. He discovered a misdiagnosis of an infection that our son developed from dental work. So, I know God can and will use doctors and healthcare professionals to bring healing to people.

I'm also not anti-denominational. I was raised Baptist, and my wife was raised in a Catholic household. My relationships include wonderful Christian people from many different denominations. I believe in the unity of faith in Jesus Christ for all believers. In that, I mean we should put our denominational and doctrinal issues aside to love each other and prepare the church to become the bride of Christ, without spot or blemish.

I realize I'm probably overdoing it with the disclaimers. It's just that I have come to learn through the years that people who write books like this tend to get labeled improperly. I can't stop that from happening, but I feel it's important to say up front that I am not looking for a demon under every bush. Every negative issue in life is not always a demon. I am not a demon hunter. Within these pages, you'll see a playbook of the enemy's tactics, but I'm not glorifying the enemy. Instead, I seek to use God's Word to expose the devil and his wicked ways—so you can be free.

The truth is, outside this book, demons aren't a frequent topic of conversation for me. I don't even give the devil credit for all the bad things that happen in the world. I recognize that we live in a fallen world, and sometimes, bad stuff just happens. The words "always" and "never" can get us in a lot of trouble with our word choices. I do not want you to assume that I always attribute negative thoughts or situations to demons. Sometimes accidents happen. Sometimes people die, and we do not completely understand why. But I also know that the devil is real, and he does have an agenda. Jesus said the enemy has come to steal, kill, and destroy, but "I have come to give you life, and give you life abundantly." Through the years, I've discovered that it's difficult to receive His abundant life when we're in bondage to the one who steals, kills, and destroys.

Hence, the necessity for this book.

You are about to embark upon a journey of the heart, mind, and soul. I hope that this book gives you a clear report on what the enemy has been up to, is up to, and what he will be up to as you move forward in this thing we call "life." After all, it should be lived well, and the Bible says that we have the victory. The final score has already been locked in. Now it's up to you to decide how you want to live in between this world and the next.

—Danny

Walking In Freedom

I grew up as a Southern Baptist, served as a deacon in a large Baptist church and even served as an executive with the largest Southern Baptist state organization in the United States. I had no doubt as to the existence of the Holy Spirit, believing in Him just as I did in God and Jesus. But I never experienced His healing power until I was fifty-eight years old.

After some life-changing events, I left the Baptist church and found a church that believes in the power of the Holy Spirit involving freedom and healing. I asked Pastor Danny to take me through freedom from generational curses I had carried for fifty-two years. As a result, one evening I was completely healed from severe asthma, having lung functions of less than 65% after fifty-two years. After years of taking inhaled steroid medicine twice daily and rescue inhalers three to four times daily, I have never taken any more medicines or treatments since. More importantly, generational curses were broken. My son had suffered from severe asthma as well, but when the generational curses were broken, his children had no asthma.

— Randy, Texas

CHAPTER ONE

What You Don't Know
Can Hurt You

"Freedom is from within."
– Frank Lloyd Wright

You were created to be free!

Looking at the world today, you might not realize that. Our society talks about the right to free speech and the freedom to make choices, but, in practice, most people live anything *but* free.

This book is about spiritual freedom. In the following pages, I am going to explain to you what spiritual freedom is, as defined by the Bible, and I am going to help you lay out a plan to walk out your freedom in Christ. If you deal with consistent negative patterns in your life, then this book may very well be your answer. Only you can come to that conclusion. However, you have to read the book in order to know whether or not there are answers for you. You are responsible for making your own choices in life. My role with this book is to simply provide you with information that I believe to be true, and you get to process that information and decide whether it is information that you wish to apply to your life.

This book contains a lot of insights about demons. Demons are real, and they have been stalking the human race for thousands of years. Their intention is to steal, kill, and destroy your life and keep you from any kind of healthy relationship with God. Consider this like a scouting report on the enemy. When I was a head football coach, my assistant coaches were gathering intel and data on our opponents at least two weeks in advance before we played the upcoming opponent. After our Friday night games, we would meet as a staff on Saturday and Sunday to process all of the data we had gathered on our opponent prior to facing them that next Friday. We would watch film, break down statistics, look for each player's strengths, patterns, and weaknesses from the opposing team. We would try to identify everything we could to give us the advantage to defeat our opponent the following week.

After we finished processing our information, our staff would take the scouting report and formulate a game plan to give us the best chance of winning. On Monday, we would share the scouting report with every player by giving them a copy of the report. We would go over the report, sharing in detail what kind of strengths and weaknesses our opponent had. We would expose to our players any tendencies the other team had, as well as individual tendencies, strengths, and weaknesses. In other words, our players deserved to know exactly what kind of adversary they were going to be lining up against on the field of battle on Friday night.

At this point, we would spend the rest of the week implementing the game plan by practicing the plan all week. This would prepare us for the game, where we would either experience victory or defeat. Without a scouting report, our chances for victory would always be lessened.

Thus, you have the *Freedom* book in your hands. This is my version of gathering the intel to which I have been exposed for the past twenty years. I have been studying the Bible, listening to testimonies of others, reading books, watching videos, listening to tapes, cd's, and online teachings for two decades now on this subject. Because I consider myself a "freedom fighter," I want everybody to be free, to feel free, and to walk in freedom. In order to do so, you need a scouting report. Why? Because what you don't know can hurt you!

If you do not know how demons operate and how they infiltrate people's lives, you could find yourself walking right into their traps. Demons do not play fair. Their master is Satan, who intends to destroy you. Everybody needs a scouting report on their real enemy ... everybody.

This same principle holds true in every type of military warfare. The acquisition of intel on the adversary is paramount in order to develop a strategic plan to fulfill a successful mission, limit casualties of war, and achieve victory.

Therefore, in the following pages, you are going to be going through a pretty comprehensive scouting report on your adversary, the devil. It is not an exhaustive report, meaning it is not all of the information about your enemy that is available to us today. In fact, I do not know every single thing there is to know about our adversary, the devil. It is a basic yet very comprehensive gathering of information to assist you in your quest for peace, happiness, joy, love, and victory in life.

I will also give you a game plan. Every player wants to know how they can obtain the best chance to win. This is the game of life. This is the most important game that you will ever play, and you must know who your enemy is and what his tactics are. In many ways, it is more like a manual. This is why it is not a short read. At the end of this book, you can pray to Almighty God, the one true living God, and ask Him for wisdom on how to proceed with what you have learned. I am not God, and I do not have all of the answers. I do know I will face Him at the judgment, and I will be held accountable for everything I teach. I do not take this subject lightly. My goal with writing this book is to give you a comprehensive version of what demons are, what they do, how they operate, how Jesus dealt with them, and how He taught us to deal with them. In addition, I want anyone in the world, regardless of geographical location, to be able to learn how to apply the knowledge in this book immediately to his or her life. Obtaining knowledge is great, but feeling confident about putting that knowledge into action is vitally important to me. I hope you can read this book and feel confident about putting Jesus in charge of helping you walk in total freedom for the rest of your life. The good news is I have over 1,500 advanced reader's copies that have already gone out, and I have heard many testimonies of people who have read this book and immediately took action on their better future, right where they lived.

Ideas Have Consequences

Anytime our life requires change, new challenges can arise. This is a book about change. For things to change, you have to change. In the process of change, there will always be things that can challenge your current beliefs, your thinking, and your mindset. This is exactly why you get to decide what you believe, how you are going to think, and what you are willing or not willing to do to change.

Many people, like me, have grown up in a world where they've been taught to believe only what they see, therefore, refusing to comprehend what they don't see. I grew up placing all of my trust in what I heard repeated to me for my first three decades of life versus exploring real truth that had the potential to change the course of my life and, ultimately, my destiny. In doing so, I was stuck in generational patterns of failure, sickness, disease, and dysfunction.

Rather than seeking wisdom on how to break these unhealthy patterns, we tend to stick to what we have been taught. In many instances, we've been taught that we have been dealt a specific hand in life that we cannot change, or we have inherited things genetically that cannot be altered. Although there is some truth in things being inherited genetically, there is so much more to the story. In this book, you will have a better understanding of the difference between something inherited genetically versus something inherited generationally.

Seeing Is Believing, or Is Believing Seeing?

What we need to learn is, in order to see, we must believe. We are too worried about seeing in order to believe instead of believing in order to see. Sometimes you haven't seen because you have yet to believe. Thus, you get caught in the vicious and detrimental cycle of life that is restricted to seeing in order to believe. This is a process that requires no faith. Since it doesn't require faith, you have no need for a God. When you choose to live by faith, you are choosing to need a real, tangible, living God that will show you things because you believe. If you want to see spiritual freedom in your life, you are first going to have to believe that spiritual freedom can occur in your life.

In fact, Jeremiah 33:3 states, "Call upon Me, and I will answer you, and show you great and mighty things, which you do not know." Have you ever taken time to pray a prayer like that? Calling upon God to show you great and mighty things that you do not know is one of the greatest challenges in life. Too many times we trust only in what we have been taught about

God's Word from a pastor, our parents, or our grandparents, while every other possible revelation gets rejected under the guise of, "I would have already learned that by now; therefore, it must be false." I have seen much of God's Word rejected by Christian men and women who turn away from personal revelation merely because it defies or goes beyond anything they have learned up to that point from the people who have either raised them or had consistent input into their lives. I am certainly not attempting to offend you or your family. However, I know firsthand what it is like to experience some of this. My dad was my hero. I absolutely loved my dad, but my dad was not all-knowing. I am a father of three boys, and I am not the source of all of the truths they discover. I have raised them to look beyond me and look to God. In doing so, they will read books I haven't read, have conversations and interactions with other Christians whom I do not know, which may greatly impact their lives for the better. In fact, this has already happened in my boys' lives. Also, there are short-sighted pastors and even some theologians, who do not believe that all of God's Word applies to your life today. I am here to proclaim the whole Bible is true, and it is God's living word. That means the Bible is alive because Jesus is alive, and it is applicable to our daily lives. Nothing is impossible for God!

An Unexpected Revelation

In the early part of 2000, Diane and I received a newly published book called *The Prayer of Jabez* by Bruce Wilkinson as a gift. It was an amazing little book that would change the course of our lives forever. The whole book centered around one particular verse from 1 Chronicles 4:10, which reads, "And Jabez called on the God of Israel saying, 'Oh, that you would bless me indeed, and enlarge my territory, that Your hand would be with me, and that You would keep me from evil, that I may not cause pain!' So God granted him what he requested."

We were desperate for more. We were desperate to go further with God than ever before. We had consistently been praying the prayer of Jabez throughout the remainder of the year when God dropped "the package" into my lap in December of 2000. It did not look like the answer to our prayer. However, God had surely brought us our answer, which is the subject of this book, *Freedom*.

As we move on, it is important to remember these words from 1 Corinthians 2:9, "But as it is written: 'Eye has not seen, nor ear heard, Nor have entered into the heart of man the things which God has prepared for those who love Him'."

Just think about yourself for a moment. Whether you love God or not, there are things He has prepared for you that your eyes have yet to see. There are things God has prepared for you that you have not yet heard. There are things God has prepared for you that have not yet entered your heart. If you don't know Him or love Him yet, consider what you are missing out on. If you already love God and have a relationship with Him, think about what you will miss out on if you are not willing to enlarge the territory of your mind and heart as Jabez did. It is vital that you keep your eyes, ears, and heart open to new revelation of things that God might be preparing for you.

Are you desperate for more?

Key Points
- God created you to be free.

- You need to know the scouting report on your adversary.

- You have to first believe you can be free in order to see it come true in your life.

Ask Yourself
- What does it mean to be free?

- What does freedom look like to you right now?

- How can you position yourself with God to expand the realm of what you are currently seeing?

For Further Study
- *The Veil* by Blake K. Healy

TESTIMONY

Empowered Through Spiritual Freedom

Growing up, I had a very skewed, misguided foundation concerning the demonic realm and spiritual freedom. I had many questions, but I was never given a solid answer to my question, "Why do we not believe those things happened anymore?"

The first time a friend gifted me with a book on freedom, I was in my thirties. After reading the first chapter, I tossed the book aside in disbelief. However, the seed that was planted as a result of reading that chapter became a hunger for the absolute truth. I prayed, asking for a complete understanding and experience of the power of the Holy Spirit, and that's when my journey to freedom began.

In February 2014, I attended a women's corporate freedom session and was changed forever. Struggles I had wrestled with my entire life, such as a quick temper, a flirtatious personality, need to control, and bulimia, were immediately broken off my life. I also experienced freedom from many demons I didn't even know I was bound by. Afterwards, I was filled with the Holy Spirit.

Experiencing spiritual freedom left me empowered, free from bondage, and full of love for those around me. My physical hearing exponentially improved, which was something I never even realized needed healing. Since then, I have been able to take my children through freedom and help others become free. Now I can recognize spirits that try to deter my destiny and cast them out so I can live a life of freedom and victory!

— Tonya, Arkansas

CHAPTER TWO 2

My Story... Looking Back at The Journey

"It is difficult to free fools from the chains they revere."
— Voltaire

My walk with Christ began at the age of ten when I gave my life to Him in a Baptist church and was baptized in water that night at the 6:30 p.m. service. I had a genuine conversion experience that day. I knew Jesus had entered my life, and, at that moment, I knew I was going to Heaven. But just like the parable of the seed and the sower, the seed of my salvation fell among the thorns. The thorns sprung up and choked them out over time.

I grew up in a very dysfunctional home, full of screaming, fighting, and chaos. There was rarely peace, joy, or happiness in our home. It wasn't violent or physically abusive, just chaotic. My parents had a very unhealthy relationship, and it was not restricted to just their bedroom. The strife and chaos seemed to be on public display at all times. We went to church every time the doors opened, but nothing matched up at home for most of my first twenty-four years of life.

Letting Jack Out of The Box

When I went to college, I rebelled from the moment I checked into my dormitory. I immediately began to embark upon a massive spiritual landslide. I know all of the rebellion was in me before I got to college, but my college days provided the first real opportunity I had to unleash it. It was very similar to a children's toy called a Jack-in-the-Box. If you're not familiar with it, it's a toy that looks like a box with a crank on the side of it. As you turn the crank, a melody plays until the crank has been turned enough times to cause the lid to come open and a surprise (usually a clown or jester referred to as Jack) to pop out of the box. In my life, Jack was there in many forms. All the box needed was to be wound up so that the lid would finally come open, and Jack would spring up and start to show his ugly head. While I was at home, the thorns were growing inside of me. My thought life and my heart were consistently focused on things that I am not proud of, but the lid had been on all of it until I got to college.

God at Work ... In Spite of Me

The next twelve years were full of sexual immorality, alcohol, recreational drugs, stealing, cheating, lying, and manipulating people and situations in order to get what I wanted through my life of self-absorption. My wife and I met in a bar in Austin in 1990 on a really fluke kind of night. Looking back, I can see how God was working behind the scenes on our behalf, even in our unrighteousness. I have no doubt that God gave me Diane, and He prepared her for me. The fact that we were both living a rebellious lifestyle meant that He had to work through our rebellion to get us together. Even if you disagree with that, our union became the will of God when we got married. God has blessed us immensely, but it wasn't that way in the early years.

Searching for God's Way

In 1996, due to a series of setbacks in every area of life, I decided to give God the attention He deserved. I always knew God, but by that time, I had been rebelling against Him consistently for many years. Diane and I were in financial bankruptcy, and my career was a mess. We had been living in rundown low-income houses and driving a beat-up station wagon for way too long. I had enough, and God was the only person I had to turn to for help, so I did. We bounced back and forth from a non-denominational church to a Baptist church for several months. Diane was raised in a very traditional Catholic upbringing, and her family was deeply committed to that way of life. To her, if we were going to serve God, we had to claim that we were Catholics. It made for quite an interesting development in seeking out what God wanted for us. Even in our spiritual immaturity, we would pray and ask God to lead us to a church where we could grow closer to Him. He soon guided us divinely to a Lutheran church that had a "contemporary" service on Sunday mornings. At this Lutheran church, Diane and I began to grow together in our spiritual walk with God.

God's Amazing Grace

Although wonderful things began to happen in our lives at that Lutheran church, the tipping point for my recommitment to living for Jesus Christ was in the summer of 1998. I attended an event called Promise Keepers, where men filled the Houston Astrodome. As the stadium full of men were singing Amazing Grace, Jesus came rushing into my body and grabbed ahold of my heart once again. My heart was pounding. I was crying. I was overwhelmed by Jesus' love in a way that was beyond description. At one point, I remember jumping up to the row behind me where my dad was seated. In one jump, I leaped into my dad's arms and said, "Dad, I'm saved! I'm going to Heaven!" He replied, "Son, I've been praying for you every day for thirteen years."

On the way home from Houston to Austin, I asked God to take away my desire for alcohol. I was addicted to beer, and I told God that He would have to take that craving away so that I would quit drinking, and He took it away instantly. In no way am I implying that drinking alcohol is a sin. I was a drunkard, and I was sinning. Therefore, I needed to be set free from my addiction. I also asked God to take away all of my profanity because I had a problem using filthy language consistently. He did just that, and I have rarely used a vulgar word since 1998 because of the grace of God.

Searching for Answers

Diane and I became more and more hungry for the things of God. We had both had enough experiences in the world to believe that God must have more power than what we had seen in our worldly experiences. What I mean by this, when we drank alcohol excessively, we were doing so to escape. We were attempting to break into another dimension looking for pleasure, only to be let down on the backside and find out what kind of stupid things we did in our attempt to break into that elusive dimension of pleasure. When I experimented with drugs, I was doing so to break into another dimension so that I could see beyond what I usually saw and experience things beyond what I would typically experience. Although this could be accomplished, it came with a price. The price was setbacks, defeats, failure, and destruction. Now as we prayed, we knew God must have some pretty cool stuff in store for us in some new dimensions. However, we had yet to see any of that in or around our Christian life.

For the next two years, Diane and I consistently asked God to direct our next move. God soon led us to a non-denominational, seeker-friendly church in Austin, Texas. It was what a lot of people call a megachurch. We really did enter into a new dimension of praise and worship, and the pastor was preaching messages better than anyone I had ever heard up to that point. It was a place where we were growing at a fast rate together.

Preparing for The Journey

So, when reflecting upon what you just read, it is hard not to notice all of the different denominations that positively impacted our lives. It wasn't one particular denomination that had the corner on Jesus. It was the body of Christ as a whole that impacted our lives, and we were willing to be open to what God was doing through members of His body, regardless of what Christian denomination they heralded from. I did not even mention the Church of Christ because we never attended the Church of Christ, but I am an ancestor of the founders of that denomination. My middle name carries their name, and my oldest son has their surname as his first name. God didn't use denominations to shape and mold us. He used Christians to influence our lives. He used a Catholic priest to teach my wife that God is the one true living God. She believed in Him because of her Catholic upbringing. He used a Baptist preacher to lead me to salvation at the age of ten. God used a coach from a charismatic background to pray for me and invite me to church. He used a Charismatic pastor to plant new seeds of the Bible back into our lives. He used a Lutheran pastor to disciple us and lead us back on God's path for our lives. God used a multi-cultural, multi-denominational event to bring me back to Christ. He used a Charismatic Hispanic pastor to stick a book in my hands that would lead to you reading what you are reading right now. The book happened to be written by a Baptist minister and his wife, whom you will learn about in the next chapter. God also used a Baptist deacon and his wife to take us beyond where we were on to a new journey of freedom in Christ that we had yet to experience. He used great Christian men and women from different walks of life to lead us down the path of an incredible journey that we are still on today. He wants to take you on an amazing spiritual journey as well. Are you ready?

Key Points
- Our environment greatly affects our beliefs.
- Our environment greatly affects our behaviors.
- If we turn to God, He will draw near to us.
- Crying out to God for our children has a lasting effect.
- God uses Christians from all walks of life to influence us.

Ask Yourself
- Have you let any areas of your upbringing negatively influence your life?
- Do you have any "Jack-in-the-boxes" in your life that come to your mind instantly?
- Have you rejected other Christians because of their denominational affiliation?

TESTIMONY

A New Creation in Christ!

I recently experienced inner healing and deliverance. Since that day, my life has never been the same. I am a new creation in Christ! Previously, I suppressed all the hatred I had toward people, which led to depression. I didn't know it was depression at first. I just didn't understand why I was sad. I had thoughts like, "I am a leader, or I just came from a mission trip." Yet, I always found myself praying to God to take me home to Heaven.

That depression went to its worst days last February, the lowest I had ever felt! In that low place, I read the book *FREE-DOM*, which I received from a pastor and his wife from Thailand. The moment they gave me the book, I knew God was about to do something in me. I finished reading it as fast as I could so that I could find the cure for this situation. Truly, it was God who prepared me and ordained everything.

I thank the Lord Jesus for this life-changing freedom! I enjoy the simple things in life again ... my food, serving my family again as I once did, conversing with people, appreciating them, and telling them, "I love you." Now I have so much joy! I am starting to dream again about my future. I love Jesus so much! I want to tell everyone how He has set me free.

The Lord has blessed me with many work opportunities, including being an accredited TESDA trainer in one of the most prestigious culinary schools in the Philippines. The enemy still tries to lie to me, but he chose the wrong woman because I am free!

—Joana, Philippines

My First Encounter With Demons

"I prefer dangerous freedom over peaceful slavery."
— Thomas Jefferson

Looking back on the year 2000 when *The Prayer of Jabez* was put in our hands, my wife and I could never have imagined the monumental changes that would take place in our lives. These changes have brought us to where we are today. When you pray for God to expand your territory as Jabez did, watch out because when you are bold enough to pray like this, you must also be courageous enough to lay hold of how and when God answers your prayer. You must also be humble enough to accept the package. Our problem as human beings is we expect the package and its delivery to be a certain way. We treat God like we are ordering from Amazon Prime. In other words, we already have formed in our mind what the package is going to look like, and we have determined a delivery date that our God better deliver ... preferably overnight.

Recognizing God's Answer to Your Prayers

Jeremiah 33:3 says, "Call to Me, and I will answer you, and show you great and mighty things, which you do not know." When God delivers things that we do not know, this also means that we have no idea what it is going to look like. This is where the problem lies with most Christians. They forget what they pray for, and their eyes are not wide open to see what God is putting in front of them, nor are their ears attentive enough to hear what God may be saying to them. Therefore, some miss the actual answer to their prayers by wearing the same old lens of life; thus, remaining stagnated in their spiritual and family life.

Here's what God has to say about keeping our eyes wide open and our ears attentive to what He is bringing our way, "For the eyes of the Lord run to and fro throughout the whole earth, to show Himself strong on behalf of those whose heart is loyal to Him" (2 Chronicles 16:9).

The eyes of the Lord are literally on you, and if you are loyal to Him, He will show Himself strong to you. You won't miss it when your heart is right. When I say heart, I'm not referring to the organ that pumps blood through your veins. Instead, in most cases, the heart refers to the set and center focal point of your spiritual and physical being. It comes from the root word "kardia," which means "core." It is translated over hundreds of times in the Bible as the set and center focal point of your spiritual and physical being.[1] That means the core of your body, your soul, and your spirit and not just your fleshly or physical heart. In this case, it comes from the Hebrew word "lebab," which means "inner man, mind, will, heart, soul, understanding." Therefore, it is interesting that God desires to show Himself strong on behalf of those whose inner man, mind, will, heart, soul, and understanding are loyal to Him. God has things to show you if the inner core of your being is really devoted to Him and desires to know Him and all of His ways.

A Life-Changing Book

Our answer came in the form of a book with a very unappealing cover. In my opinion, the cover of this book is still one of the least attractive book covers I've ever seen. I thank God that I did not judge this book by its cover! In fact, I believe the cover of this book is so uninviting that the devil is probably happy about it because the cover itself turns a lot of people away from reading it. However, at that time, it already had over 1,000,000 copies in print! The devil would not want you, me, or anyone else to read books like this because it exposes his tactics. In December of 2000, I opened up the cover of the book and began to read it. What I read on the pages of that book changed my life forever. I literally felt like the gospels were leaping off the page into my heart. I don't remember if every single thing in that book was 100% accurate Biblical teaching. What I do remember, it was the first time in my thirty-five years of life that I began to understand the fullness of the gospel of Matthew, Mark, Luke, and John. The message contained in the book started to teach me about the real ministry of Jesus, how He made disciples, and how He commanded us to live out our lives and become disciple-makers. The book gave me Biblical solutions for my human problems.

Keep in mind that book is not the Bible. I firmly believe there is only one timeless book of truth, and that is God's Holy Book. Every other book, including mine, has the potential to have unintentional errors. One of the strongest statements that has influenced my life is the phrase that we've probably all heard, which says, "Eat the meat and spit out the bones." This should be your philosophy in reading any book, except for The Bible, God's Holy Book.

Dealing With The Darkness

At the age of thirty-five, I finally realized demons had tormented me for much of my life, living inside of me for many years. Some since childhood and others had come in through open doors of opportunity because of my rebellious lifestyle. Either way, there were unarguably demons in me, and I was finally aware of it. I had lived a life of complete and total fear. My childhood was marred by fear of the dark and fear of "monsters" under my bed. I feared all kinds of confrontation and could have been easily labeled a coward. I was bullied growing up and never fought back. I had just about every type of fear and phobia you can name. The fear had mostly been passed on generationally by my mother because she was extremely overprotective. Her overprotectiveness became a gateway to spirits of fear, which I will cover more in-depth at a later point. Yet, there were other spirits that I had invited in due to my own actions or sin. While in fourth grade, my next-door neighbor introduced me to Playboy magazines stashed in hiding by his big brother. From that point, sexual fantasies of all types permeated my innermost being, and I became completely infatuated with anything having to do with women and sex. Having acquired new knowledge about the demonic realm, I had to deal with the reality of what I could not see in the natural but what I now believed.

Based on some of the consistent patterns that were part of my life, I absolutely knew I had unclean spirits influencing my life. At the time, I was in a hotel room in Atlanta, Georgia, attending a business conference. Armed with this new understanding and insight about the demonic realm, I was eager to get home and do something about my findings. As I contemplated what to do, it quickly came to my mind that there was no minister I knew who would help me with my situation when I got back home! My thought was, "Surely if someone I know has this revelation, they would have already tried to help me get set free from any demonic oppression."

Doing What Jesus Did

Since I didn't know where to turn for help, I began to do what Jesus taught His disciples. In Matthew 17, Jesus rebuked a demon in a boy, and it came out. After witnessing the scene, His disciples came to Jesus privately and asked, "Why couldn't we drive the demon out?" Jesus answered them, "Because you have so little faith. For truly I tell you, if you have faith the size of a mustard seed, you can say to this mountain, 'Move from here to there,' and it will move. Nothing will be impossible for you" (verses 18-19).

I began to call upon those unclean spirits that had harassed me for years, rebuking them in the name of Jesus. I remember having my eyes closed as I commanded these spirits to identify themselves and come forth out of my body. Before the first spirit came out of me, I saw a crystal clear picture in my mind of huge white letters on a dark background like a billboard, and the letters spelled "ANGER." Instantly I said, "Anger, you come out of me in the name of Jesus," and the demon came up through my throat. My jaw opened up very wide, and I began to let out a prolonged yawn that released the spirit of anger.

The Road to Freedom

After the first spirit came out of my body, I rose up in my hotel bed and paused to reflect on what had just taken place. I felt like two tons of weight had just come off of my life! There was such a peace within me I could not quite explain it. All I knew, I was going to lay back down and see how many more spirits I could cast out of me. I wound up casting several unclean evil spirits out of my body that night, and my life would never be the same again. I woke up the next morning, and I wanted the whole world to know where demons were, what their plan was, and how to defeat them. Little did I know that people are not always ready to get rid of the demons they don't know anything about. There's a lot more to the story of my deliverance, but the beautiful side of it is I had a new testimony. I was also coming home to my family as a different man.

When I got back home, I held my regular men's Bible study on Wednesday morning, and one of my friends brought a guest. Other than the guest, all of these men were close in my life. So, I decided to tell my testimony of dealing with the demonic oppression I had discovered. As I shared my testimony, most of my friends were a little puzzled since this was an entirely new revelation for them. However, our guest kept nodding his head in agreement with me about everything he was hearing. Later that morning, I got a call from my buddy that brought the guest, and he filled me in on some information regarding this new acquaintance. His friend went home and told his dad all about my story. His dad wanted to arrange a meeting with me. He was a deacon at a Baptist church in town, and he had been helping people get set free for the past thirteen years. I learned that he and his wife had been praying for God to bring new leaders to help minister this kind of freedom to people in our local area.

Starting a New Chapter

The days immediately following my experience in that Atlanta hotel room felt like I was starting a whole new chapter in my life. The man I was going to meet was a multi-millionaire who had a large home, a thriving business, a wonderful family, and was a deacon at the local Baptist church! It was no coincidence that four days after I returned home from this freedom experience, God put me in contact with a minister of the gospel of Jesus Christ who believed in all of the gospel, not just part of it. Only God can do things like that. I knew it wasn't by chance.

Visible Evidence of a Change

My wife recognized the difference in me too. She kept seeing the excitement on my face and this new attitude about life. She found it quite interesting when I even had some different mannerisms. In fact, she began to try to push the right buttons to trigger frustration or anger in me. Those tactics would not work. After three weeks of observing the fact that my testimony was bearing fruit, she decided to go through freedom as well. She wound up visiting the deacon's wife and her friends. They took her through spiritual freedom one day. Just like mine, her life was never the same. Past hurts, emotional wounds, and oppression that had haunted her since childhood were now gone ... completely. She was renewed just like I was and set free from the things of the past.

Following her experience, I went back over to their home. I had the privilege of being ministered to on a much deeper level than my first experience in the Atlanta hotel room. Because I had rebelled against God in so many ways, I had a lot of unclean spirits in me. These wonderful people took time out of their personal lives to help me get set free from things I had been oppressed by for many years! Yes, things that had been inside me since I was a baby; things passed on from my parents. The world calls these things hereditary, but I refer to them as generational. I also refer to them as our enemies. Why? Because they are enemies of God; therefore, they are enemies of ours too.

A Work in Progress

The freedom my wife and I experienced was life-changing. It changed our home, and it changed our family. We already had children, so we knew they would come next in the process. I'll talk more about that later.

The remainder of this book is dedicated to helping you understand, from my perspective, what I have seen, learned, and experienced about the unhealthy influence which demons can have upon someone's personal and family life. This book isn't intended to be an exhaustive teaching on the subject of deliverance from demonic oppression. Consider it more of a layman's teaching so any person desperate enough for real, tangible, Biblical change can see the simplicity of the gospels and apply the teachings of Jesus to their situation. If you want to learn from a scholar, I suggest you study Derek Prince's book, *They Shall Expel Demons.* My goal is to give you my perspective based upon twenty years of experience, both living it out and ministering to hundreds, if not thousands, of others in the process. Your job is to be open-minded and trust in God.

Here's what God has to say in Hosea 4:6 about rejecting Him, "My people are destroyed for lack of knowledge. Because you have rejected knowledge, I also will reject you from being priest for Me; Because you have forgotten the law of your God, I also will forget your children."

Trust God in The Process

It is imperative that you pray to God and ask the Holy Spirit to reveal His truth to you. I am not God. I am just one of His royal ambassadors, and I strive to please Him in all I do to represent Him. I fear Him and want to do what's pleasing in His sight. Therefore, my appeal to you is to really dig in and trust God to reveal new knowledge and understanding to you that His word can validate. I've seen far too many people over the years reject new revelation from the Lord before they got the whole revelation. They began reading part of the story, and when everything doesn't match up to their personal beliefs instantaneously, they shut the book or turn off the teaching. Without allowing themselves to read or study the entire message, they miss the revelation.

I believe what James wrote in Chapter 4 of his letter has significant meaning to pursuing the rest of this material and finding the real truth behind oppression, depression, anger, rejection, fear, insecurity, pornography, unforgiveness, pride, and many other issues Christians commonly face.

James 4:1-10 says, "Where do wars and fights come from among you? Do they not come from your desires for pleasure that war in your members? You lust and do not have. You murder and covet and cannot obtain. You fight and war. Yet you do not have because you do not ask. You ask and do not receive, because you ask amiss, that you may spend it on your pleasures. Adulterers and adulteresses! Do you not know that friendship with the world is enmity with God? Whoever therefore wants to be a friend of the world makes himself an enemy of God. Or do you think that the Scripture says in vain, 'The Spirit who dwells in us yearns jealously?' But He gives more grace. Therefore He says: 'God resists the proud, But gives grace to the humble.' Therefore submit to God. Resist the devil and he will flee from you. Draw near to God and He will draw near to you. Cleanse your hands, you sinners; and purify your hearts, you double-minded. Lament and mourn and weep! Let your laughter be turned to mourning and your joy to gloom. Humble yourselves in the sight of the Lord, and He will lift you up."

Will you join me on the journey?

Key Points
- A good book is meant to point us to truth, which is only found in God's Word.

- The first step to freedom is recognizing where a spirit has been operating in your life.

- Doing what Jesus did really works.

- Your testimony opens doors for both you and for others to be set free.

- Humility is the key to God responding to us quickly.

Ask Yourself

- Can you read a book that challenges everything you've ever known or not known … and learn from it?

- Do you really trust the fact what Jesus did is meant for us?

- Can you draw near to God and ask Him to reveal to you anything He wants to deal with in your life?

For Further Study

- *Humility and Absolute Surrender* by Andrew Murray

TESTIMONY

Radically Liberated to Walk in Freedom

I was part of a denomination that taught the gifts of the spirit were not for today. I was even fearful of people who preached such things. In 2009, Danny called to check on my husband. He sensed he needed some prayer, and he was right. My husband had been battling anger and discouragement. Danny came over and shared his deliverance story. To my surprise, my husband exclaimed, "Do that to me... I want that!" My husband was freed that night, and Danny left us with some scriptures so we could better understand what just happened.

Over the next two days, the Holy Spirit convicted me this was real, and I needed deliverance. I asked my husband to do what Danny had just done to him. "If this is God," I thought, "ALL believers have the power to help set someone free." My deliverance was radical as I felt things go one after another ... next thing I knew, we were taking people through deliverance left and right and teaching others to do the same. This included my friend who was freed from bipolar. She had been on meds since the 8th grade and in and out of mental institutions. She's been free for over ten years now!

— Shawna, Oregon

Why Jesus?

"Take the words of Jesus and let them become the
Supreme Court of the Gospel to you."
— John G. Lake

Do you really know Jesus? The one thing that matters most
to any of us is whether or not we really know Him. Jesus told
us in John 14:6 that He is the way, the truth, and the life, and
that no one can get to the Father but through Him. Jesus is the
gateway to the Father, and the Bible tells us in Romans 10:9-10,
"If you confess with your mouth the Lord Jesus and believe in
your heart that God has raised Him from the dead, you will be
saved. For with the heart one believes unto righteousness, and
with the mouth confession is made unto salvation."

There is only one way to Heaven, and that is through Jesus.
Peter said in Acts 4:12, "Nor is there salvation in any other;
for there is no other name under Heaven given among men by

which we must be saved." When we come to salvation, Jesus is both our Lord and Savior. The thing to realize is what one needs to do to get to Heaven is to be saved by grace through faith. Paul writes in Ephesians 2:8-9, "For by grace you have been saved through faith, and that not of yourselves; it is the gift of God, not of works, lest anyone should boast."

The Great Exchange

Salvation is a free gift that is available to all humanity by the grace of God. There is nothing we can do to earn the right to go to Heaven. On the cross, Jesus, the sinless Lamb of God, became our sin so you and I could be made righteous. When we confess with our mouth and believe in our hearts that Jesus is who He said He is, the grace of God will save us through our faith in Jesus Christ. Through the selfless act of His death on the cross, Jesus paid the price completely for all mankind ... not only for our sins but also to set us free from the consequences of our sin. Because of Jesus' shed blood on the cross, this timeless exchange of God's love and forgiveness is sufficient and available to all who will come to Jesus (Revelation 22:17).

The Great Commission

Once you have been forgiven of your sin and made righteous by God's grace, God has a plan to work with you and through you to reach others for Christ while you are still on this earth. Most of us were drawn to God through the lives and testimonies of other Christians who were committed to prayer and evangelism of some sort. Now that we have been redeemed by Jesus and are reconciled and restored in relationship with God, how can we keep the good news to ourselves? Jesus commissioned us to spread the news when He said, "Go into all the world and preach the gospel to every creature. He who believes and is baptized will be saved; but he who does not believe will be condemned" (Mark 10:15-16, NKJV).

Doing Our Part

Paul tells us in the scriptures that we are sowers of seed and the "fertilizers" of evangelism on the earth, as he described in 1 Corinthians 3:5-9, "Who then is Paul, and who is Apollos, but ministers through whom you believed, as the Lord gave to each one? I plant, Apollos watered, but God gave the increase. So then neither he who plants is anything, nor he who waters, but God who gives the increase. Now he who plants and he who waters are one, and each one will receive his own reward according to his own labor. For we are God's fellow workers; you are God's field, you are God's building."

Make Disciples

Jesus even told us to "go make disciples" as one of His last mandates while He was on earth before His ascension to the Father. The point is that we have work to do. Although the work is not going to earn our entrance into Heaven, we are expected to fulfill God's plan for our lives as we live out our God-given destiny on this earth. This is why Jesus is also called our Lord. He is not just our Savior, but He is also our Lord. He is our Master. This means that He has the right to give us marching orders, including His mandate to share the gospel with the world, which may be in our neighborhood or our workplace. We are commanded to make disciples.

In Luke 6:46-49, Jesus says, "But why do you call Me 'Lord, Lord,' and not do the things which I say? Whoever comes to Me, and hears My sayings and does them, I will show you whom he is like: He is like a man building a house, who dug deep and laid the foundation on the rock. And when the flood arose, the stream beat vehemently against that house, and could not shake it, for it was founded on the rock. But he who heard and did nothing is like a man who built a house on the earth without a foundation, against which the stream beat vehemently; and immediately it fell, And the ruin of that house was great."

Jesus wants us to understand He is the master, and we are to pay attention to hear His sayings and do them. Hence, the Christian life is about obeying the commands of Jesus and doing the things pleasing in His sight. Ask any soldier what is expected of him when an officer of a superior rank has issued him a command. Also, ask the soldier what happens if he does not obey the given command. How much more should we pay attention to the commands of the highest-ranking official in the universe?

Let's take a look at what Jesus did. In Acts 10:38, the Bible says, "… God anointed Jesus of Nazareth with the Holy Spirit and with power, who went about doing good and healing all who were oppressed by the devil, for God was with Him."

Here's the summation of what this passage says about Jesus' life:

1. God anointed Him with the Holy Spirit

2. He went about doing good

3. He healed all who were oppressed by the devil

4. God was with Him

Why Did He Come?

Jesus came to destroy the works of the devil. The devil altered the harmonious relationship between God and Adam by his deceptive tactics with Adam and Eve. They disobeyed God and hid from Him due to their rebellion and sin. The enemy has been at odds with God and man since the beginning, and God's plan to bring Jesus to the earth to reconcile us back to Him required Jesus to destroy the works of the devil. 1 John 3:8 reads, "He who sins is of the devil, for the devil has sinned from the beginning. For this purpose, the Son of God was manifested that He might destroy the works of the devil."

For us to be reconciled back to God, the enemy of our lives had to be conquered. Thus, Jesus came to sacrifice His life on the cross to reconcile us back to God. The blood of Jesus, which was shed for us, also redeems us or reconciles us back to God. Jesus essentially destroyed the works of the devil, saving us by His grace and giving us authority over the devil to fight the good fight of faith. Remember, the Word of God says in Ephesians 6:12, "For we do not wrestle against flesh and blood, but against principalities, against powers, against the rulers of the darkness of this age, against spiritual *hosts* of wickedness in the Heavenly *places*." Therefore, our purpose on this earth is to destroy the works of the devil by walking in our authority as a believer who is determined to fulfill the Great Commission.

What Did Jesus Do?

If we wanted to sum up the life of Jesus as it is described in the New Testament, it would go something like this. Jesus woke up each morning and prayed to the Father. He would reach into the unseen realm, or spiritual realm, in order to hear His instructions from the Father each day. When I refer to Jesus reaching into the unseen realm, remember that He existed just as we do today. Therefore, Jesus lived in our natural realm, but He knew there was an unseen realm that He also existed in and had access to. One can have access to something but never use it. For example, you may have access to a shovel in your garage, yet you never use it. Having access to something and taking advantage of the access are two different things. On that note, Jesus would take time to listen, so He knew what the Father wanted Him to do. He would then go about doing good and healing all those who were oppressed. On a consistent basis, Jesus would pray, and then He would go out and preach the Kingdom of God. He would cast out demons from those who were oppressed. He would heal the sick. He would sometimes raise the dead or cleanse lepers. He did all of these things on a consistent or daily basis. In fact, John 21:25 states, "And there are also many other things that Jesus did, which if they were written one by one, I suppose that even the world itself could not contain the books that would be written. Amen."

One could say this was the daily method of operation in the ministry life of Jesus Christ. To be more specific, let's take a look at what Jesus proclaimed about Himself as He came out of Galilee after performing numerous miracles and entered the synagogue in Nazareth to address his hometown.

If we were looking for Jesus' job description, Luke 4:18-19 would describe it in detail. "The Spirit of the Lord is upon Me, Because He has anointed Me to preach the gospel to the poor; He has sent Me to heal the brokenhearted, To proclaim liberty to the captives And recovery of sight to the blind, To set at liberty those who are oppressed; To proclaim the acceptable year of the Lord."

If we were to break this down in simple terms, Jesus did the following:

1. Preached the gospel to the poor
2. Healed the brokenhearted
3. Proclaimed liberty to the captives
4. Gave sight back to the blind
5. Set at liberty those who were oppressed
6. Proclaimed the acceptable year of the Lord

When we study the gospels, the common threads are very clear. Jesus had a simple yet powerful message. Jesus had a simple yet powerful ministry, and He would instruct us to do the same things as Him. Prior to His crucifixion, Jesus spent some intimate time with His disciples, preparing them for what was to come. In that time, He gave them instructions about how they were to imitate Him, although it was probably extremely difficult for them to comprehend at that moment. Yet, over 2,000 years later, we should be able to understand it more easily, without overcomplicating it. In John 14:12-18, Jesus said, "Most assuredly, I say to you, he who believes in Me, the works that I do he will do also; and greater works than these he will do, because I go to My Father. And whatever you ask in My name, that I will do, that the Father may be glorified in the Son. If you ask anything in My name, I will do it. If you love Me, keep My commandments. And I will pray the Father, and He will give you another Helper, that He may abide with you forever— the Spirit of truth, whom the world cannot receive, because it neither sees Him nor knows Him; but you know Him, for He dwells with you and will be in you. I will not leave you orphans; I will come to you."

Greater Works

Jesus made it perfectly clear. We were to do the same works that He did but even greater by using His name to do them. The hard part for most people is the passage says "greater works than these" instead of "some of the same things that I've done." It is hard for our ordinary minds to imagine seeing something more miraculous than Jesus Himself did. The revelation we are not understanding is that He is the one doing the greater works anyway. He wants us to carry the works out by faith using His name so that the Father can be glorified. He was letting us know He was going to include us in the ministry model so He could duplicate Himself all over the world. When He was on the earth, He acted alone, so to speak, and could only preach the gospel and perform miracles in the situation where He was present. Now, He tells us that we can use His name, perform even greater works, and the Holy Spirit will help us. This, in turn, would allow people all over the world to conduct the ministry of Jesus at any given time in any given place. So, you must ask yourself, "Have I seen greater works done? Do I believe that greater works can be done?" If you can't answer "Yes," you must keep forging ahead with an open heart and open mind. In order to see God's plan fulfilled, you must discover the incredible promises God has in store for you and so many others.

What Did Jesus Tell Us to Do?

If this is what Jesus did on a daily basis, and He also told us that we would do greater works than these, we must examine exactly what He told us to do as believers. As a believer in Jesus Christ, we all have a general calling. A general calling applies to the life of every believer because it is based on foundational principles and instructions. The general calling we have is usually summed up in what we call the Great Commission, which we briefly discussed earlier in this chapter and will look more closely. We also have a specific calling that is unique to us as individuals or groups. For example, you might be a believer, and you are confident that God has mandated for you to work specifically in the area of rescuing people from human trafficking and getting them saved, healed, and free from oppression and wounds of their past. You may be confident that God has called you to be a high school football coach so you can be a light and a father figure to so many young men who need a male figure in their lives. In either of these settings, your general calling would be related to preaching the gospel, but your specific calling would be in the area of high school kids or to those caught in the web of human trafficking. Perhaps you feel you are called to be a surgeon so that you can have a platform to glorify God in the area of working with people who need surgical procedures performed in their lives. Your general calling would be to be like Jesus and do what He did, yet your specific calling resides in the field of medicine.

Our Calling as Believers

It is vital for us to examine the true nature of our general calling. There are three key areas of scripture that clearly state what the normal, everyday Christian life is to look like. The first example is seen in Matthew 10, where Jesus had spent a great deal of time engaging the culture and equipping them for the ministry. Jesus always engaged the culture. He did this to model what we are to do as well. He also spent time establishing foundations in their beliefs to equip them for real ministry. He had been doing this up to a point in Matthew 10 where He decided to send His disciples on to the mission field by empowering them to engage the culture themselves. This is where the first example of a general calling may reside in the New Testament. Matthew 10:1 says, "And when He had called His twelve disciples to Him, He gave them power over unclean spirits, to cast them out, and to heal all kinds of sickness and all kinds of disease."

Let me reemphasize that this is the first time we see disciples being sent into the mission field to do the ministry of Jesus. If this is the first time we see on record that Jesus sent His disciples out, wouldn't it seem as if His words and commands would be of the utmost importance for all of history?

First, Jesus gave them power over unclean spirits and power to heal all kinds of sickness and all kinds of disease. He had not ascended to the Father yet, for He had not been crucified and resurrected. Therefore, He had to equip them by giving them His power at this time. Now they were empowered to walk in His power!

Then the Bible explains in Matthew 10:5-8, "These twelve Jesus sent out and commanded them, saying: 'Do not go into the way of the Gentiles and do not enter a city of the Samaritans. But go rather to the lost sheep of the house of Israel. And as you go, preach, saying, 'The kingdom of Heaven is at hand.' Heal the sick, cleanse the lepers, raise the dead, cast out demons. Freely you have received, freely give'."

Let's break this general calling down that Jesus gave His disciples:

1. Jesus sent them and commanded them
2. Go to the Jews
3. Preach the gospel
4. Heal sick people
5. Cleanse the lepers
6. Raise people from the dead
7. Cast demons out of people

He made it very clear what He so freely gave to His disciples in the process of establishing Biblical foundations in their lives and equipping them for the work of the ministry. They were to give to others freely. He also made it clear to us as believers. We are also to give out what we have so freely received from God through the saving grace of Jesus Christ. It is not to be withheld.

Chosen For a Reason

Jesus is the most powerful force in the universe! You cannot contain the power of Jesus because His power was not meant to be contained. His power is like rivers of living water that spring forth from your innermost being. It is like a moving force that has an origin, such as a wellspring, and erupts into the atmosphere with the kind of power that can transform a culture. It is the type of power that can turn a home inside out and turn a city upside down. It is not a power that is meant to be bottled up and put on a shelf as if you have access to a genie. We only uncork the bottle when we need our genie to come out and make a new wish. As Jon Bon Jovi used to sing, "Oh, we're halfway there, oh, oh, we're living on a prayer!" I'm okay with living with a life of prayer, but my general calling is not just hanging in there and living on a prayer. My general calling and your general calling are to walk in power and authority and perform the things that Jesus commands us to perform. That's why He chose us! He chose us because He desires to flow through us and use us as vessels of honor, handling His name and His power with humility and with authority so that we can do the work of the ministry. Why? For the sake of others.

We do it for the person who was not born over 2000 years ago and got to walk with Jesus twenty-four hours a day, seven days a week for three years straight. There are multitudes of people living on this earth today who know absolutely nothing about Jesus, much less anything about evil spirits. They know even less about sickness and disease or the fact that there are actually cures for all of these things. Jesus is giving us a general mandate to preach the kingdom and be prepared to heal the sick and cast out demons in the process. I'm not dodging the cleanse-the-leper or raise-the-dead issue. However, this book is intended for you to get a better understanding of how God wants to set you free from oppression, sickness, or disease. Odds are there is not a leper or a dead person reading this book, but people are getting raised from the dead all over the world, in case you were wondering. I know of an American man from Louisiana who has seen well over 100 people raised from the dead in his ministry alone. I also have a missionary friend, originally from Alabama, who has seen several people raised from the dead in Mexico and Central America through God's power. Lepers are getting cleansed as well. The fact is that we just don't run into many situations in North America where we see lepers, but they are out there. Their stories are real. They are getting healed by the power of Jesus Christ. When a believer decides to walk in his or her general calling, these things become common.

You Can Do It!

Like anything else in life, it's about repetitions. When we put things into practice, we get better with each repetition, each and every day. It is commonly known that if you put 10,000 repetitions into any skill you are trying to acquire, you will have become an expert after 10,000 repetitions.[1] Michael Jordan's greatness on the basketball court came from 10,000 plus repetitions in every area of shooting. Pele' was so great at soccer because he practiced dribbling, passing, and shooting soccer balls most of his life. The same principle holds true in golf, tennis, cricket, rugby, baseball, chess, pool, bowling, or any other sport. The same principle especially holds true in evangelism and discipleship. When we obey Jesus and do what He commanded us to do, we get more confident with each encounter. We become more skilled at helping others win in life.

I can't hit a golf ball straight because I do not practice hitting golf balls. That doesn't mean that golf balls can't be hit straight. Someone is out there every day proving that golf balls can surely be hit straight. The same holds true with the ministry of Jesus. Only believe! First, you must believe, and then you have to choose to step into your general calling.

Our Mandate

The second example I want to use is what most people call the Great Commission in Matthew 28:16-20. Jesus had been back and forth, appearing in various places for forty days following His resurrection, and He was preparing to ascend to Heaven to sit at the right hand of God. This is Matthew's account of the last words of Jesus spoken to His disciples, "Then the eleven disciples went to Galilee, to the mountain where Jesus had told them to go. When they saw him, they worshiped him; but some doubted. Then Jesus came to them and said, 'All authority in Heaven and on earth has been given to me. Therefore go and make disciples of all nations, baptizing them in the name of the Father and of the Son and of the Holy Spirit, and teaching them to obey everything I have commanded you. And surely I am with you always, to the very end of the age'."

It's always good to break down the key instructions and list them so that we might see the value of what our assignment from Jesus is:

1. All authority has been given to Me (Jesus)
2. Go ... and make disciples of all nations
3. Using My authority to do it (partner with Jesus)
4. Teach them to obey everything I have commanded you
5. I will be with you always (My authority and power will accompany you)

As you can see, even out of the disciples that were alongside Jesus for three straight years, some doubted! This sounds really crazy, but it is an interesting thing to consider.

Picture yourself walking with Jesus this intimately for three years. You saw Him die, and then you saw Him resurrected. You saw Him make random appearances for forty days after His resurrection, and you still are doubting. If this can happen to some of His own personal disciples, you could be having your doubts as well. However, I want to encourage you to live on the side of faith. Live on the side that would describe you as, "They worshiped Him." The enemy has craftily and cleverly been devising schemes for thousands of years to bring doubt into the minds and hearts of God's people. Let's take the Bible at its face value, as Christians, and believe that Jesus was giving instructions that were supposed to lead to a transferable and duplicable model of ministry that would be passed down through generations. After all, isn't that part of the reason why He came?

Jesus' Example

Think about this. Did Jesus need to get baptized? Technically, He did not. He was already the reigning king of the universe. He was perfect and sinless. He allowed Himself to be baptized to model to us what it would mean as Paul describes in the book of Colossians 2:9-12, "For in Christ all the fullness of the Deity lives in bodily form, and in Christ, you have been brought to fullness. He is the head over every power and authority. In him you were also circumcised with a circumcision not performed by human hands. Your whole self ruled by the flesh was put off when you were circumcised by Christ, having been buried with him in baptism, in which you were also raised with him through your faith in the working of God, who raised him from the dead."

Jesus did this to model to us that we should be baptized. Being baptized through immersion in water symbolizes dying to ourselves and identifying with Christ's death, burial, and resurrection. When we come up out of the water, this signifies we have been raised up as a new person with Him through our faith in God..

After this occurred, the Holy Spirit descended from Heaven and came down upon Jesus. Did this need to happen? Technically, it did not because Jesus was already God. Jesus was the most powerful force in the universe. I believe this was a sign that modeled what life would be like as a Christian when Jesus departed from the earth. God would send the Holy Spirit to endue us with power from Heaven. It would be the Holy Spirit who would come from Heaven and anoint us with His Spirit and allow us to live out our Christian lives in victory and minister as Jesus ministered.

Jesus' Instructions to His Followers

Going back to my point, it is important to see how Jesus gives the instructions that we are to follow if we really call Him our Lord. If we have confessed with our mouth that Jesus is Lord, and we have believed in our heart that God raised Him from the dead, then we are saved. Since I confessed with my mouth that He is my Lord or Master, my role is to listen and adhere to His instructions. He told His disciples, which means He is telling us, "Teach them to obey all that He has commanded us."

What did He command us to do? All we have to do is look at what He commanded the disciples to do to discover what He also commanded us to do. Therefore, let's look at the third and final example of what Jesus commands us as believers to do. I often refer to this passage of scripture as "The Last Words of Jesus" before He left this earth to be seated at the right hand of the Father.

Last Words

Now, I am going to ask you to imagine that you know for a fact you are going to no longer be on this earth tomorrow. You only have one day to live! What would you say to those whom you are closest? If you are a parent, would you gather your spouse and children and tell them the most important words you have ever spoken, and would you want them to remember? You might think about grabbing a video device and recording your last words on this earth so that your closest family members would have it long after you're gone, to review. Regardless of your particular situation in this natural life, you would be thinking about who you need to talk to and what you need to say. Jesus Christ, the Son of the Living God, was the same way. He was about to ascend to the Father, and He knew that He would not be returning until God sends Him back in the end times. So far, it has been well over 2,000 years, and God still hasn't sent Jesus back. His commands to His disciples are of paramount importance because they are a mandate for every generation to follow, obey, and teach. This occurs in the last passage of the gospel according to Mark 16.

Jesus shared His last words to His disciples in Mark 16 as they were eating dinner together. "Later He appeared to the eleven as they sat at the table; and He rebuked their unbelief and hardness of heart, because they did not believe those who had seen Him after He had risen. And He said to them, 'Go into all the world and preach the gospel to every creature. He who believes and is baptized will be saved; but he who does not believe will be condemned. And these signs will follow those who believe: In My name they will cast out demons; they will speak with new tongues; they will take up serpents; and if they drink anything deadly, it will by no means hurt them; they will lay hands on the sick, and they will recover'."

Now, let's break down the last words of Jesus:

1. Go and preach the gospel to all creation
2. Baptize new believers
3. Cast out demons
4. Speak in (unknown) tongues
5. Take up serpents (power over darkness)
6. Deadly poison will not harm you
7. You will lay hands on the sick, and they will recover

Here is a question to ask yourself if you consider yourself a believer in Jesus. Are you a believing believer? If you are a believer, Jesus said that certain signs would follow you. This means that part of the evidence of your Christian life will be the fact that these signs will follow you to indicate that you are really one of His disciples.

THE REAL QUESTION IS
DO YOU BELIEVE?

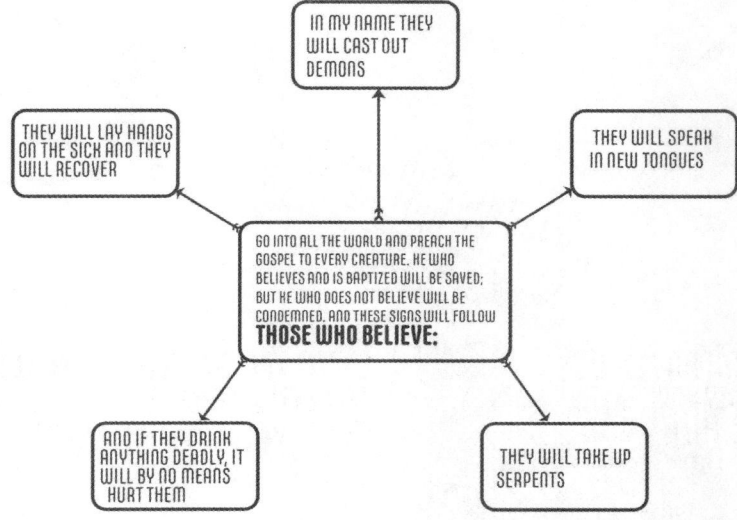

IN MY NAME THEY WILL CAST OUT DEMONS

THEY WILL LAY HANDS ON THE SICK AND THEY WILL RECOVER

THEY WILL SPEAK IN NEW TONGUES

GO INTO ALL THE WORLD AND PREACH THE GOSPEL TO EVERY CREATURE. HE WHO BELIEVES AND IS BAPTIZED WILL BE SAVED; BUT HE WHO DOES NOT BELIEVE WILL BE CONDEMNED. AND THESE SIGNS WILL FOLLOW
THOSE WHO BELIEVE:

AND IF THEY DRINK ANYTHING DEADLY, IT WILL BY NO MEANS HURT THEM

THEY WILL TAKE UP SERPENTS

AND HE SAID TO THEM, "GO INTO ALL THE WORLD AND PREACH THE GOSPEL TO EVERY CREATURE. HE WHO BELIEVES AND IS BAPTIZED WILL BE SAVED; BUT HE WHO DOES NOT BELIEVE WILL BE CONDEMNED. AND THESE SIGNS WILL FOLLOW THOSE WHO BELIEVE: IN MY NAME THEY WILL CAST OUT DEMONS; THEY WILL SPEAK WITH NEW TONGUES; THEY WILL TAKE UP SERPENTS; AND IF THEY DRINK ANYTHING DEADLY, IT WILL BY NO MEANS HURT THEM; THEY WILL LAY HANDS ON THE SICK, AND THEY WILL RECOVER.

MARK 16:15-18

These are the things that Jesus commands us to do as His disciples. From all three passages, scripture is clear. We are to preach the gospel. We are also commanded to cast out demons from oppressed people and lay hands on the sick so that Jesus can heal them. As His disciple and follower, are you ready to obey His command?

DO YOU TRULY BELIEVE?

LAY HANDS ON THE SICK AND THEY WILL RECOVER

DRINK ANYTHING DEADLY AND IT WILL NOT HURT YOU

TAKE UP SERPENTS

SPEAK WITH NEW TONGUES

CAST OUT DEMONS

"AND THESE SIGNS SHALL FOLLOW THOSE WHO BELIEVE..." MARK 16:17-18

Key Points

- Jesus is both Savior and Lord. We choose to believe and to obey.

- Jesus tells us in several ways to "Go"... tell the good news of your testimony and make disciples.

- Jesus came to destroy the works of the devil (1 John 3:8).

- Jesus has given us the authority to do the same.

- Jesus commands us to preach, heal and cast out demons.

Ask Yourself

- What parts of the complete Great Commission sound new to you?

- What does it mean to destroy the devil's works?

- What does it mean to have authority given to you by Jesus?

For Further Study

- *They Shall Expel Demons* by Derek Prince

TESTIMONY

Understanding The Authority Jesus Has Given Us

Many years back, I had a gastritis problem, and one particular day as I was praying alone in my room, I had this sudden urge out of nowhere to command the spirit of gastritis to come out in the name of Jesus. And as I continued commanding it to come out again and again, I literally felt something traveling upwards from my stomach towards my mouth, and then something came out. From that day onwards, I have been set free from gastritis. But back then, I couldn't understand why do Christians have sickness?

But after reading *Freedom*, it made me more clear that God is not just after salvation or saving people, but He is also after sanctifying His people from glory to glory and setting them free from every kind of demonic oppression. All we need to do is claim what Jesus has already done on Calvary.

For me now, when I pray, I make sure that none of the demons are controlling me or stealing and destroying the plans that God has for me. Also if necessary, I am able to do self deliverance on my own. How cool is that to know and understand that Jesus has given us authority in His name to cast out demons and have victory over every oppression, disease, sickness, sin, and even death.

Thank you, Pastor Danny, for being obedient to God and for having written such a wonderful book. It indeed has blessed me and so many others.

— Sunita, Nepal

Foundational Cracks Are Dangerous

"The time has come, I believe, to clear away the rubble of
religious tradition that has obscured the clear revelation of the
New Testament, and to reestablish the Church's ministry on
the bedrock of Jesus and the gospels."
– Derek Prince[1]

Every contractor, as well as every homeowner, knows that
their house is supposed to be built upon a strong foundation.
Arguably, there's nothing more important in the process of
building a home than laying a strong foundation that doesn't
lead to cracking and shifting. Jesus had clear instructions regarding laying the proper foundations of a house as well. He
said in Matthew 7:24-27, "Therefore whoever hears these
sayings of Mine and does them, I will liken him to a wise man
who built his house on the rock: and the rain descended, the
floods came, and the winds blew and beat on that house; and it

did not fall, for it was founded on the rock. But everyone who hears these sayings of Mine, and does not do them, will be like a foolish man who built his house on the sand: and the rain descended, the floods came, and the winds blew and beat on that house, and it fell. And great was its fall."

Facing The Challenges

Jesus was clear in His message that storms will come. There will be a variety of situations we will have to face in life that will determine whether our own life is built upon the foundations of the Word of God or if our life is a representation of a self-centered life built on sand. This particular scripture will begin to help you understand you are a spiritual house, whether you believe in all of Jesus' teachings or not. You have a spirit, a soul, and a body which are a representation of a spiritual temple.

Equipped to Stand

In his quest to equip the body of Christ properly to fulfill its destiny, the Apostle Paul gave the church more revelation regarding this spiritual temple. In 2 Timothy 2:19-26, Paul wrote, "Nevertheless the solid foundation of God stands, having this seal: 'The Lord knows those who are His,' and, 'Let everyone who names the name of Christ depart from iniquity.' But in a great house there are not only vessels of gold and silver, but also of wood and clay, some for honor and some for dishonor. Therefore if anyone cleanses himself from the latter, he will be a vessel for honor, sanctified and useful for the Master, prepared for every good work. Flee also youthful lusts; but pursue righteousness, faith, love, peace with those who call on the Lord out of a pure heart. But avoid foolish and ignorant disputes, knowing that they generate strife. And a servant of the Lord must not quarrel but be gentle to all, able to teach, patient, in humility correcting those who are in opposition, if God perhaps will grant them repentance, so that they may know the truth, and that they may come to their senses and escape the snare of the devil, having been taken captive by him to do his will."

Paul begins by encouraging the church to depart from iniquity. The people he is addressing are already believers. He refers to a great house which is the individual believer. He says there is honor (gold and silver) and dishonor (wood and clay) in every believer. The remarkable statement that he made following this is for the believer to "cleanse himself." Some versions of the Bible use the words "purge himself" from the latter (dishonor). In other words, I believe Paul was saying, "You purge yourself! You get it (dishonor) out of you. You can pray all day and ask God to help you, but Jesus gave you the power to get it out of yourself. Therefore, take the authority that Jesus established for you at the cross and use it." This doesn't mean that God isn't sovereign and that He will not take things away from us without us personally purging ourselves. God is, after all, God. He can do anything. He took profanity away from me when I asked Him. He took my craving for beer away from me so that I wouldn't get drunk anymore. But, overall, this illustration is what I believe Paul meant.

Sanctified and Set Apart

The result of the believer purging himself from unrighteousness is that he becomes sanctified. It is imperative that every believer understands the meaning of the word sanctified. Sanctified means "to be set apart and made holy." This is part of the process of living out the rest of our Christian life as long as we are on this earth. Since we are already saved, our objective is to become sanctified. Why? Paul said it was because we would be good for use, and we would be prepared for every good work that God calls us to. Most people in the secular world even understand the power of being good for use and being prepared. Our mandate as Christians is to purge ourselves from any dishonor so that we can become sanctified, set apart, and useful for God and prepared for every good work.

Once again, Paul is writing to believers about sanctification beyond the point in which they were saved. Sanctification is literally a lifelong process. If you ever meet someone who is fully and completely sanctified, that is someone you want to hang around for the rest of your life. That means that person spends a lot of time with God, and they are probably near perfect, and figuratively speaking, without sin. Our entire life, we are learning how to love better, how to forgive quicker, how to live in peace, how to have joy, how to love our neighbor, and how to live in the fullness of the spirit.

In 1 Thessalonians 5:23-24, we read. "Now may the God of peace Himself sanctify you completely; and may your whole spirit, soul, and body be preserved blameless at the coming of our Lord Jesus Christ. He who calls you is faithful, who also will do it."

Learning to Cooperate With God

In writing to believers at Thessalonica, Paul teaches them about the sanctification of their body, their soul, and their spirit. He also reminds them that God is faithful to do exactly that if they become blameless in their bodies, souls, and spirits.

Think about being a treasure hunter. If you were looking for treasure, you would not go walking around expecting gold and silver to be lying all over the ground so that you can become instantly rich. People who have found great treasures have had to dig for that gold or silver. In the same way are the treasures in your great house, the temple of the Holy Spirit. Throughout our lives, especially if we have not had proper teaching, we accumulate wood and earth that pile up on all of the rich treasures that God has put in us. It is not God who tries to cover these treasures up; it's the devil and his demonic forces. Once we find out where these treasures are, is it not worth it to dig out all the wood and the earth for the treasures to rise up in us and flow out of us? This understanding will lead us to the point of digging. First, you must understand why you are digging, what you are digging for, and what tools you are going to use to start digging.

Key Points
- Hearing Jesus and obeying Jesus leads to a rock-solid life.
- Obeying Jesus' teachings prepares us for the storms of life.
- As Christians, our entire lives are learning how to become "fit for the Master's use."
- Sanctification means to be set apart and made holy.

Ask Yourself
- Is it difficult for me to do what Jesus tells me to do in God's Word?
- Are you at a point where you feel like you could withstand a major storm in your life?
- Can you purge yourself from unrighteousness?

For Further Study
- *The Purple Book* by Rice Broocks and Steve Murrell

TESTIMONY

From Bondage to Freedom

Imagine trying to run the good race with your appendages in shackles, the chains of Houdini internally wrapping you, and your mind as enemy number one. That is the kind of bondage I experienced. Doctors' "solutions" were never-ending with no real remedies, and psychologists recommended the mental asylum.

But Jesus.

Jesus does not operate in the confines of the physical and seen. He prescribes spiritual solutions that last. I had a prejudice toward deliverance rooted in the world and tactics of the enemy, but I praise God for opening my eyes to His truth. It was one of the most peaceful experiences I have ever had and an incomprehensible display of His love.

He delivered me from countless spirits that kept me from any kind of physical activity, from spirits destroying my internal organs, and from spirits that kept my mind in agreement with serving the enemy. Aside from inviting Jesus into my heart, it was one of the most pivotal choices I have made in my race, and I would encourage anyone and everyone to allow Him to set them free too so they can live a life of freedom.

— Eric, Texas

Preparing For Battle

"Today we will discover how God is training His army.
Whether we realize it or not,
we are in a war against unseen forces."
— Derek Prince[1]

The problem with most people is that they never truly understand where the real battle is. Regardless of what one believes, every person lives in two basic realms. We live in a spiritual realm, and we live in an earthly or natural realm. This natural realm can also be described as a seen realm because we can see it with our natural eyes. When I teach this, I use two hula hoops to represent the two distinct realms in which we reside. I can place both hula hoops over my body, down to my waistline, and pull them completely away from each other. This represents my mere existence in both realms. I have essentially one foot in the unseen realm and one foot in the earthly realm.

Jesus was God in the flesh, as most Christians understand. God came down from heaven and became man in the form of Jesus Christ. He lived the life that we should have lived. He died the death that we should have died, by dying in our place. Three days later He rose again, proving He was the Son of God and offering us the free gift of salvation to all those who repent and believe in Him. This is the good news of the gospel of Jesus Christ.

YOU EXIST IN TWO REALMS

Jesus, Our Example

Since Jesus was modeling to us each day how we are to live, we must look at His daily activity. It began with prayer, as we see in John 5:19-20, "Then Jesus answered and said to them, 'Most assuredly, I say to you, the Son can do nothing of Himself, but what He sees the Father do; for whatever He does, the Son also does in like manner. For the Father loves the Son, and shows Him all things that He Himself does; and He will show Him greater works than these, that you may marvel'."

Jesus explained to religious leaders that He could do nothing on His own but only what He had received from His Father. In essence, Jesus would pray to His Father and seek counsel. This required Him to enter into another spiritual dimension via prayer and come out of prayer to perform the work of the ministry. As each day went by, according to the gospel accounts, we see Jesus preaching the gospel, healing the sick, raising the dead, and casting out demons, in no specific order.

Jesus existed in both realms. He was able to fully exist in the unseen realm and fully exist in the seen realm. He was able to do this perfectly because He was God. The Bible says that He was perfect. For the sake of illustration, imagine if Jesus were holding the hula hoops over His waist, He would be holding them perfectly together, one on top of the other, and His body would be in the center of the hula hoops with a hula hoop "halo" around Him. This represents perfect existence in the spiritual realm and the natural realm.

HOW JESUS EXISTED IN
BOTH REALMS

SPIRITUAL
PHYSICAL

Preparing for The Real Battle

Our life is about choices. You cannot avoid living in both
realms. How you choose to live in those realms will make all the
difference. If you run from the spiritual realm, it will still find
you. The devil and his demon forces also exist in the unseen
realm, and they take great pleasure in chasing down people

who remain ignorant of learning how to operate in this realm. One must not forget that the devil and his demons have been stalking people for thousands of years. They are not dead. He has been defeated, but he still has authority to roam about the earth until Jesus returns to deal with him. The devil knows that he and his minions' days are numbered, and he is doing everything he can to take as many souls to hell with him as possible. If Satan can't take souls with him, he will attempt to torment Christians and make their lives as miserable as possible during their stay on earth. This was not God's plan for your life, and Jesus paid the ultimate price at the cross for you and me to be able to use His name to defeat the devil and his demon forces on every occasion. You must work hard to understand the kind of battle you are in and what the battleground is.

Paul explains very clearly in Ephesians 6:10-18 what kind of battle we are in and the type of armor we need for the battle to prevail over the enemy. He writes, "Finally, my brothers, be strong in the Lord and in the power of His might. Put on the whole armor of God that you may be able to stand against the wiles of the devil. For we do not wrestle against flesh and blood, but against principalities, against powers, against the rulers of the darkness of this age, against spiritual hosts of wickedness in the Heavenly places. Therefore take up the whole armor of God, that you may be able to withstand in the evil day, and having done all, to stand. Stand therefore, having girded your waist with truth, having put on the breastplate of righteousness, and having shod your feet with the preparation of the gospel of peace; above all, taking the shield of faith with which you will be able to quench all the fiery darts of the wicked one. And take the helmet of salvation, and the sword of the Spirit, which is the Word of God; praying always with all prayer and supplication in the Spirit, being watchful to this end with all perseverance and supplication for all the saints—."

Recognizing The Enemy

The battle is not against people! The fight we are in is a supernatural battle that requires us to have a keen understanding and awareness of the unseen realm. There is so much revelation in these verses regarding the unseen realm that we are called to understand, in order to be equipped for this battle. I have met so many Christians throughout the years that were utterly stubborn and afraid to acknowledge the spiritual realm, much less talk about demons or principalities or powers. Yet, these same people will quote scriptures about the full armor of God, teach their children what the armor of God is, but will never teach them why we must put on this armor. We put on armor to protect ourselves from penetration of the fiery darts of the wicked one. Fiery darts penetrate the flesh, bleed into the soul, and can affect the spirit of a man. One must clearly understand that darts and arrows are meant to penetrate. The devil does not carry around arrows with little rubber stoppers that he purchased from Wal-Mart. The enemy also doesn't care if you are a Christian or not. Paul was teaching us Christians to put on this armor to avoid fiery darts that penetrate our bodies. I will say much more about this issue in the following chapters.

Armed for Battle

When it comes to our weapons to fight this battle, Paul states the following in 2 Corinthians 10:3-6, "For though we walk in the flesh, we do not war according to the flesh. For the weapons of our warfare are not carnal but mighty in God for pulling down strongholds, casting down arguments and every high thing that exalts itself against the knowledge of God, bringing every thought into captivity to the obedience of Christ, and being ready to punish all disobedience when your obedience is fulfilled."

We must engage in warfare that entails pulling down strongholds, which are not to be confused with footholds. They are strongholds. Webster's Dictionary describes a stronghold as such:

1: a fortified place

2: a) a place of security or survival; b) a place dominated by a particular group or marked by a particular characteristic[2]

Seeds of a Stronghold

Paul's direct teaching about pulling down strongholds relates to the fact that we are warring against fortified places, both in the unseen realm and sometimes in our own lives. That is why he goes on to say we are to take every thought captive unto the obedience of Christ, casting down arguments and every high thing that exalts itself against the things of God. We are to take every thought captive and ask ourselves, "What would Jesus do with this thought?" If the thought is not worthy of absorbing, it must be cast down. If we do not think this way, thoughts will enter our minds and hearts, and they will begin to become things. Never forget, thoughts and ideas become things! Wrong thoughts not captured and cast down become wrong things in our hearts. This is how strongholds begin to form. They first come into our minds and our hearts as little footholds. They're just little thoughts or minor occurrences. However, when those seeds take root in our minds and hearts, they usually get watered with more of the same thoughts and occurrences leading to strongholds. Even Webster's Dictionary describes a stronghold as a place dominated by a particular characteristic.

For example, when a boy engages with pornography and allows those images to sink in rather than cast them down, the seed begins to take root in his mind and heart. He then has the urge to go back and view more pornography. This waters the seed, and its roots begin to strengthen. He starts to be more consistent with his viewing, and it becomes an addiction, which leads to a stronghold developing in his body. The stronghold is in his body because his mind and heart are in his body. This affects his entire being: spirit, soul, and body.

Equipped for The Fight

We must have some weapons available to us to fight this battle. Remember that these are teachings from Paul the Apostle, after the death, burial, resurrection, and ascension of Jesus Christ. Jesus had already gone to the cross to take the curse for us and make the ultimate sacrifice for our salvation, including our victory over sickness, disease, death, and hell.

Jesus foretold this in the Gospels when He asked His disciples, "Who do men say that I, the Son of Man, am?" When Peter replied to Him that He was the Christ, the Son of the living God, Jesus' response begins to give us clues as to what kind of weapons we would be fighting with after He was gone. Matthew 16:17-19 says, "Jesus answered and said to him, 'Blessed are you, Simon Bar-Jonah, for flesh and blood has not revealed this to you, but My Father who is in Heaven. And I also say to you that you are Peter, and on this rock, I will build My church, and the gates of Hades shall not prevail against it. And I will give you the keys of the kingdom of Heaven, and whatever you bind on earth will be bound in Heaven, and whatever you loose on earth will be loosed in Heaven'."

I am amazed at how many Christians are never taught what Jesus was clearly trying to foretell here. He told His disciples, which also includes us that He would be giving them the keys to the Kingdom of Heaven. This speaks of the authority His disciples would be granted in the unseen realm. He went on to say whatever is bound on earth will be bound in Heaven. Picture a person with their hands tied behind their back, or picture a horse tied up to a hitching post. Those things are bound in the natural realm. Jesus said that whatever you bind up in the natural realm, the same will be done in Heaven. He knew the disciples understood He was referring to binding up negative, counter-productive, or evil things. They also understood this would be done with words.

The Power of Words

Our weapons of warfare are not carnal but mighty in God. Proverbs 18:21 states, "Death and life are in the power of the tongue, And those who love it will eat its fruit."

Your words either bring life, or they bring death. Your words have the power to bind things on earth that will be bound in Heaven. Consequently, Jesus said whatever is loosed on earth will also be loosed in Heaven. Now picture untying a person's bound hands or loosing a horse from the hitching post. You are freeing the person or horse to function like they were designed to function. Learning how to loose things in the natural realm with our words is pivotal for fighting the warfare that we have been called to engage in while living upon this earth.

To engage in the unseen realm, we need proper access and authority. Jesus makes it clear to us where we get this access and authority in the entire chapter of John 14. I am going to highlight verses 12-14 where He says, "Most assuredly, I say to you, he who believes in Me, the works that I do he will do also; and greater works than these he will do, because I go to My Father. And whatever you ask in My name, that I will do, that the Father may be glorified in the Son. If you ask anything in My name, I will do it."

The Name of Jesus

Jesus said, "Whatever you ask in My name that I will do," which is a precise reference to the keys to the kingdom. Jesus gave His life and shed His blood for us. He did all of this in order for us to use His name as an access point into the unseen realm to gain proper authority in things that pertain to the will of God for our lives. Jesus didn't do it so that we could use His name as a key to enter the unseen realm to get whatever we want to fulfill our self-centered dreams and lifestyle. He did it so that we would have access to the Father like He had access to the Father, and He gave us the key to bring the unseen realm into the natural realm to manifest.

Earlier in John 14:6, Jesus told Thomas, "I am the way, the truth, and the life. No one comes to the Father except through Me."

Jesus' Name is The Key

Jesus is now making it clear that He is the key to the Father. He holds the keys to the kingdom, which is unseen to us at this point. Here is the key being offered to you and me. I hold the keys to my house, and you cannot get into my house unless I give them to you to gain access to my home. Unless you have a key to my house you will never know what my house looks like unless you enter my house. If you take the key, access the house, and enter into that new realm, you will see what my house looks like.

The key that Jesus is giving you is the authority of His name. It is the name above all names that has already defeated Satan. When we use the name of Jesus to defeat the devil, we are not fighting for victory; we are fighting from victory! Philippians 2:10 assures us that every knee will bow to one name, the name of Jesus. Every knee will bow in Heaven, on earth, and beneath the earth to the name of Jesus.

In Revelation 3:7-8, Jesus was speaking to the faithful church, the church of Philadelphia. He said this, "And to the angel of the church in Philadelphia write, 'These things says He who is holy, He who is true, He who has the key of David,

He who opens and no one shuts, and shuts and no one opens. I know your works. See, I have set before you an open door, and no one can shut it; for you have a little strength, have kept My word, and have not denied My name'."

Jesus has the key of David, and He opens doors and closes doors with that key. You and I have access and authority to enter into new dimensions with the name of Jesus. The "key" to using the key is to honor God in all that you do, bring honor to Jesus as you use His name for proper access, and use the authority of Jesus' name in faith.

The Difference Between Victorious Living and Mediocrity

The name of Jesus is powerful. If you do not learn how to use His name as a key to fighting spiritual battles to pull down strongholds, you will succumb to an ordinary life of defeat, set-backs, and unfulfilled circumstances throughout the remainder of your life here on this earth. You may very well get to Heaven because you are saved, but you will be one of those weak, tattered, and defeated soldiers who never really engaged in the good fight of faith.

You might have become one of those people who just believes that God is sovereign, and we are saved by grace. You may have settled for believing there's nothing we can do to change anything while we are here on this earth because our sovereign God is on the throne. That is partially true because we are saved by grace. It is partly true because God is sovereign, and He can do whatever He wants, whenever He wants, and however He wants. So if you find yourself believing that God's sovereignty means that you have no role to play and do not partner in the plans of God, consider the following:

Why in the world do you go to church? Based on that kind of reasoning, you don't need church. You're already going to Heaven, aren't you?

Why do you pray? Your prayers don't mean anything because God is sovereign, and your requests aren't going to change a thing.

Why do you put on the full armor of God? You don't need armor. Your enemy was defeated at the cross, and he is not allowed to attack Christians. He only attacks non-believers. You're already saved! You're fully sanctified. You're set apart and made holy. Your spirit is perfect; therefore, you do not need any such armor.

If God had not intended that through our relationship with Him, we become actively involved in His plans and purposes, then Paul's instructions would have been ludicrous. It is imperative that we understand both who we are in Christ and what we are to do to fulfill the calling on our lives.

Avoid Deception

As silly as this all sounds, some people really buy into many of these teachings from well-meaning Christians. Some of these men and women have prominent names throughout North America and the world. Some actually named God's Holy Book after themselves and market their false doctrines to people who choose to stay bound up in traditional mindsets. Just like Saul of Tarsus, these people believe what they are teaching their Christian brothers and sisters is so right, yet Saul found out one day that he was so wrong. Jesus had to even show up on the scene, smite Paul with blindness to put him in his place, give him a new lens, and set him on the course for his destiny. This shows that even those we hail as the most brilliant scholars of our time can be very wrong. Saul was one of the most brilliant theologians of his time, yet he ordered Christians to be persecuted and executed.

Be careful who you exalt to be the expert in Biblical teaching. Jesus said this in John 14:25-26 about who would teach us what we need to know, "These things I have spoken to you while being present with you. But the Helper, the Holy Spirit, whom the Father will send in My name, He will teach you all things, and bring to your remembrance all things that I said to you."

Jesus, while on this earth, taught His disciples all things. The Bible says Jesus is the Word. In the Word, we learn so much about how we are to walk out the ministry of Jesus. Once Jesus left the scene, and God sent the Holy Spirit to us, the Holy Spirit was present to teach us all things. The Holy Spirit's job is to manifest, or reveal Jesus to us. Everything that the Holy Spirit does is done to reveal Christ to you, to me, and to all the world. The Holy Spirit is a teacher. He is a better teacher than any man, including myself.

Jesus has made His name available to you to fight the battle. His name is the most powerful weapon available in the spiritual realm. When you pray "in the name of Jesus," you have all the authority of His name available to you because you ask in prayer with His authority. Will you, by faith, step into that realm of power and authority today?

Key Points

- We live in a visible and an unseen realm—the area surrounding us in the spiritual world.

- Our battle is not against people. It's against principalities and powers in the unseen realm.

- A stronghold is a fortified place the enemy tries to create in us.

- The name of Jesus is our greatest weapon.

- Jesus gave us the power to bind and loose and use His name. We do that with words.

Ask Yourself

- Is there any area of your life where you believe the enemy may have a stronghold?

- What is more in control in your life—your spirit or your body?

- Do you use the name of Jesus boldly in prayer?

- Do you know how to speak the name of Jesus to effectively bind or loose things around your life?

TESTIMONY

Fifty-Nine And Did Not Know

It all started with a simple question, "Have you ever gone through deliverance?"

My head tilted, and my mind asked, "What is he talking about?" I was fifty-nine years old and had no idea such spirits actually existed even though I had been in church the majority of my life. I listened as the conversation continued and heard about the process of breaking free of the influences of the negative forces we allow to guide and direct our lives.

Over the next few months of deliberate study, I learned pride, prejudices, and low self-esteem are all weapons the enemy (Satan) uses to disrupt and destroy our lives. Then came the question we all must ask, "Who is in control of my life, my spirit or the enemy?" I knew God had given me dominion over my life, but I had not taken hold of that gift.

Freedom happened for me the moment awareness, desire, and action took place. The pressures of life became less because the enemy knew I was aware of his destructive plans. When you recognize your enemy and take hold of your rights given to you by God, the freedom promised by God becomes a reality.

— Larry, Texas

7

Spirit, Soul, and Body

"When a Christian tries to live by reason he is moving out of God's country into the enemy's land. We belong in the miraculous and the supernatural realm."
— John G. Lake

You are a person with a spirit, soul, and body. It is imperative that you have a general understanding of your three-part being. You are a human being. In that being, you have a fleshly body. You also have what I believe to be a replica of the fleshly body that we call your soul, and you have a spirit that dwells in you.

Many teachers believe the soul consists of your mind, will, and emotions. Although this is true, the other parts of your being are active in these functions as well. Here is a quick excerpt from Paul's teaching in 1 Corinthians 2:11 for you to consider,

"For what man knows the things of a man except the spirit of the man which is in him? Even so no one knows the things of God except the Spirit of God." You have a spirit in you, and your spirit actually thinks; therefore, it is operative in the area of the mind, will, and emotions. Regarding emotions, here's one excerpt from God's Word about one's spirit from Luke 1:46-47, "And Mary said: 'My soul magnifies the Lord, And my spirit has rejoiced in God my Savior.' Mary's soul magnified the Lord; however, her spirit rejoiced, which is a display of emotions."

Here's why it is essential for one to have a general understanding of our spirit, soul, and body. The Apostle Paul spoke of the war that occurs between the spirit and the flesh in Galatians 5:16-18, "I say then: Walk in the Spirit, and you shall not fulfill the lust of the flesh. For the flesh lusts against the Spirit, and the Spirit against the flesh; and these are contrary to one another, so that you do not do the things that you wish. But if you are led by the Spirit, you are not under the law."

The Never-Ending Tug of War

If you can picture three people standing side by side, locking arms together, this is what the war looks like. Your soul would represent the person in the middle. The flesh would be the person on one side and the spirit on the other. In essence, the spirit and the flesh are playing tug of war with the soul. The flesh and the spirit are continually warring against each other in the quest to affect the soul. Picture how much the flesh is pulling on the soul to obey its lusts, and on the other side, how the spirit is pulling on the soul to refrain from disobedience and to keep being fed by the things of the Spirit of God. The health of the soul is determined by the number of victories the spirit wins in the tug of war with the flesh.

THE BATTLE OF FLESH VS SPIRIT

FLESH

BATTLE FOR
YOUR SOUL

SPIRIT

What Are You Feeding?

Another picture to imagine is this. Envision three people lined up, one behind the other. The person in front is the flesh. The person second in line is the soul, and the person lined up behind the soul is the spirit. In this picture, if the flesh is out in front, the flesh is going to be fed or be in the lead role. If we feed our flesh, we focus on carnal things (and I'm not just talking about food). What we feed becomes the entry point to the soul. Paul talks about this also in the verses just beyond Galatians 5:18,"Now the works of the flesh are evident, which are: adultery, fornication, uncleanness, lewdness, idolatry, sorcery, hatred, contentions, jealousies, outbursts of wrath, selfish ambitions, dissensions, heresies, envy, murders, drunkenness, revelries, and the like; of which I tell you beforehand, just as I also told you in time past, that those who practice such things will not inherit the kingdom of God" (Galatians 5:19-21).

When we consistently feed our flesh these things, our soul can become contaminated by those particular strongholds. As they are practiced, the sin grows larger inside of us, and it crowds out our spirit, leaving no room for it to grow and flourish. Therefore, what will flow out of us are the very things in which we are partaking or feeding upon.

WE BECOME WHAT WE TAKE IN

ADULTERY
FORNICATION
UNCLEANNESS
LEWDNESS
IDOLATRY
SORCERY
HATRED
CONTENTIONS
JEALOUSIES
OUTBURSTS OF WRATH
SELFISH AMBITIONS
DISSENSIONS
HERESIES
ENVY
MURDERS

SPIRIT
SOUL
BODY

The Right Order

On the other hand, if you move the person (spirit) in the back to the front, and you move the front person (the flesh) to the back, this is what a visual picture of a healthy Christian life should look like. We are to be led by the Spirit. If your spirit is in the front of your daily life, your focus on prayer, God's Word, resting in Jesus, and the like are feeding your spirit. Thus, your soul is getting fed what is healthy and good. This will lead to a life lived on a daily basis that will provide you with the maximum opportunity to walk in the spirit in all that you do.

Because of this, your flesh would be in the back, taking a lesser position, and have to follow the marching orders of the spirit and soul. Being led by the Spirit requires our spirit to be out in the forefront so that we can walk in the nature of the Spirit of God. Consequently, if our flesh is out in the forefront of our life, we will tend to obey the appetites of the flesh.

Paul's final instructions on the matter of the war between the flesh and the spirit are in Galatians 5:22, "But the fruit of the Spirit is love, joy, peace, long-suffering, kindness, goodness, faithfulness, gentleness, self-control. Against such there is no law. And those who are Christ's have crucified the flesh with its passions and desires. If we live in the Spirit, let us also walk in the Spirit. Let us not become conceited, provoking one another, envying one another."

Where Do You Stand?

When we have our spirit at the forefront of our everyday life, we have a real shot at displaying this kind of fruit to the world in which we live. When it comes to your daily walk, evaluate how much of this fruit you believe is on display throughout your life. Ask two or three other people close to your life to make the same honest evaluation of you.

Here's a checklist of the fruit of the Spirit. Circle which answer applies to your life currently:

NKJV	THE MESSAGE		
Love	Affection for others	YES	NO
Joy	Exuberance about life	YES	NO
Peace	Serenity	YES	NO
Long-suffering	A willingness to stick with things	YES	NO
Kindness	A sense of compassion in the heart	YES	NO

NKJV	THE MESSAGE		
Goodness	A conviction that a basic holiness permeates things and people	YES	NO
Faithfulness	Involved in loyal commitments	YES	NO
Gentleness	Not needing to force our way in life	YES	NO
Self-Control	Able to marshal and direct our energies wisely	YES	NO

How do you fare right now? If you circled "No" to any of the boxes above, it doesn't necessarily mean that you are under a lot of demonic oppression. It does, however, help you gauge how your daily walk is in the spirit. This is how we have been taught to live as Christians, and this is the fruit which we are supposed to produce. Therefore, we must make sober judgments of ourselves and figure out what might be holding us back from being able to circle "Yes" in every area. I know people like this! They are amazing people, and they practice living like this on a daily basis. I know that their lives are grounded in prayer, God's Word, and having a healthy love for their neighbor.

Watch Out for The Fiery Darts

Everything you have read so far has been presented to help you develop a clearer picture of life's battles. For instance, if your flesh has been winning the war against the spirit in your personal life or in your past, you know the fiery darts of the enemy were obviously penetrating your life by way of the unseen realm. Those fiery darts were attacks from the enemy to send unclean spirits into your life to try to get you to create a consistent pattern out of their assigned attack. For example, if you were shot with a fiery dart of the enemy related to sexual perversion, that unclean spirit, once in, will begin to work on your mind to persuade you to keep practicing that particular act. As you practice the sin, that spirit develops a stronghold in your flesh and your soul.

Proverbs 25:28 says, "Whoever has no rule over his own spirit is like a city broken down, without walls."

One should always think spirit, soul, and body instead of body, soul, and spirit. We must learn to rule over our spirit to keep our spiritual house fortified with the right things. Ruling over our spirit is learning self-discipline, and we learn self-discipline from loving and acknowledging our Father in Heaven. Through loving Him and fearing Him, we learn and develop the self-discipline to rule over our spirit and keep it at the forefront of our daily life, thereby keeping our spiritual house strong.

Key Points

- Your spirit is meant to be at the forefront and lead your life.

- Your spirit and your flesh battle constantly to affect your soul.

- What you feed your soul is what will reflect your behaviors.

- The fruit of the spirit is a reflection of being led by the spirit.

Ask Yourself

- Have you been more led by your flesh or by your spirit lately?

- What does it look like to feed your spirit daily?

TESTIMONY

Learning To Walk in True Freedom

I learned about freedom through Pastor Danny McDaniel. Freedom is a process. It took me several times to truly lay it all at Jesus' feet. I was so full of pride and ego and immersed in fear, doubt, loss of identity, anger, guilt, shame, remorse and had a debilitating panic and anxiety disorder. I was raised by an alcoholic mother and verbally abused by older siblings. I was controlled, manipulated, and cheated on in my first marriage.

Pastor Danny and his ministry team walked me through a deliverance process to start a healing process. So often, I looked at what was wrong with everyone else when what I needed to work on was myself. I learned about spirits that took root inside me and discovered I had nothing to be ashamed of. So much of it comes from how we were raised and what we were exposed to growing up. I am still working on full healing. I was freed from a twenty-year smoking addiction and healed completely from my panic and anxiety disorder. I regained my true identity. I was extremely afraid of death. I no longer fear death. I found forgiveness for those who had hurt me and spoken death over my life, even though I never received an apology. I learned how to forgive myself for my mistakes and how to walk in true freedom.

I am very thankful for everything Pastor Danny sowed into our lives. My husband and I celebrated twenty-four years of marriage, and our son is thriving while advancing through the highest levels of the hockey world. This would not have come to pass if we were not obedient and sought help and did the work to continue the process of freedom. Thank you, Jesus, for the healing in my life.

— Shannon, Michigan

CHAPTER EIGHT

What Are Demons and Where Are They?

"...Scripture teaches us that Satan and his demons are very real. Nothing is comical about them and we need to take their existence very seriously."
— Robert Morris[1]

Very few people talk about demons unless a sports announcer talks about a fallen sports hero who couldn't "exorcise their demons." At times, it's a television show that is actually putting the demonic realm on display through various forms of media, sometimes in very accurate portrayals. This is how the devil works. He is not wise, but he is clever and crafty. He knows if he can hide in plain sight, most people will ignore him. That's what happens with all of the television, cinema, and gaming exposure in our society. Because of the weird, twisted, or completely distorted depictions of our enemy and his satanic kingdom through these mediums, most people do not even acknowledge their authenticity when there are real portrayals. Little do these people know that spiritual gateways, or portals, can be opened as a result, leading to demonic entry into people's lives. This, in turn, leads to spiritual oppression which is what we are about to dive into.

If you open your Bible and read Matthew 15 and Mark 9, you will notice it was common for ordinary people to refer to demons. Not only did they refer to demons, but these common people could also identify demons! The scriptures validate that it was and still is completely normal to refer to and identify demonic activity in and around our lives.

Demons are real, so the question I want to ask is, "Where are all of the demons that are supposed to be getting cast out?" Are they all down in hell torturing lost souls for eternity? Many demons, too many to number, are down in the depths of hell torturing the lost souls who have condemned themselves to hell by their disobedience to God. So the answer to demons being in hell is simply "yes," but they are not all confined there. Many other demons, too many to number, are traveling around in the unseen realm stalking mankind. Their objective is to steal, kill, and destroy just as Jesus said in John 10:10. The devil has access to an army of evil spirits and rules over them, just as God has an army of Heavenly angels and rules over them. I don't believe anyone really has any idea how many any of these two armies are in total numbers, but I do know it is more than you and I can probably estimate. One day we will all find out; however, for now, we can merely fight the fight based on how much intel we have. There is enough intel from the Bible and experiences validated by God's Word to determine how we are dealing with numerous forces. They roam throughout the whole earth, and they are attacking all people groups around the world.

What Is a Demon's Purpose?

One should know three keywords to comprehend better the purpose of demons roaming about the earth. (The third keyword will be covered in the next chapter.)

First, the term "devil" is derived from the Greek word "diabolos." The word diabolos means false accuser or slanderer.[2] In Ephesians 2:1-3, Paul describes the devil as such, "And you He made alive, who were dead in trespasses and sins, in which you once walked according to the course of this world, according to the prince of the power of the air, the spirit who now works in the sons of disobedience, among whom also we all once conducted ourselves in the lusts of our flesh, fulfilling the desires of the flesh and of the mind, and were by nature children of wrath, just as the others."

The Prince of The Power of The Air

Paul referred to him as the prince of the power of the air, meaning he is the ruling unclean spirit that wars against God and His angels to try to bring as many people to hell with him as he can. Jesus described the devil to His disciples as "the ruler of this world" in John 14:30. I believe what He meant by this was the ruler of this world was coming and had permission to rule over disobedient people. However, Jesus is also teaching us that, in Him, the ruler of this world cannot penetrate us. Therefore, it is important as a Christian to learn the power of living in Christ and living each day clothed in the full armor of God.

The devil is like a prosecuting attorney. He wants to bring you and me to the throne of God and present a case before the Lord so that he may gain access into our lives. If he has a legitimate cause, he can gain access. If he doesn't, he will do everything in his limited power to falsely accuse you. Remember, he is a slanderer and has been since the beginning.

Demons ... Satan's Minions

The next word that is important to learn is the word "demon," derived from the Greek word "diamonion." It is a noun that means unclean spirit or evil spirit.[3] The words demon, unclean spirit, and evil spirit are interchangeable in relation to the subject of demons and how they operate. It is quite simple to understand that a demon is an unclean spirit operating under the command of Satan. Satan has a hierarchy of demons, and his army has a structure to it. I don't care to get into the whole theology of how demons became demons because that is not very relevant to understanding a demon's role. What is important to know is that the word demon or unclean spirit is used 156 times in the Bible. The word pastor is used once. No one is running around denying the fact that pastors are real, yet that title is used only once in the Holy Scriptures. Demons are very real, and they have been hunting and stalking humanity for thousands of years. The devil is a master hunter. Although he doesn't have the wisdom of God, he does know a lot about laying traps and snares successfully to cause man to stumble and fall into temptation. Look at the success he had with Eve in the Garden of Eden.

Unmasking The Enemy

Since Satan desires to steal, kill, and destroy, according to John 10:10, he wants to do it by using his well-planned and organized army of unclean spirits. We do not know every single thing about Satan's complete army of demons, just as we don't know every single name and rank of God's Heavenly army. The good news is that the Bible gives us some great insight into what Satan's army of demons is up to. We have also been given a straightforward, effective, and powerful plan to implement in order to achieve victory.

Higher ruling demons have assignments related to geographic regions and cities, and they attempt to rule and establish strongholds over these places. For example, when Daniel had been praying to God and fasting for twenty-one days to get an answer from God, an angel finally showed up on the twenty-fourth day. In Daniel 10, there is the depiction of the battle the angel had been facing. Daniel 10: 12-14 says, "Then he said to me, 'Do not fear, Daniel, for from the first day that you set your heart to understand, and to humble yourself before your God, your words were heard; and I have come because of your words. But the prince of the kingdom of Persia withstood me twenty-one days; and behold, Michael, one of the chief princes, came to help me, for I had been left alone there with the Kings of Persia. Now I have come to make you understand what will happen to your people in the latter days, for the vision refers to many days yet to come'."

The Battle Between Good and Evil

Not only was there a high-ranking demon ruling as a prince over the geographical region of Persia, but also the angel refers to Michael, one of the chief princes and top officers of the Heavenly army who had come to help him fight. The angel that showed up on the scene to meet Daniel had apparently battled for over twenty days to get from his starting point in the unseen realm to arrive at Daniel's aid. It was all due to the battle between good and evil, the principalities and powers of the air. The angel even described having been left with the Kings of Persia, meaning he had to deal with battling several high-ranking demons in the principalities.

The Real Battlefield

Remember, our battle is not against flesh and blood. It is against spiritual wickedness in high places (Ephesians 6:12). We may not know all of the names of every demon that exists, but the Bible points us in the direction of making sure we understand who our enemy is and what our enemy is up to. One cannot say, "If it is not in the Bible, it does not exist." Nor can one say, "If I don't see it in the Bible, then I can't have any part of it or the so-called knowledge thereof." If that were the case, we could not use electricity because electricity is not in the Bible. We could not fly in an airplane because that wasn't taught in the Bible. We also could not get many of the surgeries that are afforded us today because most of them did not exist in Biblical times. Nor could we acknowledge many of the sicknesses and diseases today as being real because they are not named in the Bible. ADHD is not in the Bible anywhere, yet it is highly recognized and accepted as a condition that affects people's behavior today. Here are some examples of unclean spirits (by name) revealed to us in the Bible that we know to exist:

Mark 5:8	Legion	**Numbers 5:30**	Jealousy
Mark 5:8	Beelzebub (ruler of the demons)	**Deut. 2:30**	Hard heartedness
Luke 11:14	Mute spirit	**Judges 9:23**	Ill will (Divisive)
Mark 9:24-25	Deaf and Dumb spirit	**1 Samuel 1:15**	Sorrowful spirit
Acts 8:7	Paralysis and lame spirits	**1 Samuel 16:14**	Distressing spirit
Revelation 2:20	Jezebel	**1 Kings 22:23**	Lying spirit
Revelation 9:11	Apollyon	**Ecclesiastes 7:9**	Anger
2 Timothy 1:7	Fear	**Isaiah 19:3**	Egypt
Isaiah 61:3	Heaviness	**Hosea 4:12**	Harlotry
Isaiah 19:14	Perverse spirit	**Luke 13:10**	Infirmity
Isaiah 27:1	Leviathan	**Luke 16:13**	Mammon
Romans 8:15	Bondage	**Acts 16:16**	Divination
Job 7:11	Bitterness	**Romans 11:8**	Stupor

Leviticus 20:6	*Familiar spirits*	**1 John 4:3**	*Anti-Christ*
1 Samuel 15:23	*Rebellion Witchcraft Stubbornness Idolatry*	**1 John 4:6**	*Error*

Identifying Demons

These scriptures are glaring proof that there are numerous unclean spirits roaming the earth, each with different names, ranks, and assignments. The purpose of this book is to identify the activity of demons, or unclean spirits, which are meant to personally attack your life. I also want to give you insight into how to overcome those demons that have affected you and/or your family.

It has often been taught that for every action there is an equal and opposite reaction. Where there is hot, the opposite is cold. Where there is light, the opposite is darkness. Where there is right, the opposite is wrong. Where there is true, the opposite is false. The list goes on. The same holds true for the Heavenly versus the demonic. The world tends to label things and classify them according to medical or clinical standards, or they label things as positive or negative behavioral issues. While there is some truth in these classifications, the reality is that unclean spirits have names and assignments.

Look a Little Further

Let's take a lying spirit, for example. Is a lying spirit of Heavenly form or demonic form? Of course, it is demonic. The opposite of a lie is truth. Is a spirit of love Heavenly or demonic in nature? It is Heavenly in nature; therefore, it is not demonic. We know that the opposite of love is hate. Many names of clinical diagnoses and behavioral diagnoses carry demonic origins, and they usually have an unclean spirit working behind the scenes through the individual. This means many medical or clinical diagnoses have elements of truth in their assumptions, but there can be much deeper meanings attached to them that happen to be of spiritual origin.

The Root of The Problem

I had issues with frustration and anger. As a dad, I could lose my temper too quickly over the silliest little things with my boys. There were consistent patterns of anger and frustration in my life, which were demonic in nature. The Bible instructs us to be angry without sinning. Therefore, one can get angry and it not be demonic. However, consistent patterns of negative human behavior usually have demonic origins. If I were to display consistent patterns of anger, it would be very easy for people to recognize I have an anger issue. If we were conducting spiritual CSI, we would want to get to the root of the problem and find out how the consistent anger pattern originated. Anger is the effect; we are searching for the scene of the cause. Another way to understand the concept is taking a look at fever. Infections cause most fevers. The fever is evident on the surface of our skin, but the underlying cause is a virus within our body. In the same way, consistent patterns of anger result from something deeper. It is the virus within. We must get to the root.

Is depression Heavenly? Are you happy or depressed? How about fear? Are you courageous and fearless, or are you fearful? Is insecurity Heavenly or demonic? Do you have a strong sense of self-worth and identity, or do you worry about what others think about you? What about pride? Would you call pride Heavenly? It has to be one or the other. You are either prideful or humble. Is bitterness Heavenly? You are either sweet and kind to people, or your bitterness leaks out as cynicism, negativity, and hatred towards others.

Demons on Assignment

The list could get very long because there are a whole lot of demons roaming the earth with various assignments, and their job is to get inside a person's body and carry out that assignment. An unclean spirit of alcoholism focuses merely on driving a person to have another drink. A spirit of destruction working in someone's life is focused on causing that person to experience painful moments of failure or cause accidents to happen, leading to setbacks and destruction. A spirit of infirmity has the assignment of producing sickness and disease in one's body. There are spirits of rejection that cause a person to distrust in most relationships. It is like having a dirty filter in your air conditioning system. The spirit of rejection is filthy, and it takes things that people say and filters it through a dirty, twisted lens, so the person on the hearing end completely distorts what is being said to them. Its assignment is to twist words coming from other people's mouths and cause an offense. That spirit causes one to feel rejected, even though the other party was saying nothing offensive or condemning.

A spirit of fear has the assignment of bringing torment to a person's mind by causing them to fear the dark, fear what others think, fear confrontation, or many other types of fear. A spirit of lust gets inside of a person's mind and continually provokes the person to fantasize about people in whom they should not be fantasizing about. For example, I was exposed to pornography in fourth grade, and not long after that, I wanted a Farrah Fawcett poster more than anything else in life. With over 12 million copies sold, the Farrah Fawcett poster is the top-selling poster of all time. My parents allowed me to buy the poster, and I pinned it on the wall right next to where I laid my head on my pillow. I went to bed every night and woke up each morning to Farrah Fawcett right in front of my face. The little voices inside my head taught me how to imagine things that young boys should not imagine at the age of nine. Farrah

Fawcett wasn't speaking to me each day, nor was there a demon on the wall speaking to me. A voice inside my head spoke to me to facilitate lust in my heart and fantasy in my mind.

Huggy, The Labrador

Once we know that demons have real names and assignments relating to those names, it is quite easy to figure out what their role truly is. Unless they are a territorial-type demon, most other demons have the assignment to find a body to get inside and wreak havoc upon. Unclean spirits want to be in a human body preferably, so I will primarily focus on human beings. There are exceptions where I have personally seen animals with unclean spirits in them. In 2007, my mom was struggling with severe alcoholism, and she was living by herself, except for her labrador retriever named Huggy. My mom had a lot of issues at the time, with bitterness, unforgiveness, and many other emotional wounds that were quite extensive. Huggy had been a normal acting Labrador and was probably around four years old. As the year 2007 went on, Huggy came down with crippling arthritis and could barely sit up, and he had difficulty using his back legs to walk. I concluded through my discernment that Huggy was just full of spirits of infirmity, sickness, disease, and arthritis stemming from my mom's bitterness and misery. She was in a very low state, and I believe Huggy had taken on her pain as well.

One day, I had Huggy over at our house, and I decided to simply cast those spirits out of him and pray for healing in his body. It only took a few moments to cast those spirits out of the dog and pray for healing, and Huggy was quickly back to normal. When I say quickly, I mean he was immediately back to being 100% functional. He was able to run around that day.

Cunning, Deceptive Spirits

When Legion asked Jesus if He would allow all of the spirits that would come out of the demoniac to go into the pigs nearby, he would have preferred a human body. However, he was willing to settle for pigs rather than being sent back down to the abyss or to dry and arid places. One time, I was ministering alongside two married couples, and we were helping another lady get set free from oppression. I was a guest in one of the married couple's homes, and I forgot to inform the unclean spirits they were not allowed to transfer into any animals in or around the home or neighborhood. I would normally tell them this and inform them that they will go exactly where the Holy Spirit and His angels intend for them to go, but they will not transfer into any living being in the area. About halfway through the ministry time, I was casting out a certain spirit from this woman. I just happened to say, "You are all going to come out peacefully and quietly right now in Jesus' name, and you will not transfer into any other person or animal in this house." Within two to three seconds of my command, the dachshund sitting on the couch about four feet away from us vomited on the couch. We all knew exactly what happened. Some spirits had left this lady and decided they were just going to take advantage of going into the dog. They didn't have the option of transferring into anyone in the home because we were all suited up in the full armor of God and covered by the blood of Jesus. The homeowner stated that her dog doesn't get sick, doesn't throw up, and knew precisely it was a spirit that had transferred from the lady to the dog.

Recognizing Demons at Work

It's not just pigs and dogs that demons want to get inside of. The ultimate objective is to steal, kill, and destroy God's people. It is human bodies where demons have the most fun because this is where they have the best shot at carrying out their assignments in their attempt to destroy mankind. They can certainly work through an animal, but they are much more effective working in humans. If you've never seen an animal with a bad spirit, which would be an unclean spirit, you may not have seen very many animals in your lifetime. If you've never seen a person with a bad spirit or an unclean spirit, it is time to keep forging ahead and learn how to recognize how unclean spirits get inside of humans and cause them harm.

Key Points

- The devil acts as a prosecuting attorney in our lives, constantly trying to find a way to accuse us of wrongdoing before God.

- Demons are unclean spirits that operate under Satan's command.

- Demons have real names and assignments that relate to those names. Their ultimate objective is to steal, kill, and destroy.

Ask Yourself

- What did Paul mean when he called Satan "the prince of the power of the air?"

- What did Jesus mean when He called the devil "the ruler of this world?"

- What are some examples of demons' names that you have seen influence your life thus far?

For Further Study

- *Shadow Boxing* by Henry Malone

TESTIMONY

Something Had To Change!

My freedom story began in July of 2011. At the time, neither my wife nor I knew what life could be like as "captives that were set free" as talked about in Luke 4:18. If asked if we were Christ-followers, we would have said, "Absolutely!" But where was our fruit? Our marriage was on the rocks; our lives were riddled by sabotage, anger, betrayal, deceit, and confusion. A "normal" conversation about plans for the day consistently turned into an argument. We couldn't get anywhere meaningful as a couple.

As a family, life was rocky too. Our kids were young, with our daughter turning five and our son just shy of his eighth birthday. One day after a shouting match, my wife and I turned and saw our son standing there. With tears in his eyes, he cried, "There is no peace in this house." This was a moment I will never forget! He was right, and I had no clue what to do. All the prayer in the world could not get me past this evil operating in my life, my marriage, and my family. Something had to change, and then it happened! We were introduced to Danny McDaniel and our new church. Within a week of meeting these wonderful people, our lives were radically changed as we learned how to live a victorious, abundant life like Jesus talked about in John 10:10.

Today, everything has changed. Now I understand that a life of victory doesn't mean things can't go wrong. I still deal with the ups and downs of life, but at the same time, I am experiencing win -after-win. And as you begin to walk in freedom, I believe the same will occur with you as you discover a life that is focused on building Jesus' Kingdom and not your own.

—Christian, Texas

CHAPTER NINE

9

Can a Christian Have a Demon?

"The influence of spiritual evil is more common than we think. Spiritual snakes can slither in to open doors and windows of our lives. They need to be dealt with. We need to grapple with this idea that spiritual oppression can happen to anyone. Even you and me."
— Robert Morris[1]

Is it possible for a Christian to have a demon? This seems to be a modern-day question more than an age-old question. The enemy has deceived our modern-day culture of Christians by convincing many that it is impossible for a Christian to have a demon of any kind. Yet, so much of it can be answered with common sense. On the other hand, I could recopy a large portion of the gospels and include it in this book to make it very long with accounts of how demons come inside of people and how they manifest in people, including believers.

Is Demon Possession Real?

This leads us to the third key term associated with demons so that you can understand how Satan attacks Christians. The third key term to understand regarding demons is the Greek word "daimonizo," which means to be "demonized." It also means to "be subject to demonic influence." This Greek word daimonizo was mistranslated into modern English.[2] Our Bibles usually refer to this word as "possessed" or "demon-possessed." This can lead to a very controversial subject if not understood.

When it comes to the word "possession," this word portrays ownership. Only one entity can own you. Either God owns you, or Satan owns you. Jesus said that you could not serve two masters. In John 8:44, Jesus said to the Jews who did not believe Him, "You are of your father the devil, and the desires of your father you want to do. He was a murderer from the beginning and does not stand in the truth because there is no truth in him. When he speaks a lie, he speaks from his own resources, for he is a liar and the father of it."

I believe that God owns a person or the ruler of this world owns them until they surrender their life to the Lordship of Jesus Christ. I do not believe that Satan can own nor possess a Christian. However, I do believe that Satan can own and possess a non-Christian, even if they don't personally claim allegiance to Satan. Most people would not want to claim allegiance to the lordship of Satan; however, their lifestyle does so and speaks for itself. Satan doesn't care whether one pledges his or her allegiance to him because he is a deceiver. Satan seems to be quite pleased with people serving his purposes when they have no clue that they are even doing it.

No Trespassing

Any person who believes that a demon cannot possess a Christian is absolutely right. A demon cannot possess (or own) a Christian. To be under the subject of a demon or to be demonized is better described as being trespassed. The enemy is always trying to gain ground in a Christian's life, and he can trespass if allowed. He looks for openings or chinks in the armor, where he can fire a dart and penetrate a Christian's life in order to get a foothold. If the enemy can gain a foothold, it has the potential to become a stronghold in one's life.

The Bible says the following about strongholds in 2 Corinthians 10:3-6, "For though we walk in the flesh, we do not war according to the flesh. For the weapons of our warfare are not carnal but mighty in God for pulling down strongholds, casting down arguments and every high thing that exalts itself against the knowledge of God, bringing every thought into captivity to the obedience of Christ, and being ready to punish all disobedience when your obedience is fulfilled."

Let's break this down in simple terms:

1. We do not war according to the flesh

2. Our weapons are not physical weapons

3. Our weapons are spiritual from God

4. These weapons pull down strongholds (inside of us as well as outside)

5. These weapons bring every thought (inside of us) captive to the obedience of Christ

6. These weapons drive back all disobedience when we obey

The Christian's Arsenal

So, what are these weapons? These weapons are the Word of God. Jesus told the devil, "Man does not live by bread alone, but by every word that proceeds out of the mouth of God" (Matthew 4:4). These weapons are the name of Jesus and the blood of Jesus. They are spiritual weapons. The Word comes out of your mouth, and it is not physical. It wars on your behalf, and it causes angelic forces to war on your behalf, under the authority of an almighty God. The name of Jesus is spiritual. He is seated at the right hand of God; therefore, the Holy Spirit is present to manifest the power of Jesus in and around our lives. The blood of Jesus was shed over 2000 years ago, but it has spiritual power that causes the enemy to flee. There is power in the blood of Jesus!

Our Authority

I used to own a ranch in North Texas. My ranch was completely fenced, as most Texas ranches are. I owned the ranch. It was mine, and I had sole rights to it. However, that did not mean I kept all the trespassers at bay. If I wasn't out at my ranch at all times, my 209 acres was left somewhat unfortified. One would think the fences and locked gates would be enough. Thieves do not care about fences or locked gates. I had to deal with the possibility of trespassers who would want to steal my livestock or others who might want to poach a deer from my property. As a landowner, if I were to spot a trespasser, I would have full authority to kick that trespasser out. If they refused to leave, I could use force in order to remove them from my property. Why? Because I owned the property, and the trespasser was coming to either steal something or kill something on my property. Jesus said, "The thief does not come but to steal, kill, or destroy." This is what being demonized, not demon-possessed, really means. God owns you. You are His property, and the enemy is constantly attempting to trespass into your life so that he can get some kind of access to the property. He is trying to steal from what is rightfully yours! Although God is the ultimate surveillance over His property, He gives you the right, the power, and the authority to lock and unlock the gates to your property each and every day. He gives you the right, the power, and the authority to check your fence lines. He also gives you those same rights to check your entire property internally and see if something has penetrated the heart or the core of your property.

Dealing With Squatters

I have some dear friends who purchased eighty-one acres in the mountains where he and his wife had a dream of building a ministry and leadership retreat center. Sometimes, we can build dream homes too quickly and then realize that God may want us to move somewhere else and live for Him. When it became a reality that it was not God's timing to build a re-treat center, they put the property up for sale. Eventually, they received a generous offer on the property that would yield them a profit on the sale of the property. During the course of the closing procedures, the prospective buyers found that there were some structures in the back corner of the property. When my friend went to the back of the eighty-one acres to find out what might be happening, he found a huge problem. He found a large shanty, a bunch of old cars, and other junk scattered around the back of his property. Sometime after my friends had purchased this beautiful acreage in the mountains, trespassers had come on to the property and decided to put up a structure. These squatters became so comfortable they built a shanty and brought all of their junk with them.

This is a picture of what happens when we don't take care of our property. If we leave areas of our life unattended, the enemy will come in, trespass, and fill any voids. He will build a nest right under our noses in the unmonitored areas of our soul. My friend got his bobcat dozer, took it to the back of the property, and did a number on the stronghold that had been established. Unfortunately, the buyers backed out of that deal, and my friends eventually had to take a loss on the sale of the land. This is another example of how God's economy works. He can redeem us and cleanse our property, but there still may be consequences stemming from the process of removing the stronghold and re-establishing a clean property.

My Journey to Freedom

Let's go back to the question, "Can a Christian have a demon?" I'll answer it from my personal experience. From a practical standpoint, I was saved in 1998, and I knew I was going to Heaven. It was a true conversion that was supernatural and very real. I was set free from demonic oppression two years later, in December of 2000. Unclean spirits came right up through my body and out of my throat, and it was very real. The effects were very real, and the fruit of my life validated the reality of the matter. If a Christian can't have a demon, how could I have been a man on fire for God from 1998 to the end of 2000, yet go through a process of freedom from demonic oppression that led to even greater transformation?

I know for a fact I was saved in 1998 as I stood in the Houston Astrodome with my heart pounding in my chest and asked Jesus to be my Lord and Savior. I was bawling like a little baby as I threw myself into my dad's arms and told him I was saved and going to Heaven. Yet, in December of 2000, I read a book about spiritual freedom that rocked my thinking in such a way I could see my whole life of setbacks, misfortunes, and unhealthy character traits. It finally made sense to me. I could see real spiritual answers to the consistent negative patterns in my thought life and my actions. I addressed those issues the way Jesus commanded us to address them, and my life has never been the same. The point here is I was genuinely saved in 1998, and I had some additional and authentic spiritual experiences two years later, which led to incredible new levels of freedom in my life. My experiences matched up with the scriptures. It is very Biblical, and it is vividly taught in Matthew, Mark, Luke, and John.

Armor for The Fight

I would pose the question, "If a Christian can't have a demon, why did Paul instruct Christians to put on the whole armor of God?" Armor is for battle, and the armor we are instructed to put on is to extinguish the fiery darts of the enemy. Why does a football player put on his gear? He does so to avoid bodily injury, externally and internally. Why does a hockey player put on his gear? He does so for the same reasons. Why does a police officer put on armor? He does so to prevent the enemy from killing him with a gunshot to his vital organs. How about a soldier? He wears armor into battle, not to get on an airplane and fly home. Throughout all of history, all armor has been solely utilized for the protection of the human body, externally and internally. Armor is used to keep one from being penetrated. Armor does not keep a monkey from jumping on your back. Armor protects you from things designed to penetrate your body and wreck you on the inside; thus, killing you from the inside out. If you are a Christian, and the Bible instructs you to wear armor, there is a reason for it. The reason is there is an enemy who fires away at your life, looking for a way to penetrate your body in order to get to your soul and destroy both soul and body in the process.

The Battle Within

Does alcoholism not destroy both soul and body? What does the Bible say about the drunkard and his soul? What does your knowledge of alcoholism tell you about what it does to the body? Does sexual perversion destroy both soul and body? What does the Bible say about fornication and adultery and how it affects the soul? What does the Bible say about how it affects the body? It can get pretty ugly. Does unforgiveness not destroy both soul and body? Jesus posed a question something like this, "If you cannot forgive your brother, how can your Father in Heaven forgive you?" We cannot enter Heaven with unforgiveness. Jesus died on the cross and sacrificed His life to forgive us as we forgive others. He told us to pray like this, and the caveat happens to be, "...as I forgive others."

When we hold on to unforgiveness and become bitter, it literally leaks out of us towards others. Have you ever seen an authentic Christian who had unforgiveness in their life or bitterness in their life? I have seen plenty. The real question is, have you ever known a Christian that did not deal with having to "let go" of someone or forgive someone for something that had been done to them? Some Christians have held onto this for too long, and it becomes a demonic issue that creates a hold on their life. The battle is within. It is in the heart of a man or woman.

If a Christian can't have a demon, why are so many believers addicted to pornography? Why do pastors and worship leaders have affairs with other women in the church? Why do Christians take antidepressants? If the Bible says, "I did not give you the spirit of fear, but of power and love and of sound mind," then why would a Christian need to take anti-depressants? God can heal mental conditions just as easily as He can heal physical ones. Why do Christians die from cancer? Is cancer Heavenly or demonic? God doesn't give us cancer. God heals us of cancer. The enemy is the one who brings sickness and disease to us. God is not responsible for us eating unhealthy things that have cancer-causing agents in them that could potentially stack up against us and begin to grow. This doesn't mean that if a Christian dies from cancer, they were a bad person or living in sin. I cannot explain all of the mysteries of God. I have seen great Christians die from cancer, and I have seen scores of people miraculously healed of cancer. I just know that cancer is evil.

God says in Matthew 8:16-17, "When evening came, many who were demon-possessed (oppressed/trespassed) were brought to him, and he drove out the spirits with a word and healed all the sick. This was to fulfill what was spoken through the prophet Isaiah: 'He took up our infirmities and bore our diseases'."

The Ultimate Weapon

On the cross, Jesus took up our infirmities and our diseases. Literally, this means, on the cross, Jesus exchanged His wholeness for our sicknesses and diseases. That doesn't mean we aren't or won't be under attack throughout our lifetime. It does require each of us to get a real revelation of God's Word and claim what Jesus did for us on the cross. God never intended for you to hold on to something that Jesus took on the cross on your behalf. If the enemy tries to put things on you that are demonic instead of Heavenly, your job is to recognize it and use the name of Jesus to overcome. Jesus loves to be reminded that you know the rules of the spiritual game or battle in which we are in. He loves it when you use your authority in His name to declare victory over sin, sickness, disease, and death. He went to the cross for it! He did so to reconcile you back to God so that you could obtain the relationship with Him like Adam once had. That was true friendship. That must have been some kind of intimacy. We all must recognize the simplicity of these things that are clearly laid out in God's Word.

The Battlefield of The Mind

It merely takes common sense to figure out that the voice inside of our head is not coming from the outside! It should not be hard to figure out that the wicked thoughts residing in our mind continually are not coming from outside of our body but from the inside of our heart. Yes, demons do exist and function in certain assignments outside of people's bodies. However, our focus is on the demons assigned to get inside people and wreck their lives.

As I stated earlier, the word "heart" in the Greek is "kardia," which means the "core." It refers to the set and center focal point of one's spiritual and physical life. It is used many times in the Bible in reference to this description, being the set and center focal point of one's spiritual and physical being.[3]

Jesus said in Mark 7:21-23, "For from within, out of the heart of men, proceed evil thoughts, adulteries, fornications, murders, thefts, covetousness, wickedness, deceit, lewdness, an evil eye, blasphemy, pride, foolishness. All these evil things come from within and defile a man."

Evidence of What Is Within

When you look at these descriptions, it is relatively easy to assume that these are demonic characteristics. Jesus describes all of these things as evil things, and they come from within a man and flow out of the core of his being. That means there is demonic activity that flows out of a man, Christian or non-Christian. You and I both have seen these things flow out of people we know to be Christian people. To say that a "true Christian" is incapable of being consistently prideful is almost ludicrous. To say that a Christian person has never committed adultery or fornication is virtually insane. This happens all of the time throughout the world. It was happening when Paul was alive. He had to address the believers in the church of Corinth on issues pertaining to the things above. He brought to them necessary correction that would lead to a sanctified life in Christ. He called them brothers, and at the same time, corrected them for their sin. One cannot say, "Well, they weren't Christians then." If that's the case, the Holy Spirit would have directed Paul not to call them brothers in Christ.

The Operator's Manual

We must remember that approximately one-third of the New Testament addresses salvation, and the other two-thirds address the issue of sanctification. There is clear instruction in the New Testament on how to live out the Christian life once one is saved. Part of this includes being set apart and being made holy. The other part entails making disciples of all people throughout the world.

I have never really understood the argument against a Christian having a demon. When we read the scriptures and see that Jesus was clearly the only One who ever lived without sin, it just seems pretty straightforward. Jesus was the only One who could ever say, "The devil has nothing in me." Who else has really ever been able to say that truthfully? I would sure like to hang out with that person! I've met a few who have been very close to this standard, and I loved being around them!

The Battle Within

Going back to my reference to common sense, I believe we have to use common sense in evaluating the question regarding a Christian having a demon. When we read the Bible, we see incredible stories of people overcoming dark and evil forces on a daily basis. However, we don't stop for one moment to think about the fact that we are not experiencing any of those victories over the forces of darkness in our own lives. Do you think there is a spirit of addiction sitting on a tree limb shouting to you, "Hey, you need a drink"? No! That spirit is inside of someone's body, talking to them through their thoughts in the classic battle between the spirit and the flesh. How about sexual fantasy? Do you believe there is a demon standing on your front porch shouting out to you, "Hey, you need to click on this website and look at this pornographic video"? No! That spirit is inside of a person, causing them to have lust of the eyes and lust of the flesh which is flowing from within to get them to succumb to the pornographic viewing and fantasy.

The enemy did not go away 2,000 years ago, nor did all of his minions. We have become joint-heirs with Jesus Christ and are recipients of a new and better covenant. In addition, we are given authority and power over our enemy in the name of Jesus to defeat Satan and his minions in every situation throughout our lives. It is only in our unbelief that we limit our authority to which we have been given access through Jesus Christ. Unbelief and faith do not work together at all. Our unbelief brings us into agreement with the enemy about what he says about us, versus being in agreement with Jesus and what God says about us and our circumstances. When we see defeat, we can trace things back and eventually find unbelief operating somewhere in the midst of our situation. God gets blamed for too many things that we allow to happen in our lives due to our own lack of faith or our unbelief. Most of the time, people have a hard time admitting that they struggled with fear, unbelief, or lack of faith in a situation of defeat.

The point is that the enemy is still roaming about seeking whom he may devour, and he is using his entire army of demons to assist him. His plan and methods of operation have not changed. And Jesus' plan and His methods of operation have not changed either! The good news is that once you understand the playbook, which is the Bible, and put the game plan into action, you win!

Key Points

- True Christians cannot be possessed by demons—but they can be oppressed.

- When an unclean spirit enters a Christian, this is trespassing.

- Demons are attempting to penetrate our spiritual armor to get inside our hearts.

- We are instructed to take every thought captive and examine it.

- Jesus said evil flows out of the heart, from within a person.

Ask Yourself
- What do you think the difference is between demons' assignments today versus 2,000 years ago?"

- Have you seen any other instructions in the bible about how to handle demons differently today versus 2,000 years ago?

- Have you ever felt like a demon has entered your life, specifically causing you trouble in some area?

- Is there anything flowing from within, out of your heart, that you desire to change?

For Further Study
- *Protection from Deception* by Derek Prince

A Divine Appointment

My first experience with deliverance was in 2005. My best friend asked me if I wanted to come over to his house for a deliverance session. The criteria were we had to fast and pray until the night of the event. I met Danny McDaniel that night, and as soon as we stepped into the house, you could feel the presence of the Holy Spirit.

Danny started the night just talking about what Jesus did here on earth. At the end of the night, Danny prayed over me and called out pornography and heart disease. He also grabbed my foot and put oil where I had a heel spur. It felt like a hot poker hitting my foot. He said, "Satan will try to kill you through heart disease, but you will not die!" That night my heel spur was completely gone! Since then, I had a heart attack in 2015, with no heart damage at all! I am grateful for Jesus and the freedom I experienced that night through a man I call my friend.

— Mike, Alabama

CHAPTER TEN

What Did Jesus Do?

> "Because I am committed to the truth of Scripture, I must try
> to understand what Scripture says, even if it transcends my
> own experience."
> — Craig S. Keener[1]

The question is not "What would Jesus do?" The question
is, "What did Jesus do?" Before we discover what Jesus did, it
would be wise to look at a couple of terms that will help us
better understand the teachings of Jesus. The first term is a
Greek word called "sozo." Sozo is a word that appears in the
Bible numerous times throughout the New Testament. Anytime you see the word "saved," the word "healed," or the word
"delivered," it is referring to the Greek word "sozo." Basically,
sozo is a verb that carries out the action of salvation, healing,
and deliverance. Translated in English, it means "salvation" or
"to save." It also translates in English as "to heal," "to make

well," or "to restore." Another translation into English of the word sozo is "to deliver," "to deliver from danger or suffering," or "to deliver from the bondage of sin."[2]

An example of sozo can be found in Mark 16:16, "He who believes and is baptized will be saved, but he who does not believe will be condemned."

Faith is The Key

This passage could also read, "He who believes and is baptized will be healed." It also means, "He who believes and is baptized will be delivered." The Bible says in Romans 10:17, "Faith comes by hearing and hearing by the Word of God." When one receives a revelation from the scriptures that he or she did not have previously, it should lead to an increase in faith. In this case, it would be a greater measure of faith to believe that healing comes with Jesus and that freedom from oppression comes with Jesus.

Another example can be found in Romans 10:13, "For whoever calls on the name of the Lord shall be saved."

Knowing that this word was translated from the Greek word sozo, now insert the words "healed" and "delivered" into this passage. Read the passage aloud to yourself with each of the three words, and listen to yourself as you read it. What does this say about healing? Whoever calls upon the name of the Lord shall be healed. What does this say about your guarantee to be set free from things that oppress you? Whoever calls upon the name of the Lord shall be delivered. That includes you, me, and anyone who calls upon the name of the Lord for deliverance.

One final example is found in Philippians 2:12, "Therefore, my beloved, as you have always obeyed, not as in my presence only, but now much more in my absence, work out your own salvation with fear and trembling."

Believe and Receive

The English word "salvation" is translated from the Greek word "soteria," which means "deliverance." Strong's concordance defines it as rescue or safety (physically or morally): deliver, health, salvation, save, saving.[3] I encourage you to do the same thing with this verse as the last one. Read it by interchanging all three words translated from the Greek and listen to how the passage reads. The revelation that I get from this passage is that we are to walk out our salvation for the rest of our lives, obeying Jesus' commands and abstaining from practicing sin. I also understand that sometimes healing has to be walked out. Sometimes healing is the "process of recovery," as the Bible describes. My job is to receive and believe. If I do my part, God says that He will do His part. It also shows me that I am to walk out my freedom from demonic oppression for the rest of my life.

The Maintenance Plan

Almost everything we acquire in life, including vehicles, appliances, computers, cell phones, and more, has a maintenance plan that accompanies it. I have to change my HVAC filters in our home periodically because the air filters get too dirty to filter clean air efficiently. I have to change out the oil filter on our cars periodically because the oil filter cannot capture any more toxins than it is designed to capture to keep my engine running efficiently. I have to cleanse my body periodically so that I can purge the toxins from my liver and kidneys due to all of the junk that I either breathe in or ingest through food choices. The same principle holds true in our spiritual life. Our goal is to keep the full armor of God on, stay consistent in God's Word, and have a healthy prayer life. If we let our guard down for too long, the enemy could slip a toxin in, and it will eventually need to be addressed.

As you dive into Matthew, Mark, Luke, and John, you will now notice the many accounts of Jesus casting demons out of people. He commanded His disciples to do the same thing, and you have already read that He expects us to teach and to obey all that He commanded as well. The English translation for casting out demons comes from the Greek word, "ekballo." Ekballo means "to cast out" or "to drive out."[4] One gross misunderstanding of how Jesus dealt with demons comes from both Hollywood and the rest of secular society. When the average person thinks or hears about demons, they usually correlate "exorcism" with the word "demon." The devil is probably very pleased about this correlation because it usually strikes fear or uncertainty into the heart of the listener or viewer.

The word "exorcism" is an English translation from the Greek word "exorkizo," which means "to expel evil spirits from a person or place by prayers, adjurations, or religious rites."[5] This word is only used one time in the New Testament. In essence, Jesus was talking about casting out demons from people's lives, or driving them out of people's bodies on command. It is not a prayer. It is a command. The only difference between then and now is that we use Jesus' name by saying, "In the name of Jesus" when we give the command. When we give that command, we have access to all the authority and power connected to the name of Jesus based on God's Word.

One of the first accounts of Jesus casting out a demon occurs in Mark 1:23-28, "Now there was a man in their synagogue with an unclean spirit. And he cried out, saying, 'Let us alone! What have we to do with You, Jesus of Nazareth? Did You come to destroy us? I know who You are—the Holy One of God!' But Jesus rebuked him, saying, 'Be quiet, and come out of him!' And when the unclean spirit had convulsed him and cried out with a loud voice, he came out of him. Then they were all amazed, so that they questioned among themselves, saying, 'What is this? What new doctrine is this? For with authority, He commands even the unclean spirits, and they obey Him.' And immediately His fame spread throughout all the region around Galilee."

Jesus had just begun gathering His new disciples, Simon, Andrew, Phillip, Nathanial, James, and John. They had traveled to Capernaum. He drove the demon out of the man because that was going to be the nature of His ministry. He was modeling to His disciples how they, as well as we, would all minister under this New Covenant that was being established. This is a classic example of the ministry of Jesus.

Authority Through Jesus' Name

I remember ministering to a man one time who had just been released from prison. He was hungry for God, and he wanted to be free from all the things that had held him down for so many years. A friend of mine who had also been in prison introduced us and wanted to help this man get set free. The first thing that happened in our ministry time was that an unclean spirit spoke to me through this man's mouth and said, "I am the spirit of idolatry, and I am not coming out!" Now, I can't replicate the voice that I heard, but it was not this man's voice. I had been in conversation with this man for over an hour before ministering to him. The voice that spoke to me was very demonic. I simply responded, "Yes, you are coming out of him, in Jesus' name; therefore, Idolatry rise up and get out of this man in Jesus' name!" The spirit came out of the man. I was not looking to have a conversation with an unclean spirit, just as Jesus was not particularly looking to have a conversation with an unclean spirit. But when a spirit speaks to me, I just tell it to be quiet and come out of the person in Jesus' name.

When Jesus came out of the wilderness and began to teach in the various synagogues, He came to his hometown of Nazareth. On the Sabbath, Jesus entered the synagogue, and He made a declaration of what His ministry model would look like for the rest of the history of mankind. Luke 4:17-19 says, "And He was handed the scroll of the prophet Isaiah. And when He had opened the scroll, He found the place where it was written: 'The Spirit of the Lord is upon Me, Because He has anointed Me to preach the gospel to the poor; He has sent Me to heal the brokenhearted, To proclaim liberty to the captives And recovery of sight to the blind, To set at liberty those who are oppressed; To proclaim the acceptable year of the Lord'."

This might seem a bit redundant; however, we must break this down into a list to capture the essence and the simplicity of what the ministry of Jesus would look like. In doing so, keep in mind that one person would not come to the earth to do what is described above and not want to see it taught and duplicated throughout the earth for generations to come.

1. God's Spirit was on Him (We need God)
2. He was anointed (analogous to smearing with oil) by God for this purpose
3. To preach the gospel (no favorites)
4. To heal broken hearts (emotional wounds)
5. To proclaim freedom to people taken captive (could be prison and/or religious systems)
6. To open blind eyes (healing)
7. To set free people who are oppressed (demonic oppression)
8. To proclaim that the time is now to believe (in Jesus)

Following Jesus' Example

This is pretty eye-opening because it is Jesus 101. By this I mean, Jesus did nothing His Father did not instruct Him to do. In turn, Jesus expects us to do only that which He commands us to do. Therefore, preaching the gospel, healing emotional wounds, healing people physically, and setting people free are all just part of the Christian way of life. One might ask, "Why is that just part of the Christian way of life?" We walk all around each and every day and witness people who are lost, emotionally hurt, physically ill, and demonically oppressed. With this being the case, life ought not to be that way for people, and we have the power to change it. It is the resurrection power of Jesus Christ who lives in us and gives us the authority to preach this message, as well as use His name to see people healed and set free.

There is a point in this process of gaining new revelation about the ministry of Jesus where you will have to open up the Bible and begin to reread the gospels. In reading the gospels, you will begin to see that Jesus cast out many demons and healed many diseases. You will sometimes notice Jesus had to cast out the demon before the healing could occur. Here is an example from Matthew 9:32-33, "As they went out, behold, they brought to Him a man, mute and demon-possessed. And when the demon was cast out, the mute spoke. And the multitudes marveled, saying, 'It was never seen like this in Israel!'"

Deliverance and Healing

Many times people want to be healed, but they do not realize there may be demonic oppression attached to the physical bondage from which they are suffering. I have a close friend who had come to me for the ministry of deliverance, which is simply the ministry of Jesus. As I prayed for him and cast out spirits that he had carried throughout his life, he had a really neat supernatural encounter with God. During this ministry time, he felt what he thought was fire coming out of his left ear and blew his ear open. You see, he had been 95% deaf in his left ear since he was a tiny boy. Over forty-five years later, God completely opened up his ear. As unclean spirits were getting driven out, healing began to occur in his body. He went on to be healed of color blindness. Through this process of healing, one day, he just began to see all of the colors that he had never been able to see his whole life! He called me on the phone as soon as this happened and was celebrating the miraculous power of God he had just experienced simply through the process of what the scriptures say to do. "They will lay hands on the sick, and they will recover" (Mark 16:18).

In Luke 13, Jesus healed a woman who had been bent over for years with a bad back. Have you ever seen people walking around in public hunched over, knowing that they have a severe back problem? Have you ever thought about the fact it could very well be a spiritual problem causing the physical suffering? Here's how Jesus dealt with this woman's bad back in Luke 13:10-12, "Now He was teaching in one of the synagogues on the Sabbath. And behold, there was a woman who had a spirit of infirmity eighteen years and was bent over and could in no way raise herself up. But when Jesus saw her, He called her to Him and said to her, 'Woman, you are loosed from your infirmity'."

Personal Experiences

I have prayed for numerous people throughout my years in ministry who have had moderate to severe back problems. I have also seen many people miraculously healed. I have been privileged to witness God straightening the backs of people with scoliosis. I have seen God heal people's backs of vertebrae issues and slipped discs. I have seen God heal people who had suffered from chronic back pain without ever being able to pinpoint the origin. In many of these instances, if not almost all, there was a spirit of infirmity involved in the process. The spirit of infirmity had to be cast out in order for healing to be able to take place. It is the unclean spirit that is wreaking havoc from the inside, and I have to obey Jesus' teachings and drive the unclean spirit out of the person to give them a fighting chance to walk in healing.

One time, one of my dear friend's wife received a doctor's report diagnosing her with breast cancer. Here was this beautiful, kind, ultra-successful businesswoman who had just received a report that can literally strike fear in the heart of any human being. My buddy was a close friend I had been mentoring for less than a year. He was raised as a Catholic and grew by leaps and bounds in our Bible study each week. When I heard the news, I told him to get his wife and come to our house as soon as possible. They came immediately, and my wife and I took them up in our theatre room and witnessed to them about the ministry of Jesus for about an hour. During the course of our conversation, I asked her if she had any issues with her mom or sister. I have learned that sometimes breast cancer can be rooted in failed mother/daughter relationships or sibling rivalries that exist in a family. In this case, it was confirmed that these things did exist.[6]

I went on to tell her that Jesus wanted to heal her and set her free from a spirit of bitterness, and then she would be healed of cancer. At the end of my wife and I sharing stories, my buddy responded to all of our teachings and recommendations. He basically said, "The whole time I've been sitting here, I knew this was 'of God,' and I know this is her answer. We are going to get this done, and we are going to get this done right now! The devil is not going to win here, and the devil is not going to take her life! So let's get this done!" This was slightly paraphrased, but it exemplifies the boldness and faith that Jesus wants us to have when we get a revelation of truth!

The Victory

What followed this moment of revelation was a time of prayer for her. We cast out several demons that were networking together to bring sickness and disease into her life, and we commanded healing to occur in her body. Some of those spirits were cancer, infirmity, sickness, disease, death, destruction, bitterness, jealousy, and strife. The results of this were deliverance and healing! She went back to the doctor, received her report, and she was completely cancer-free! This couple soon started their own ministry, which was wildly successful. They still minister to the hearts of people today. They pay it forward. What Jesus did for them, they do for others.

As you read all of these accounts, you should notice that there is no particular formula that Jesus is trying to get you to adhere to, other than to believe in the power of God and use the name of Jesus to do what He did. John testified as it is written in John 21:25, "And there are also many other things that Jesus did, which if they were written one by one, I suppose that even the world itself could not contain the books that would be written. Amen."

Follow The Road Signs to Your Destiny

There are plenty of stories and accounts in the Bible for you to capture the essence of what I am attempting to describe to you. If I used all of these accounts to try to make a point, I would merely be including the four gospels within the pages of this book, and there is no need to do that. This book coincides with the gospels only as a signpost on the road pointing you in the right direction to get to your destination. Sometimes, we need guidance because we have been given too many directions from too many people, which has caused confusion in our lives. As a result, we can occasionally get a little off track from the road to our destiny. I do not know what each reader's particular destiny in life is. However, I do know each of us is to be conformed into the image of Christ throughout our lifetime. Are you ready to discover how that can happen in your life?

Key Points

- The Greek word sozo means salvation, healing, and deliverance.

- Jesus cast out demons to heal people and to model to His disciples.

- Jesus was anointed to preach the good news, heal people, and set captives free.

- Sometimes a spirit has to be cast out before healing takes place.

- We are also Jesus' disciples.

Ask Yourself

- What does it mean to ask, "What did Jesus do?"

- You believed God by faith for your salvation. How much more difficult is it to believe Him for your healing or deliverance? Should it be more difficult?

- Do you believe that Jesus' methods of ministry are to be carried out by you?

TESTIMONY

Getting Rid of The Black Cloud

I found myself battling frustration, anger, and self-imposed guilt on-and-off from past financial and business mistakes that led to an economic spiral. Recovery was taking far longer than I ever anticipated or could imagine, and it was taking a toll physically and emotionally. Every time I started to gain financial traction, setbacks quickly followed like a black cloud and at an odd, unexplainable frequency. I felt stuck and trapped. However, quitting to regain economic stability and freedom for my wife and I was never an option.

The message shared in *Freedom* challenged and stretched my perspective and beliefs. The biblical insights and truths served as powerful keys that unlocked new revelation. Suddenly, everything started to make sense and became crystal clear! I was in a spiritual battle that I would never overcome without God's loving protection, guidance and grace. I gained a deeper understanding of the critical importance of the apostle Paul's teaching in Ephesians 6:10-17 and since then, have experienced real and tangible freedom, not only in financial breakthrough but also emotionally and spiritually.

— Todd, Florida

CHAPTER ELEVEN

How Do Demons Come In?

"...most victims of demonic oppression have been left to suffer without any offer of practical help from the Church."
— Derek Prince[1]

There are various ways that demons can enter into a person's life, but their goal is to get inside of a person, one way or another. Our job is to gain understanding and insight into how these things occur in order to equip ourselves to keep them out of our lives. As I am writing this book, I am in a wonderful little cabin in Moravian Falls, North Carolina, sitting next to a warm fireplace. However, I can hear a little scurrying in the attic space above me. I know for a fact it is either a squirrel or a rat nesting in the attic above. As I listen to the activity in the attic above me, I'm not sure if the owner of the cabin, who graciously allowed me to use it, really wants any varmints nesting in his house. Most people don't, and I count myself among those who do not!

The Unwelcome Attic Dwellers

In 2007, we moved to the Dallas/Ft. Worth area where we leased a house for nine months prior to purchasing our home. During that time, after all of the lights would go out and we would all get quiet in our beds, we would begin to hear noises in the attic. For quite some time, I would just tell my wife, "Oh honey, it's just squirrels, and it's cold, so we won't bother them because they aren't bothering us." There are a couple of problems with this kind of thinking. First, I did not own the home; therefore, I did not care enough about the problem. I was willing to compromise due to my lack of ownership in the property. Secondly, I failed to consider that small varmints usually multiply quickly. In this case, the nighttime noise got louder and louder, so I ventured into the attic to discover that our entire attic was full of rats!

I went to Ace Hardware and bought rat traps immediately, and I went to war with the rats in our attic. I wanted all of those rats gone because they were nasty, full of diseases, and the nastiness was being passed on through the atmosphere of our home. The rat urine would penetrate the ceilings, and elements of their nastiness would be spread through our HVAC system. It took months of me battling to catch one rat at a time. During this process, I also had to go outside and look for any openings in the home and seal them up with spray foam. I had to prevent more rats from getting in while driving out all of the existing rats.

If this happened to you, I would assume you would have the same attitude. No one wants rats in their attic or mice in their home. There's something that just makes you feel like your home is being defiled when these creatures find their way in and start gnawing away at your stuff. Well, this is exactly how spiritual warfare is depicted. There are unclean spirits, just like rats, looking for openings to enter your home and begin to gnaw away at your life. They work under the radar, meaning that you rarely can recognize what they are up to. They are hiding in the attic of one's flesh and soul, working covertly to bring destruction to your spiritual house. When you find out about them, are you going to treat them like you would rats in the attic? I would certainly hope so. In order to take action toward your better future, it takes a genuine hunger for truth and a real disgust for the enemies who want to defile your life.

A Generational Curse

One of the first ways unclean spirits find their way into one's life is through ancestral lines. In other words, they can find their way in through a generational curse that runs through a family lineage. This would mean that the spirits can come into a person while they are in their mother's womb. The person never asked for the demon, but the demon had permission based upon the parents' rebellion or the rebellion of other ancestors.

The Bible says this about generational curses in Exodus 20:3-6, "You shall have no other gods before Me. You shall not make for yourself a carved image — any likeness of anything that is in Heaven above, or that is in the earth beneath, or that is in the water under the earth; you shall not bow down to them nor serve them. For I, the Lord your God, am a jealous God, visiting the iniquity of the fathers upon the children to the third and fourth generations of those who hate Me, but showing mercy to thousands, to those who love Me and keep My commandments."

Before we go any further, let's take a look at the new covenant so that we don't get led astray here. In Galatians 3:13, the Bible says, "Christ has redeemed us from the curse of the law, having become a curse for us (for it is written, 'cursed is anyone who hangs on a tree')." It is clear in scripture that Jesus came to take the curse for us by hanging on the cross. In turn, this redeems us from the curse of the law.

Now let's take a look at a situation in the book of Matthew where Jesus was preaching the greatest sermon ever spoken called "The Sermon on the Mount." This was the first time Jesus was now publicly teaching and preaching to the masses, so it must have been matters of great importance. In Matthew 5:17-20, the Bible states, "Do not think that I came to destroy the Law or the Prophets. I did not come to destroy but to fulfill. For assuredly, I say to you, till Heaven and earth pass away, one jot or one tittle will by no means pass from the law till all is fulfilled. Whoever therefore breaks one of the least of these commandments, and teaches men so, shall be called least in the kingdom of Heaven; but whoever does and teaches them, he shall be called great in the kingdom of Heaven. For I say to you, that unless your righteousness exceeds the righteousness of the scribes and Pharisees, you will by no means enter the kingdom of Heaven."

Breaking it down, it looks like this:

1. Jesus did not destroy the Law (Ten Commandments)
2. He came to fulfill the Law
3. Until God sends Him back
4. Do not break the commandments or lead others to do so
5. Follow the commandments, and teach others to do so
6. Your "right-standing" with God must exceed that of the Old Testament lovers of God
7. Jesus raised the standard, but He is the standard; therefore, in Him we can do all things

A Call to Righteousness

Jesus came to fulfill the law of Moses. He preached that our righteousness was to exceed that of the scribes and Pharisees. Now, we are not to even lust after another person, or it will be considered adultery. In Old Testament times, adultery was only considered adultery if one committed the physical act of adultery. Under the law of Moses, one could only be convicted of murder if the physical act of murder took place. Now, we cannot even hold on to our anger for too long without a cause. That in itself would now be considered murder according to scripture. Therefore, this is all pointing to the fact that Jesus calls us as Christians to a higher standard of righteousness.

By hanging on the cross, He fulfilled the law of Moses. Because of His sacrifice on the cross, we are now able to be reconciled back to God, and we have the power of Jesus Christ living within us. Paul said in Romans 8:11, "But if the same spirit of Him who raised Jesus from the dead dwells in you, He who raised Christ from the dead will also give life to your mortal bodies through His spirit who dwells in you." Because the Holy Spirit dwells in us, we have the power to exceed the law of Moses. The Holy Spirit lives in us and among us in order to manifest Jesus Christ to the world, who is our standard and example. Therefore, we are expected to have exceedingly high moral standards, just as Jesus did.

Blessings and Curses in Families

This has a whole lot to do with blessings and curses because we sometimes see consistent patterns of failure in our lives or in our families that do not match up to the standard of righteousness depicted by Jesus in Matthew 5. There are entire books written on blessings and curses and what Christians need to know. The best one I have ever read is *Blessing or Curse* by Derek Prince. It is a must-read for all Christians, and it can give you so many details about how blessings and curses affect people's lives.

After I got delivered in December of 2000, I began searching online for teachings about deliverance, and the first person I stumbled across was Derek Prince. I found that he was an international Bible scholar who had written more than fifty books and some were published in over 100 different languages. He had two books of particular interest to me: *Blessing or Curse: You Choose* and *They Shall Expel Demons.* I ordered his books, cassette tapes, and video teachings to begin studying more about blessings and curses and spiritual freedom. I must say that a great deal of what I learned early on came from the things I learned from Derek Prince, as his teachings pointed me toward things in the Bible that I needed to see. Sometimes I have wondered why in the world I am writing a book on deliverance when there are materials out there to read from Derek Prince, but I also know that God instructed me to write this book, so I can't overthink the process. I can recommend that you read Derek Prince's book on blessings and curses or even go online and watch his teachings about blessings and curses.

More Than a Coincidence

On a personal note, as I learned about curses and how they affect people's lives for generations, I began to see the consistent patterns of failure that existed in my family ancestry. The same held true for my wife and her family ancestry. We learned from Derek Prince's teaching that there were seven major areas of curses (empowerment to fail) described in the Bible, and we learned that we could be subject to any or all of them. My wife and I were already Christians, and we enjoyed chasing God with every bit of our being. However, we quickly saw areas of our lives that matched up to what we could now clearly see as patterns in our ancestries. For example, I could look at my family tree and see that my entire family tree had been through divorces, including horizontally with my two sisters. They were both divorced and remarried. I was one of the only people in my ancestry not divorced, which showed me that a generational curse of family breakdown had been initiated in my family lines somewhere. Where there is a curse, demons follow. In looking at my wife Diane's family tree, there was virtually no divorce with the exception of one divorce horizontally to her.

Unclean spirits are always going to be lurking around, like hyenas on a lion's kill, waiting for the opportunity to devour someone. They can only do this if they have permission or legal right based upon someone breaking God's laws. I also looked at my family tree and noticed a lot of death from sickness and disease, such as cancer, running in my family. There was obviously a curse of sickness and disease running in my family lines. My dad eventually died of cancer, and my sister also died of cancer at the age of fifty-three. I also noticed there was a real pattern of emotional breakdown and mental illness in my family lines. I could see how it had tried so desperately to affect me through the years and how it had tried to affect my sisters as well. It was apparent in my own life that there had been spirits operating in my life since I was a little boy as a result of ancestral curses.

In looking at my wife Diane's family lineage, we noticed a significant amount of death and destruction in her family lines. Multiple suicides and multiple tragic deaths were running in her ancestral lines, yet there were no suicides or tragic deaths anywhere in my ancestry. This was no coincidence to us.

Breaking Generational Curses

Although this is not an exhaustive teaching on blessings and curses, I want to give you enough basic information to understand that generational curses can operate in a person's life. They can also be forever broken in the powerful name of Jesus

Christ! When this revelation alerted me to generational curses and their effects upon a family lineage, I prayed to break all of these types of curses in Jesus' name. Now, we have a family that lives solely under the blessing of Abraham, Isaac, and Jacob.

If you consider the fact that Jesus did not come to abolish the law, but to fulfill it, the following passage in Deuteronomy 30:11-20 will make total sense, "For this commandment which I command you today is not too mysterious for you, nor is it far off. It is not in Heaven, that you should say, 'Who will ascend into Heaven for us and bring it to us, that we may hear it and do it?' Nor is it beyond the sea, that you should say, 'Who will go over the sea for us and bring it to us, that we may hear it and do it?' But the word is very near you, in your mouth and in your heart, that you may do it. 'See, I have set before you today life and good, death and evil, in that I command you today to love the Lord your God, to walk in His ways, and to keep His commandments, His statutes, and His judgments, that you may live and multiply; and the Lord your God will bless you in the land which you go to possess. But if your heart turns away so that you do not hear, and are drawn away, and worship other gods and serve them, I announce to you today that you shall surely perish; you shall not prolong your days in the land which you cross over the Jordan to go in and possess. I call Heaven and earth as witnesses today against you, that I have set before you life and death, blessing and cursing; therefore choose life, that both you and your descendants may live; that you may love the Lord your God, that you may obey His voice, and that you may cling to Him, for He is your life and the length of your days; and that you may dwell in the land which the Lord swore to your fathers, to Abraham, Isaac, and Jacob, to give them'."

Examining The Family Tree

God has always given us a choice, and He has made it clear that we have the power to choose life and blessing by loving

Him completely, obeying His voice, and clinging to Him all the days of our lives. When we choose otherwise, we can affect future generations, as you read previously in Exodus 20. When you read "the sins of the fathers are passed down through the third and fourth generations to those that hate Him," one has to start doing some math. At the time of this book being written, four generations back in your lineage could be as far back as the late 1800s. That actually totals up to thirty ancestors! The question one has to ask is, "Do I know what my great, great grandfather (four generations ago) was up to in 1900?" He could have been a major alcoholic, drinking, gambling, and coming home to beat on his wife. He could have been an adulterer or a rapist. He could have killed someone in cold blood. He could have been a thief, stealing money and goods from business establishments and others. If any of these are true, he would have invoked a curse upon his third and fourth generations of descendants.

This vicious cycle can continue due to the sins of the next generation, thus passing down the curse to another generation, three and four levels down. All of this produces patterns in ancestries that can be easily identified. They can be identified by similarities in outcomes of failure in family trees. It's very similar to a crime scene investigation. If you are gutsy enough to conduct a "spiritual CSI" through your family lineage, you can find a lot about the root of failures that might have occurred in your lifetime. Better yet, you can find the solution for resolving these patterns of failure and turn them into blessings. With all of this said, someone else's sin is not an excuse for us to sin or an excuse for negative choices that we have made. However, spiritual forces of wickedness play a role in carrying out negative choices and patterns that allow demonic entry into a person's life, even from an ancestral curse.

The word "curse" occurs 230 times in various forms throughout the Bible, so God must want to make sure that He gets our attention in this matter. The word "curse" comes from the Hebrew word called "qelalah" or "qala" which means "cursed or lightly esteemed."[2] It is a lowered position that represents an empowerment to fail. People love to be empowered, but no one likes to be empowered to fail.

Blessings and Curses

There are seven major forms of curses that we can take from studying scripture, and I give credit to the late Derek Prince for how this is categorized.[3] The following table is taken from Deuteronomy 28:

Blessings	Curses
Exaltation	Humiliation
Reproductiveness	Barrenness
Health	Sickness/Disease
Prosperity	Poverty/Failure
Victory	Defeat
Authority (Head)	Helplessness (Tail)
Above (Strength)	Weakness (Beneath)

In addition, Derek Prince taught there are seven major marks of a curse. This is not Christian doctrine but merely a summation of what we read about in Deuteronomy. When one is trying to determine whether there is a curse operating in one's life or not, it is always best to go to God and ask Him. The Holy Spirit knows all things, teaches all things, and brings all things into remembrance. This is only information being given in order to obtain greater depths of applicable knowledge. After all, Hosea 4:6 says, "My people are destroyed for lack of knowledge. Because you rejected knowledge, I will reject you from being priest for Me; because you have forgotten the law of your Lord God, I also will forget your children."

Here are the seven major marks of a curse:[4]

1. Mental or emotional breakdown

2. Repeated or chronic sickness

3. Female problems

4. Breakdown of marriage or family alienation

5. Continued financial insufficiency

6. Being accident-prone

7. History of unnatural deaths or suicide

Once again, I will leave it up to God to reveal what He wants to reveal to you. I am merely one of His ambassadors, but I am not God. I do know that when you see a consistent pattern, over and over in one of these areas, it can be a strong indication that a curse could be in effect. Also remember, wherever there is a curse, there will be demons that have been granted permission to torment in those specific areas.

Steps to Freedom

The solution for breaking curses and sealing up your spiritual house from anything ever affecting your life or your children's lives is to pray a prayer to break curses and then deal with any demonic influences involved in those areas. Let me give you an illustration of how curses can affect a person's life. Jesus hung on the cross to take all of our sins. He became accursed so that we can be blessed. Yet, when we sin, it is as though we go to the cross where Jesus gave his life and say, "Jesus, I'll take that sin back." Now, you and I both know we would never literally do this. However, think about how many times we have figuratively done this when we lied, gossiped, stole something, murdered in our heart, lusted in a perverse way, fantasized uncontrollably, fornicated, committed adultery, hated, held on to unforgiveness, or any other sin that could be mentioned. What Jesus paid for on the cross, we take back by our actions. Jesus certainly doesn't want it to be this way, and I believe that He will gladly take every single burden of sin and ancestral sin. In turn, He desires to shower us with His mercy, grace, and blessing.

At the end of this book, you will find a prayer for breaking curses that you can read out loud to God if you are ready to apply the blood of Jesus to every situation in your life. The prayer is a general prayer covering all seven major areas of curses and all seven forms of curses. You may not feel as though all of these apply to you; however, there is nothing in the prayer that can hurt you! I would recommend that anyone who reads it to break curses reads the whole prayer just to cover "all the bases," as one might say.

This is just the first area or open door that the enemy can use to penetrate the life of a person. In the case of generational curses, these were doorways opened by a parent or another ancestor, and those spiritual issues were never resolved. Once you have knowledge of how the enemy has possibly infiltrated your life through a generational curse, you have the power of choice in how to deal with it. I, personally, choose to err on the side of using the name of Jesus Christ to pray against any legal judgments the accuser (the devil) has put on my descendants or me. Freedom from generational curses is available to you, and you have the power to deal with it through the name of Jesus. Don't wait another minute to step into the freedom that awaits you!

Key Points

- Unclean spirits are like rats in your attic—working under the radar to cause destruction.

- Demons sneak in like rats through any opening they can find in your spiritual house.

- Generational curses can operate in a family lineage.

- There are seven major areas of curses that can affect your life and family.

- Curses can be broken for good through the power of the name of Jesus and His blood.

Ask Yourself

- Have any "rats" gotten into your life through ancestral lines?

- Do you recognize any patterns of curses in your family tree?

- Do you realize that you have the ability to break any and all ancestral curses that have ever affected you or your family in the name of Jesus?

For Further Study

- *Blessing or Curse: You Choose* by Derek Prince

TESTIMONY

Liberated From Darkness

Walking through freedom has, by far, been the most significant "line-in-the-sand moment" for me. I walked in that day as a twenty-year-old girl who had struggled her whole life with addiction, chronic depression, a failing marriage, and generational baggage, which I had absolutely no idea I could actually have a life apart from them.

Every part of my life was broken, right down to my body. I had grown up around "church," yet lived completely separated from true life that was transformative and liberating. That hopelessness was devastating until freedom. There was generation after generation of things unraveled that day within my spirit, soul, and body. I walked out completely set free from a life dictated by darkness into a life radically transformed by the liberating power of Jesus. Generational cycles gone. Chronic depression gone. Completely healed from years of failed attempts of corrective kidney surgery. Twenty years later, I still walk in this freedom within my family, my body, my mind, and ministry.

— Meagan, Texas

The Rest of The Doors

"Satan rules over all rebels; thus, those who rebel against God are under the dominion of Satan. You do not have to vote for Satan. All that is required is a vote against God; the moment you do that, even if only in your heart, you elect Satan by default as your ruler."
— Derek Prince[1]

Any involvement with the occult can open spiritual pathways for a demon or multiple demons to enter your life. God is a jealous God, and He does not share Himself with false gods of any kind. He is a supernatural God, and He has no tolerance for us using wicked powers to manipulate things in the spiritual realm. He is the sole source of spiritual power.

Speaking of this, the Bible says in Deuteronomy 18:10-12, "There shall not be found among you anyone who makes his son or his daughter pass through the fire, or one who practices witchcraft, or a soothsayer, or one who interprets omens, or a sorcerer, or one who conjures spells, or a medium, or a spiritist, or one who calls up the dead. For all who do these things are an abomination to the Lord, and because of these abominations the Lord your God drives them out from before you."

Deception and Lies

I have been able to minister to many people who have had in-depth involvement with the occult. Ones who went as deep as Satanism have had a hard time believing that they can be forgiven. This is the exact lie the devil wants them to believe. They are usually told time and time again that they cannot be forgiven for all of the wicked things they have done. They are told there is no turning back, and God could never redeem them. The enemy tells them God could not and would not ever love them again. Demons lie to them repeatedly in an attempt to convince them they are condemned and have no chance of ever being saved. They hear things from demons such as, "How could God ever forgive you for all of the horrible things you've done?" The list goes on. However, God can and will forgive any person for their involvement with witchcraft or the occult because there is no limit to God's willingness to forgive. If one truly repents and believes, God forgives.

Practicing anything related to witchcraft or the occult will immediately unlock the door for demons to come into one's life. When God's Word is violated in this manner, demons know that they have been invited to the party and waltz right into one's life. In doing so, they gain a foothold in a person's life, and continued practice of anything related to witchcraft or the occult leads to a stronghold. When we were kids, we used to own a Ouija Board, which is considered by many to be a game. Like many people, we didn't know any better so we would practice speaking to the game piece on the board. Even out of ignorance, when we did this, it opened up spiritual doorways in our lives for a spirit of rebellion (witchcraft) to enter. The devil doesn't care whether you are ignorant or not. He only cares if you partake of his little schemes, and then he uses it against you. During the same time, we also used to light candles and have séances with our friends because we thought it was intriguing and fun. Little did we know at the time, we were opening up spiritual portals of evil into our homes and our bodies.

An Encounter With The Demonic Realm

I once ministered to a man who had joined a Satanic cult, and he literally entered into a vow to sell his soul to the devil as a teenager. When I got to know him, he had been a Christian for a few years, but he struggled greatly with condemnation. He continually battled in his mind whether he was really saved or not. Unclean spirits were always telling him inside of his head that he could not go to Heaven. These spirits told him lie after lie that continued to leave him feeling ashamed and condemned. On the other hand, he loved God immensely. He was faithful in his service to God, and he loved worshiping God in church. He was simply tormented by the voices working on him from within.

When I ministered to him and began to cast the first demon out of him, his eyes turned blood red, and he started growling at me like a mad animal. It would almost be a growl like you would hear on an X-Men movie. He began to lean toward me as he growled and sneered. In an instant, I knew I was either going to get attacked, or I was going to use the name of Jesus to stop that demon in its tracks. The Lord spoke through me because I immediately told the demon to be quiet, called it by name, and commanded it to come out in the name of Jesus. I commanded about three or four more high-ranking demonic spirits related to Satanism to come out of him, and after that, he was completely exhausted. He laid on the floor for a few minutes completely lifeless, just as a similar account in Mark 9:26. At the time, all of this was relatively new to me, and I did not know anything about Satanism or some of the spirits that I called out of him. The Holy Spirit definitely spoke for me and through me in that hour.

Changed In a Moment

This man went home to rest, and when I followed up with him, he was so excited. He could not stop telling people how his life was transformed in such a quick moment. He worked closely with the pastor of his church, a church with several thousand people. He tried to talk his pastor into preaching more about deliverance. His pastor, who would consider himself a charismatic pastor, was not too excited about helping people in his church get set free from demonic oppression. He was very happy for his friend, but he did not want to cause a "stirring" with any people in his church over deeper spiritual issues. He told my friend that if he addressed these deeper issues, too many men living in sexual sin would wind up leaving the church, and the pastor even mentioned how it would affect the offerings in church.

The problem I have with this situation is we are called to believe what Jesus said to believe and do what Jesus said to do. I did not write the rules; Jesus did. Seminary did not write the rules; Jesus did. Ministry is not always easy, but brokenhearted people need healing and captives need liberty.

Another Point of Entry

Another way that can open doors for unclean spirits to enter into one's life is through prenatal influences such as rejection and fear. When a pregnant woman or a couple does not want a baby and voice this, a spirit of rejection can instantly access the womb and bring torment. When a woman or couple has fears related to the pregnancy, spirits of fear can enter the womb. It may be that one or both has voiced fear of an early miscarriage, fear of birth defects, or fear of death. This can open the door for spirits of fear to gain access.

Since I have become accustomed to ministering as Jesus tells us to minister, I have witnessed so many wonderful child births and so many peaceful children. Proverbs 18:20 says, "Death and life are in the power of the tongue, and those that love it eat the fruit thereof." Our words have a serious impact on other people's lives, especially our children's. When a Christian couple ministers to a baby in the womb and speaks words of life over the child, they will usually experience a child-rearing season of peace and harmony. Parents will witness and experience better sleep patterns in their infant, as well as less sickness and strange occurrences. Parents who have spoken words of negativity over children in the womb — words of death and words related to fear — stand a chance of dealing with a much more troubled infant. There are also things like arguing, screaming, and fighting, exposing them to secular music such as rock music, industrial music, or rap music that can have serious adverse effects on an infant's behavior, once born.

When our oldest son was born, my wife and I were not serving God. We did not speak any words of death, fear, or rejection over our son. However, we did party a lot, so we listened to a lot of unhealthy rock music. I even remember going with my wife to Deep Ellum in Dallas to a bar to watch my best friend play a music gig. My best friend was a rocker, so the music was extremely loud and hard. I remember our son kicking my wife like crazy in the womb that night. We laughed about it as if he was as excited as we were about listening to my best friend play his rock-and-roll gig.

Our son had a pretty rough first year due to our unhealthy lifestyle. His nights were tough. He cried a lot and sometimes just screamed a lot, and we did not have answers. We only knew to look for medical reasons why our son was so disturbed at night. The facts were he was being tormented by unclean spirits as a result of his father and mother's sins. There was a period of time that he screamed all night long for a week straight and would only sleep during the day when we were at work. Those were tormenting spirits trying to drive us to do things parents should not do to their children. When you are tired, haven't slept in days, and your kid is screaming uncontrollably, the temptation to squeeze them and shake them is there. This happens in some kids' lives. Fortunately, we did not do that to our son, but we were certainly tempted to do so.

The Toy With No Batteries

Also, during his first year of life, I woke up one night to one of his stuffed animals playing music as the red heart on the stuffed bear was lighting up while the music was playing. The irony of the story is that when I went into our son's room to stop the bear from playing music, there were no batteries in it. And you only think it happens in the movies? When we make unrighteous choices and expose our children to our sinful ways, they reap what we sow. They, too, become victims of demonic influence due to the unhealthy choices we make. Fortunately, we have the power to change our circumstances and change the circumstances in the lives of our children.

By the time we had our third son in 1999, we had both gotten saved and were on fire for God. We only listened to Christian music, and our house always had a peaceful atmosphere. As a result, our third son had an incredibly peaceful infancy. There is a lot to be said about open doors for the enemy to take aim in the life of an unborn child or infant.

The Doorway of Soulish Domination

The next possibility of how an unclean spirit can enter into a person's life originates through the soulish domination of another. One of the primary examples of soulish domination is an overprotective mother (or parent). An overly protective mother tends to hover over her child, anticipating and directing his or her every move. The child's life is full of rules and directives such as:

"Don't do that."

"Stop that, or you are going to get hurt."

"If you do that you are going to break your neck."

"I told you to stay right here close to me."

"Come over here so I can see you." (to an extreme)

"Don't go too far because I need to see you." (to an extreme)

"Slow down, or you are going to fall and break something."

An Overprotective Mom

This list of soulish domination statements can go on for pages. The person raised in an overprotective, controlled environment can make an unending list of statements such as the ones I showed you. I know because I was one of those kids. I love my mom, and I honor my mom. However, my childhood was riddled with overprotectiveness. I am only sharing this with you to relate to you as a reader, not dishonoring my mother. My mom was psychotic for the first thirty-five years of my life. She had issues that I did not understand until I got set free and received the promise of the Holy Spirit (Acts 1:8).

I grew up as a coach's son in small towns throughout south and west Texas. I say "towns" because we moved a lot. Eventually, I learned that we moved a lot because my mom was never happy. In her opinion, every town "hated" her. She never had any friends, and she was always depressed because she felt like the world was against her. Some of these towns were so small there was only one yellow blinking caution light at the main intersection or only one red light in the whole town in others. Yet, I could not venture too far from home because of my mom's constant need to watch over me. We lived where a boy like me could have roamed about all over the countryside on foot or on a bike. I could have been an avid fisherman as a child or an avid hunter with all of the wilderness that was right out of our back doors. But my mom lived in great fear that I would get hurt if I ventured too far off. She greatly feared that one of her children might get hurt or killed. Therefore, she did everything in her power to keep us close to her side as long as she was awake. I could not even have a BB gun! This is a mild account of how it was, but you probably get the idea behind the point that I am trying to make.

Living With Fear

As a result, I lived in great fear, and I did not know why. I was scared of the dark. I believed that monsters were always in my closet and under my bed. I was so scared of the dark and monsters that I usually remained paralyzed in fear at night. If I had to go to the bathroom during the night, I was too scared to get up, so I would just pee in my bed or lean over and pee on the floor because I was so fear-stricken. I found myself constantly trying to sleep beside my dad and lay on his arm as much as he would allow me. I would even crawl into my parent's room and sleep under the bed in order to feel safe at night if I could pull it off without them catching me.

These fears grew as I got older and spilled into other areas of my life. I became terrified of heights. I feared confrontation of all kinds. I was severely bullied (which is physical and soulish domination), and as a result, I backed down when any kid confronted me with fighting. In our era, fighting was very common, and it usually sorted out all of the problems any two kids might be having. I still believe that defending yourself from bullies is highly necessary to ward off future attackers and to ward off the enemy from attacking your soul and your mind with fear. I remember being totally scared of the dark when I had to walk home at night from our school to our house, which was less than two blocks. I was also scared to go outside at night anywhere around my house. Basically, if you can name a type of fear, I had it. I felt like I was completely eaten up with fear, and I knew it. As a result, a part of me was very miserable and unhappy inside.

I had so much fear, anxiety, and worry that it robbed me from enjoying my first nineteen years of life. As you can see, this is not Godly. This scenario is demonic, meaning that demonic forces were plaguing the early years of my life. At the age of nineteen, I went through a series of very unpleasant tests with gastrointestinal specialists to find out that I had bleeding ulcers and ulcerative colitis. I was also misdiagnosed with Crohn's Disease. All of the medical disorders I was experiencing were the result of spiritual problems. Anxiety, worry, fear, and stress are major contributors to gastrointestinal disorders, and unclean spirits work inside of people to wreck their bodies internally.[2] Many physical issues are the manifestation of fiery darts of the enemy penetrating one's body and soul and spreading the poison in which they carry. In other words, they carry out their assignment.

The Power of Manipulation

Manipulation by others can open doors just as an overprotective parent can because manipulation by others wounds the soul. Suppose we allow ourselves to be manipulated by an employer or by a supervisor. In that case, it can open up areas of our lives that can allow an unclean spirit to enter and begin to get a foothold. The foothold will usually begin with frustration, and if it continues, it will lead to resentment. From there, unclean spirits work in groupings. Their role is to carry out specific assignments, and they have names and ranks that signify this particular order, which will be covered more in-depth in another chapter. When resentment grows and becomes a stronghold, it can be accompanied by bitterness, anger, hate, revenge, retaliation, and the like.

It always depends on the type of manipulation being used as to what kind of unclean spirits find access to one's life. Sometimes, a teenage girl might find herself being completely manipulated by one of her friends, who always has to be in control of her peers. She then might make decisions based out of fear rather than wisdom. This can open doors as well. This kind of peer pressure greatly affects the minds of youth. When thoughts are not taken captive unto the obedience of Christ, Satan can establish footholds in a young person's soul that can lead to wrong choices, anxiety, depression, and more, not to mention sexual sin.

Don't Surrender to The Wrong Authority

When we subject ourselves or succumb to domineering or manipulative people, we run the risk of the enemy attempting to infiltrate our lives with unclean spirits. I am certainly not saying that every time we are manipulated or dominated, we get trespassed by a demon in our soul or flesh. However, I am saying that one needs to be aware of the potential that stems from succumbing to constant manipulation, control, or domination patterns. God did not design us to be manipulated, controlled, or dominated. This is much different than being disciplined, obedient, and submitted to proper authority. There is safety in Godly obedience. There is also safety in loving discipline, and there is safety in being submitted to proper authority.

Behind Closed Doors

Pressures in early childhood are another way that unclean spirits can enter into one's life. In fact, this is an extremely common occurrence. Disharmony in the home swings the door wide open for the enemy to invade a family's home. When the enemy can invade a home, he can send unclean spirits into people's bodies and souls. A chaotic and dysfunctional home is a breeding ground for demons. There are very few things more dangerous for a child other than witnessing strife between parents. When children see and hear their parents screaming at each other, their minds begin to wonder about divorce. Stress, tension, chaos, dysfunction, disorder, abuse, screaming, and fighting in the home bring an array of possible attacks from the enemy on the home. Insecurity in the children can quickly become a factor. Children become very insecure about the family unit, the future, and even their safety. Insecurity is an unclean spirit, and along with it, that spirit tries to bring all sorts of fear and rejection. Spirits of death and suicide can even come into play at times. In my house growing up, suicide was a very common word. In fact, I heard the statement, "I'm going to kill myself," from my mom and one of my sisters scores of times growing up. I can't tell you how many times I lay in bed with a pillow over my head, hoping that the chaos happening around me would end.

The Price of Ignorance

Rebellion is a spirit that preys upon early childhood pressures. When a man does not have his house in order, he opens his castle gate to the opposing army to march right in and plunder his home. He may be doing it out of ignorance, but the enemy does not care if one is ignorant or not. All he is looking for is a legal right to enter. The apostle Paul stated in 2 Corinthians 2:11, "Lest Satan should take advantage of us; for we are not ignorant of his devices." He was teaching on forgiving others, but this statement he made to the church of Corinth happens to apply to any subject regarding unclean spirits. Please do not be ignorant of his devices because what you don't know can hurt you! Because my dad did not keep his home in order, our entire home was subject to chaos. I loved my dad and we had an incredible relationship. He was a great father to his son, but he was ignorant in several areas. It cost him much grief. It cost him grief in his marriage, and it caused him grief in dealing with the sins of his children. I could go into detail about my siblings and me; however, it doesn't require a lot of intelligence to imagine what kind of sins that kids in dysfunctional homes can get involved in. We were no different.

We went to church every time the doors opened ... twice on Sundays and once on Wednesday nights. On the home front, nothing matched up with what we were supposed to be experiencing on Sundays and Wednesday nights. When children live in a home where things don't match up, this leads to a much greater dilemma than inconsistency. It leads to outright rebellion. Kids will sit in their home and calculate how they can break free from the chaotic environment or the disorder of the home. If parents are strong enough to contain most things, the spirit of rebellion that was let into the home will be patient, knowing it will have its day. Then one day, Jack will come out of the box.

The Person Behind The Perception

For me, I was what most adults would consider a great kid. I was involved in every type of athletic and academic activity. I was in the band, and I was part of FFA. I did it all. However, there were always devious thoughts stirring inside of me. I could not wait to get out on my own so that I could explore all of the possibilities associated with my calculated deviant thoughts. The first day I left home for college, I bought a bottle of whiskey and a case of beer, and my friends and I got blasted. This became a consistent pattern in my life that led to so many other things, including sexual promiscuity, recreational drugs, stealing, lying, cheating, and all things related to them. The root of these issues stemmed from early childhood pressures.

Doors were opened early in my life that created instability in my spiritual life that could have protected my soul. My family lived in the flesh, and when a family lives in the flesh, they carry out the works of the flesh (Galatians 5:19-21).

I am not advocating that every work of the flesh will bring demonic control into one's life. The Holy Spirit will have to answer that one for you. There is a huge difference between a single occurrence of our fleshly nature acting out, versus consistent patterns. If you notice, I have used the word consistent patterns frequently in this book. I believe that consistent patterns have much to do with spiritual doors being opened in one's life, giving demons access to the flesh and soul.

God's Plan of Protection

A father's role or a single parent's role is to protect the home with Godly order. This happens through prayer, reading God's Word, obeying His Word, and learning how to love as Jesus did. Love is the greatest protection against enemy infiltration, and the home should be the greatest area of God's love being reflected toward each other. The enemy hates love, but he cannot infiltrate one's life or one's children's lives when the love of Jesus flows through that person consistently.

If a father is not protecting the home with Godly order, God's love, and loving discipline, the home looks a lot like what we see with prison. Depending upon how many children one has, we have two or three little prison cells called "bedrooms," where we imprison our children for eighteen years. Meanwhile, they are calculating and scheming how they might escape, and if they can't escape, they are devising their plans for what they will do when they finally get out of the chaotic house to which they have been imprisoned. It's really like a prison with no rehabilitation program to shape and transform a prisoner's life so that he or she can live life to the fullest, thinking righteous thoughts and making righteous choices. Righteous parenting sets an atmosphere for safety in the home, protecting the children from the massive schemes of the devil.

The Door of Emotional Weakness

Another area that makes one vulnerable for penetration by the enemy is found in moments of weakness, emotionally or physically. If someone is so tired and weary that they may feel like giving up in a situation, this can open the door to spirits that affect the mind. I refer to them as mind-binding spirits because their assignment is to bind up the mind demonically. It may start with the simple fact that one is grieving over the death of a loved one. Grieving does not bring in demonic spirits because grieving is natural. However, because of the fatigue and weariness, if one does not have a relationship with God or does not maintain an attitude of intimacy of some sort with God, demons will lurk around that situation like hyenas waiting for a slip up. If we don't allow God to bring us through this process of grieving, we can take on spirits of heaviness, depression, despair, gloom, and the like. As the days and months go by, we get to a point where we just can't shake off the frustration and depression, and we don't know why. Ultimately, if not taught where the root of the problem is and how to deal with it permanently, one is likely to begin taking a prescription for some psychotropic drug that will temporarily alleviate the pain. All the while, it is just an unclean spirit or group of unclean spirits invading one's flesh and soul. Jesus said, "Blessed are those who mourn, for they shall be comforted." He did not say, "I'm sorry you are mourning so much and feel depressed. Here is a really good pill to balance the chemical issues that are occurring in your brain."

Much sexual sin occurs in moments of emotional weakness. When someone has experienced the death of a loved one, they can be tempted to look for security, love, or affection from another person to fill the gaping hole of sadness over the death of a loved one. For example, a teenage girl can become very vulnerable to sexual predators when she has experienced emotionally traumatic things in her life. The predator knows how to say all of the right things to comfort her and seduce her into making a wrong choice.

Physical Weakness and Poor Choices

The same thing can happen with physical weakness. When our body is drained physically, we are usually weaker emotionally. Some people tend to make poor food choices when they are physically drained. If we tend to make poor food choices, we can make other wrong choices, including the things we are viewing or the thoughts we are entertaining. I study the science of the brain a lot; however, I am not going to elaborate on those things because that is not the purpose of this book. I want to stay focused on the root causes of things that attack the mind first and foremost. The thing that physical or emotional weakness can do to our bodies and souls makes us vulnerable to temptation. Just as it might be hard to resist that double meat cheeseburger at 11:00 p.m. after an emotionally or physically draining late-night event, other temptations can lead to sinful choices. It is not the emotional weakness or the physical weakness that presents the problem but the choice to sin that opens the door to demonic activity. Think about times in your life when you were being challenged emotionally or physically. Reflect on those times and see if you can recall some bad choices you might have made when you were really tired or emotionally weak.

I do know a great deal of sexual sin occurs during times of emotional weakness. When someone is dealing with a death in the family, all kinds of thoughts can begin to race in their mind, and sometimes people wind up succumbing to the temptation of sexual sin to gain temporary comfort for the grief or pain they might be experiencing. It is not just death that can trigger this response. It could be a variety of traumatic events, such as divorce, bad accidents, or hospitalization of a loved one. This can happen to Christians and non-Christians alike. The enemy shows no partiality. He is only looking for an open door or an available vessel. Every person has the choice to take every thought captive unto the obedience of Christ, then either reject or accept that temptation.

The Doorway of Sin

The last open door I want to touch on is the door we cause to swing wide open due to our own choices in life. This is the door of sin. Sin will take you further than you would ever want to go, and it will cost you more than you could ever know. Deliberate sin immediately gives the demonic realm access into your life. And yes, there is a difference between sin and deliberate sin. When I say deliberate sin, I am referring to calculated sin. For example, if a man meets a woman at a hotel bar on a business trip and she gives him the key to her room, he now has a choice. He can refuse to take the key, or he can follow her up to the room. If he chooses to follow her up to the room, he makes a conscious choice to sin.

Willful Sin Versus Ignorant Sin

On the other hand, we sin at times because we are merely humans, and we can be walking by the flesh and not by the spirit. Think about the times you have really messed up and said things you should not have said or developed jealousy or envy toward someone. You may have gossiped about someone, not realizing that you were gossiping. However, the Holy Spirit later convicted you that you were sinning against your brother or sister by talking about them the way you did. This happened to me recently. I talked about someone to a group of peers in a highly confidential meeting. For two days following the meeting, I felt deeply convicted by the Holy Spirit that I had sinned against this man. I had said things about him that I was unhappy about, but I had not even called him to tell him about my frustrations with him. I had to call this man, tell him what I had done, and repent to him. I then asked him to forgive me, and I told him that I would let every person in that room know that I had addressed this with him and repented.

At the time of my initial action of gossiping, I wasn't willfully gossiping. I was ignorantly gossiping, thinking I was rightfully sharing necessary information with my peers. The Lord had other thoughts about the matter, and He let me know about it. This is the difference between willful, deliberate sin and sinning because of our ignorance of a situation or circumstance at the time.

Here is what the Bible says about willful sin in the book of Hebrews 10:26-31, "For if we sin willfully after we have received the knowledge of the truth, there no longer remains a sacrifice for those sins, but a certain fearful expectation of judgment, and fiery indignation which will devour the adversaries. Anyone who has rejected Moses' law dies without mercy on the testimony of two or three witnesses. Of how much worse punishment, do you suppose, will he be thought worthy who has trampled the Son of God underfoot, counted the blood of the covenant by which he was sanctified a common thing, and insulted the spirit of grace? For we know Him who said, 'Vengeance is mine, I will repay, says the Lord. And again, The Lord will judge His people.' It is a fearful thing to fall into the hands of the living God."

Don't get mad at me. This is what God says. Here's a breakdown of what this means:

1. If you willfully sin after knowing Jesus, the sacrifice for that sin is nullified
2. You are now under judgment

3. You rejected the commandments

4. You trampled Jesus

5. You took His blood sacrifice for granted

6. You insulted the grace Jesus gave you

7. God will repay you (by allowing the enemy to have access)

8. It is a fearful thing to come before the Almighty God (be prepared)

The Subtlety of Sin

Sin opens the door for demons. When I went to college and began to engage in drunkenness, I opened the door for demons of all sorts to come into my life. If I engaged in sexual sin while drunk, demons of sexual perversion entered me and began to dominate my mind and attitude towards sexual promiscuity. If I engaged in acts of destruction or theft during my drunken moments, demons of destruction were allowed to enter my life. If I participated in sarcasm and the mockery of others during my drunk moments, all kinds of unclean spirits of pride, cynicism, and mockery were allowed to enter my life and influence me more negatively.

Sinful acts are like an avalanche. Once you get on a roll, they all begin to roll down the hill together. The more types of sinful acts you engage in, the more types of demons you expose yourself to. Personally, I had numerous demons inside of me at the age of thirty-five when I found out demons existed, and realized they resided in me!

If you are a parent, your sin affects your children, just as your parents' sins affected you. Demons know what they are doing, and if you aren't walking in the wisdom of God, they have plenty of traps to lay down in front of you that you will never recognize or acknowledge. If you have consistent anger in your life, it not only affects you but also all of those around you. If you have children, your outbursts of anger will unleash fear in the life of your child. It is easy to spot a child who has been exposed to an explosive parent. They are usually scared to make a move. The same holds true with parents who have to control and correct every move their child makes in public. The child becomes so scared to make a move they eventually do not do anything until the parent commands, for fear of messing up. After reading this book, just observe parents who are constantly correcting their children in front of other people and orchestrating their every move. Those children are usually skittish, shy, and generally walk in embarrassment and humiliation. Parents who shame their kids in public open all kinds of doors for the enemy to enter with mind-binding spirits.

The Wrong Kind of Inheritance

If you are addicted to alcohol, a spirit of addiction will be passed down to your children because they are not being protected by their spiritual covering. Your children will receive a transfer of any spirit you have because the devil wants to afflict your child as a result of you not having your life and your house covered by the blood of Jesus Christ. This does not mean your child will become an alcohol addict; however, the potential would certainly be there. If you are an adulterer, you run the risk of invoking curses upon your own children due to your sin. That doesn't mean that God won't forgive you and revoke the curse because He can, and He will. I cannot speak for specific consequences being carried out because I am not in charge of Heaven. I do know that God forgives those who repent. He revokes curses when we repent and ask Him to release any curses over our life due to our willful sins.

I have a friend who grew up as a preacher's kid. He also grew up loving God, and even as a middle-aged man, he still loved God. Several years before I met him, he had fallen in love with a woman at his workplace, yet he was married with children. He followed through with the relationship at work, cheated on his wife, and eventually got a divorce. He then married the woman with whom he was having an affair. A couple of years after that, his young son was diagnosed with leukemia and eventually died at the age of fourteen. Sometime after this, my friend got set free and broke all generational curses over his family's lives. The Holy Spirit spoke to him about his son. The Holy Spirit revealed to him that his son's death was a consequence of his adultery (his sin). He was forgiven, but it cost him the life of his son. This is not God's fault. The enemy had a legal right to access this man's family and attempt to bring destruction into his family. In this case, the enemy succeeded in shortening the life of his son. Read the story of King David and Bathsheba. It had a very similar outcome.

Remember, the sins of the father are passed down to the third and fourth generations of those who hate Him (God). We might not say with our mouth that we hate God, but when we willfully sin against Him, we are saying it by our actions. This is where doors in the spiritual realm come open, and "the rats sneak into the attic." Isn't it time to remove the rats from your attic?

Key Points

- Demons sneak in through many avenues, including the occult, prenatal influences, soulish domination, early childhood pressures, emotional and physical weakness, and manipulation.

- What we speak over our children in the womb matters.

- Whether it be intentional or unintentional sin, our choices can also open the door for the enemy.

- Your sin affects your children.

Ask Yourself

- Which of the "rats" listed in this chapter have you seen in your own life?

- Have you made wrong choices during times of emotional weakness?

- Can you identify a choice you made recently that may have unwittingly opened the door to the enemy?

TESTIMONY

LIFE: Living In Freedom Every Day

In 2009, we had no understanding of what living in freedom everyday really was. We were both living a sinful life in 2009. I was convicted by the Holy Spirit to quit drinking alcohol and started praying for my wife and our marriage to be saved. A year later, God restored my marriage. My wife quit drinking alcohol and was saved in August 2010. The Lord transformed our mouths from cursing and how we treated each other.

Transformation began in our lives, and we grew hungrier for the Lord. We were introduced to the process of freedom, and the experience changed us forever. We released all prior sins, unforgiveness, and strongholds from years past. We believe family curses were broken. We had been trying to conceive a child naturally for the first ten years of our marriage. After several medical treatments and two miscarriages, we were blessed to adopt our first daughter. Through freedom, we believe our bodies were set free! Praise God! My wife became pregnant after sixteen years of marriage. Through the process of healing, God remained faithful by giving us another beautiful daughter. We know it was a miracle!

— Brandon and Sarah, Indiana

Identifying Your Enemy

"The Spirit reveals, unfolds, takes of the things of Christ and shows them to us, and prepares us to be more than a match for Satanic forces."
— Smith Wigglesworth[1]

If an intruder enters your home and causes harm to you or your property, the primary job for an investigator is to identify the perpetrator and the nature of the crime. One of the first things an investigator does is go to the scene of the crime and gather all of the evidence he or she can. The same thing happens when dealing with the demonic. I call this process spiritual CSI because it is like a spiritual crime scene investigation. We often come up with way too many conclusions that we blame on God or genetic predisposition or heredity instead of researching the spiritual crime scene to identify the real perpetrator.

Although we may not be able to properly evaluate the root of every sin that led to a specific sickness, ailment, or negative situation, it sure doesn't hurt to do exhaustive spiritual research. Simply relying on the Holy Spirit for answers to root problems is a starting place. When we begin to ask God to reveal truth to us, He doesn't have a problem revealing what has led us to the point where we are. In addition, there are spiritual gifts that God allows us to use to aid in finding root causes to issues.

Tools of The Spirit

Spiritual gifts would be analogous to a crime scene investigator's kit. An investigator must have available a number of tools to gather data such as fingerprints, blood samples, fiber samples, and the like. Investigators do not just walk up to a crime scene, evaluate the situation, and come to a conclusion without tools to help gather intel. In the process of identifying where the enemy has attacked your life or your family's lives, God provides us with ministry tools to help gather intel.

A minister's arsenal supplied only by the Holy Spirit is discussed in 1 Corinthians 12:4-11 which says, "There are diversities of gifts, but the same Spirit. There are differences of ministries, but the same Lord. And there are diversities of activities, but it is the same God who works all in all. But the manifestation of the Spirit is given to each one for the profit of all: for to one is given the word of wisdom through the Spirit, to another the word of knowledge through the same Spirit, to another faith by the same Spirit, to another gifts of healings by the same Spirit, to another the working of miracles, to another prophecy, to another discerning of spirits, to another different kinds of tongues, to another the interpretation of tongues. But one and the same Spirit works all these things, distributing to each one individually as He wills."

The Word of Knowledge and Discerning of Spirits

Words of knowledge and discerning of spirits are two essential tools in helping identify root causes of demonic oppression, sickness, or disease in one's life. It is a manifestation of the Holy Spirit in us and through us that allows us to obtain knowledge or discernment that we would not otherwise have. When God uses us like this, it can bring about a remarkable change in helping someone get to the root cause of a problem. This is part of the Holy Spirit's role in our lives. He desires to help us identify activity that is going on in the unseen realm so that we can make proper correlations to the natural realm. Don't forget; we live in both an unseen realm and a natural realm, which includes things our eyes can see visibly and things that we can discern only through spiritual means. There are many great teachings on spiritual gifts, and I encourage you to read and study more about these particular ministry gifts if you are not yet accustomed to them. I knew nothing about these manifestations of the Spirit of God until after I was set free and baptized in the Holy Spirit. As soon as I received the promise of the Holy Spirit, the first book I read was a book on spiritual gifts. I will never forget devouring that book on a plane during a flight to Hawaii. It was more equipping for me, as God had called me to pay it forward in the area of freedom and the ministry of Jesus. I needed to know more about the powerful tools He makes available to us as we submit to Him and become a vessel for His use.

Because of the vast history of crimes that have taken place in our world, law enforcement agencies know a lot about the profiles of all types of criminals. They know the backgrounds that support certain criminal activities, as well as the character traits of each type of criminal. A thief is going to have a completely different profile and tendencies than a murderer. A child molester has a completely different profile and tendencies than a drug dealer. The same principle holds true with the forces of darkness. Each spirit has particular traits and tendencies, and because of the vast history of demons attacking mankind, Christians have access to a lot of insights about demonic profiles.

The demonic realm is a highly structured force, very similar to a military force. All Satan can ever do is copy and pervert what God has already established. God's army of angels has names, ranks, and assignments. Even though the Bible does not provide us with an exhaustive list of all of His angels, we do know several of their names, along with their ranks and assignments. The Bible also gives us clues into Satan's army of demons, which also have names, ranks, and specific assignments. Even though we do not know every single name, rank, and assignment for every demon, there has been a lot of intelligence gathered through the ages by ministers of God. If you battle the devil long enough, you are going to find out more and more about his team and his team's tendencies. There have been men and women who have come out of the occult and surrendered their lives to Jesus, who have extensive knowledge of Satan's kingdom and his hierarchies. I have met some of these people personally and heard their stories. I have gained very helpful and necessary knowledge from them about the enemy's tactics.

Identifying the Enemy's Strategy

When it comes to identifying unclean spirits that infiltrate people's lives by bringing demonic oppression, that list can be enormous. I have seen entire manuals, twice the size of this book depicting all types of spirits and demonic groupings, but I will use the groupings that I have commonly used throughout my years. The particular list that follows is an excellent example of how demons basically work in the lives of people throughout the world. Depending upon the culture, there could be some very unique demons that may not be prevalent in the lives of others. For example, if you come from a Hindu background, there will undoubtedly be a network of spirits that have affected your life that would not be the case for an Irish Catholic person. You need to understand that the following lists are not Christian doctrines. They are lists compiled from years of casting out unclean spirits that defy the Living God. Many are named in the Bible, but some are not named in the Bible. Don't forget there are many other sorts of names and things not listed in the Bible that we recognize as very real. Our job is to partner with the Holy Spirit and determine what is supported by God's Holy Word.

Also consider, whether a spirit listed below actually carries the exact name mentioned is not as important as the fact that the demon works in a mode to carry out a particular action. For example, there is probably not a demon with the name "Hard Heartedness." However, demons are assigned to harden one's heart and cause heart damage. There may not be a demon with an actual name called "masturbation," but I can assure you that a demon is assigned to carry out that task. There are quite a few "names" listed below that aren't actually "names" of demons, but more accurately, characteristics or actions carried out by demons. Whether all of these listed are specifically named demons or not, these are negative patterns that can be identified in one's personal life. More often than not, there is an unclean spirit behind the action. The list includes some actual names of demons, and others listed are behavior patterns influenced by demons. I repeat; all of the names listed below are not necessarily exact names of demons. The list represents consistent negative patterns that can occur in one's life. Demons attach to consistent negative patterns.

Mind Binding Spirits

Fear	Fear of Man	Fear of the Dark
Phobias	Fear of Success	Fear of Failure
Fear of Death	Fear of Losing it All	Confusion
Tormenting Spirits	Nightmares	Nightstalker
Double-Minded	Doubt	Unbelief
Anxiety	Stress	Worry
Deaf & Dumb	Fear of What Others Think	

"Self"

Self-Righteous	Self-Defeat	Self-Failure
Self-Destruction	Self-Pity	Self-Delusion
Self-Rejection	Self-Guilt	Self-Condemnation
Self-Reliant	Self-Will	Self-Accusation
Self-Deceit	Self-Mutilating	Self-Absorption
Self-Centered	Selfish	

Sexual Perversion

Whoredoms	Lust	Fantasy
Masturbation	Fornication	Adultery
Homosexuality	Lesbianism	Pornography
Incest	Rape	Lasciviousness
Lewdness	Frigidity	Coldness
Lack of Affection	Molestation	Incubus
Succubus	Tamar	

Addiction

Alcohol	Drugs	Nicotine
Gluttony	Sexual Addiction	

Witchcraft

Rebellion	Anti-Submissiveness	Control
Manipulation	Dominance	Black Magic
White Magic	Voodoo	Sorcery
Divination	Necromancy	Occult Spirits

Mental Curse Spirits

Schizophrenia	Paranoia	Bi-polar
Depression	Heaviness	Darkness
Gloom	Agony	Despair
Despondency	Guilt	Shame
Hopelessness	Insanity	

Bitterness

Unforgiveness	Anger	Hate
Rage	Revenge	Retaliation
Vengeance	Temper	Violence
Quarreling	Fighting	Backbiting

Pride

Stubbornness	Ego	Vanity
Performance	Competition	Haughtiness
Mockery	Intellectualism	Leviathan
Arrogance	Skepticism	Cynicism
Hard-Hearted		

Idolatry

Idolatry of Man	Idolatry of Money	Idolatry of Women
False Gods	Self-Idolatry	

Rejection

Insecurity	Abandonment	Withdrawal
Retreat	Orphan Spirit	Unworthiness
Timidity	Inferiority	Victim

Religion

Religious	False Doctrine	False Teachings
Legalism	False Prophecy	

Accusation

Judgment	Criticism	Faultfinding

Blasphemy

Cursing	Railing	Mockery
Sarcasm	Coarse Jesting	Belittling
Criticism		

False Identies

Masquerading	Alter Identities

Infirmity

Sickness	Disease	Heart Disease
Lung Disease	Diabetes	Leukemia
Blood Disease	Cancer	Tumors
Epilepsy	Lupus	Fibromyalgia
Mystery Diseases	Auto Immune Disease	Asthma
Ulcers	Lesions	Herpes
HIV	Spirits that harden the heart	

Death

Destruction	Destroyer	Murder
Suicide	Python	Asthma
Abortion		

Jealousy

Envy	Strife	Mistrust
Suspicion	Contentions	

Occult Spirits

Ouija Board	Séances	Jehovah Witness
Mormon	Islam	New Age
Yoga	Masons	Eastern Stars
Shriners		

Slumber

Tiredness	Laziness	Procrastination
Slothfulness	Fatigue	Weariness
Lethargy		

Pharoh System Demons

Bondage	Slavery	Containment
Insufficiency	Poverty	Lack
Fragmentation		

Ahab

Weakness	Passivity	Compromise
Indecision	Indifference	Passivity
Withdrawal	Escape	Retreat
Rebellion	Idolatry	

Jezebel		
Control	Manipulation	Seduction
Dominance	Witchcraft	Murder
False Prophecy	Harlotry	Possessiveness
Accusation	Selfishness	Conniving
Flattery		

Rebellion		
Lying	Cheating	Deceit
Stealing	Murder	

Yoga Spirits		
Kundalini	Shiva	Kali
Yogeshwara	Many More	

Because we do not know every detail about Satan and his forces, there is no arrangement or organized list of demons that one could call a perfect resource. The Bible is the only perfect source of information, and Jesus is the only perfect example of dealing with the demonic realm. The Bible is 100% truth, and, as with everything else beyond God's Holy Book, we have to "eat the meat and spit out the bones," including the great books written about this topic by anointed ministers. However, I believe the list of demons given to you in this book will be extremely helpful in assisting you to identify patterns of defeat, oppression, or destruction in your life. It should suffice as a great starting point.[2]

Demons Work as a Team

When you begin to embark upon the journey of personal freedom, you will find these demons always work in groups like a network. If a person has been holding on to bitterness and unforgiveness over a situation, that brings a whole network of demons to the party. Bitterness, hatred, unforgiveness, revenge, retaliation, vengeance, temper, anger, and even spirits in control of gossip, backbiting, jealousy, quarreling, bickering, envy, and strife can all be working together in this situation. What this person doesn't realize is that some or all of these characteristics may be part of their behavioral patterns but have yet to find any correlation or root cause of these behaviors. None of these behaviors are positive, and if they are consistent behaviors, there are unclean spirits at the root of the problem.

When one has engaged in sexual sin, one cannot escape the fact that the Bible says, "The two have become one flesh." 1 Corinthians 6:15-18 says, "Do you not know that your bodies are members of Christ? Shall I then take the members of Christ and make them members of a harlot? Certainly not! Or do you not know that he who is joined to a harlot is one body with her? For 'the two' He says, 'shall become one flesh.' But he who is joined to the Lord is one spirit with Him. Flee sexual immorality. Every sin that a man does is outside the body, but he who commits sexual immorality sins against his own body."

Sharing More Than Intimacy

For this reason, when a person has intimate sexual relations with another person outside of wedlock, they are now sharing each other's demons. Those demons now have a legal right to transfer into the other person and invade his or her life. If you have had multiple encounters with other people out of wedlock, then you have inherited things from others that you may have never wanted or asked for. The devil doesn't care whether or not you wanted the demons or asked for them. All he cares about is that you sinned against God, and he now has a legal right to send demons into your life to bring oppression to your body and soul. His goal is to make you completely ineffective, hoping that you will never surrender your life to Jesus and get set free. This is why sexual sin is so dangerous because it really does lead to a depraved mind.

In Romans 1:28-32, Paul the Apostle teaches us how God eventually reacts to consistent sexual sin among people, "And since they did not see fit to acknowledge God, God gave them up to a debased mind to do what ought not to be done. They were filled with all manner of unrighteousness, evil, covetousness, malice. They are full of envy, murder, strife, deceit, maliciousness. They are gossips, slanderers, haters of God, insolent, haughty, boastful, inventors of evil, disobedient to parents, foolish, faithless, heartless, ruthless. Though they know God's righteous decree that those who practice such things deserve to die, they not only do them but give approval to those who practice them."

Undesirable Baggage

The effects of multiple sexual encounters can be quite devastating to the soul. It brings people to the point where they carry all manners of unrighteousness, as Paul described. Why? Because demons, with all of these different names and assignments, had gained legal access to enter into that person's body when they sinned. This can certainly be overcome as in the case of myself. I had multiple sexual encounters prior to marriage, which I am not proud of. As a result, during these many years of rebellion from the age eighteen to the age of thirty-three, I carried all of the traits listed by Paul and a whole lot more! It wasn't until I learned about deliverance from demonic oppression, two years after I gave my life to Jesus, that I was able to root out all of those demons completely.

The Truth About Soul Ties

Sexual sin also brings with it soul ties, which I will discuss more in detail later. Basically, when we engage in sexual intimacy with another person, it can create a tie in the unseen realm called a soul tie. With a soul tie, there can be an unexplainable "pull" on your life toward thoughts, emotions, or actions that are not healthy or productive.

When someone carries a spirit of rejection, there is always a myriad of other spirits that run alongside this demon. The root cause could be abandonment, especially if one was adopted or a child of divorced parents. Even if this were not the case, the root of rejection could have stemmed from mental or emotional breakdowns in the family lines. For example, my mom dealt with a lot of rejection because she did not feel like she was loved as a child. She even heard phone conversations where her mom talked about her as a child. Those conversations deeply scarred her emotionally. As a result, my mom always carried a victim spirit. She constantly stated things like, "This town hates me! No one likes me! These people here are unfriendly! I hate this place! I ought to go ahead and kill myself. No one ever talks to me."

That list could go on and on. People who carry the spirit of rejection or victimization usually filter everything they hear through rejection. Another way to put it is they are usually projecting rejection toward you before you ever say anything at all to them. Because they unknowingly project rejection toward others, they take everything said and receive it as if you are rejecting them. If you are a person who feels as if you are being rejected a lot, this is probably the case. The key is to get to the root of the problem and cast the spirit of rejection out of your life, along with all of its cohorts. They actively work to completely destroy your relationships with others and your confidence in who you are called to be in Christ.

Who Are You Dealing With?

In review, when you take a hard look at all of the names of demons and how they are grouped, this does not mean there absolutely is a spirit named "Laziness" or "Hard-heartedness." However, there is a spirit or multiple spirits responsible for demonic oppression related to these issues. The key to understanding the names and groupings of demons is to get a healthy understanding of demonic activity. If I were ministering to somebody and discerned he had a hard heart, I would speak to the enemy and command any spirits assigned to attack this person's heart and make it leave immediately. I would say something like, "I don't care what your name is. I know what your assignment is, and I am commanding you to leave this person right now, in Jesus' name." The spirit or spirits have to leave when called upon.

On the other hand, many of the demons listed in the groupings of names are very specific in both name and assignment. For example, the spirit of rebellion has a very specific assignment. It is allowed to enter into our lives when we disobey God and rebel against His laws. The same is true with the spirit of python. You may or may not have heard of this spirit, but python is a serpentine spirit that usually wraps around the shoulders of an individual. Its job is to suffocate one's life and bring major oppression. In addition, that same spirit usually brings health problems, creating major tension and/or pain in the neck and shoulder area. The spirit of leviathan is the literal name of a spirit that is also serpentine in form. It wraps around the spine and creates back problems for people. It is rooted in pride, and it can be passed down through ancestors or inherited by the sin of pride in one's life. I have seen scores of people completely healed of their back issues and back pain after they are set free from a leviathan spirit.

When in Doubt, Cast It Out!

These are but a few examples of how demons can work in the lives of people who are experiencing consistent patterns in their lives that are counterproductive to God's plan for their lives. When you review this list of names, ask the question, "Is this Heavenly or demonic?" If it is not Heavenly in nature, it carries with it demonic activity. Also, if it is a part of your life on a consistent basis, it could be a demon. My wife and I certainly are not looking for a demon under every bush; however, we do live by certain principles. One of those is, "When in doubt, cast it out!" We have taken the stance that we would rather go after the possibility that something might be present in our lives rather than be prideful and assume that we are perfect.

Brutal Honesty

I once had a very close friend who had become somewhat disgruntled with our friendship. We had the kind of friendship you only have with a couple of people in your life. We shared our innermost thoughts with each other, and we did a lot of life together. When he decided he wanted to create distance in our friendship, for lack of a better explanation, he told me that I was carrying a lot of pride. I responded to him by saying something like, "Thank you for letting me know how you feel. I will certainly go to my closet and ask God if I have pride. If I do, I will deal with it." It did not feel great to have a friend say all kinds of negative things to me and top it off with the fact that I had a lot of pride! However, it is sometimes good to listen to your critics! I went to my closet and prayed. I asked God if I had any pride in my life, and He said, "Yes, you do." At that moment, I repented to God for having pride, and I then commanded "Pride" and all of his cohorts to leave my body immediately. Several small burps instantly followed this, and I had dealt with that spirit. I can also gladly say that this man is still my friend today.

I used this example to make it clear to you that we are not perfect people. This is why God's Word instructs us to put on the whole armor of God, as well as take every thought captive unto the obedience of Christ. Satan's demons are lurking around, waiting for an opportunity to pounce on us if we let our guard down as Christians. It's nothing to be concerned or paranoid about. It's just part of the good fight of faith. It's part of the battle for souls in which you are engaged. The good news is that victory is in Jesus! In addition, you will find further teaching on how to keep your deliverance later in this book.

Don't forget! Your Christian life is about the process. After you get saved, you are called to press on to your higher calling. You are called to be holy as God is holy. You are called to walk in the fruit of the Spirit. You are called to bear fruit, much fruit, more fruit, and lasting fruit, according to John 15. This all involves growth and warfare.

It's Your Decision

If you don't choose growth and warfare, you are choosing to accept lack of growth and warfare. Either way, you will have warfare. You just won't be as equipped to go from victory to victory on this earth. That's why, in Christ, you are more than a conqueror. The quest is to be in Him. Are you equipped for the challenge?

Key Points

- The Holy Spirit manifests nine different ways in and through believers.

- The word of knowledge and discerning of spirits are God-given gifts, helping you identify root causes of demonic oppression, sickness, or disease.

- Demons usually work in groups, networks, or packs.

- Demons have specific names and assignments.

- Consistent negative patterns can be an indicator of demonic activity.

Ask Yourself

- Have you ever had the Holy Spirit give you a word of knowledge or the gift of discerning of spirits?

- Looking at the reference list in this chapter, what unclean spirits do you think you might have to deal with in your life?

- What other demons might be associated with the ones you've identified?

For Further Study

- *They Shall Expel Demons* by Derek Prince

Marriage Breakthrough!

I knew in my heart I struggled with "trust issues." Really, the truth was I had some major "control issues." Before my parents received Jesus when I was young, our home was full of anger, addiction, and pain. My dad was very dominant and over-controlling. My mom was consistently doing everything she could to not ever "set him off." As a result, I began telling myself the LIE that if I'm going to avoid major drama (and trauma), I needed to make sure everything I was responsible for was done as perfectly as possible. Even after salvation and deliverance came into our family, this remained how I was "hard-wired." My thoughts were always, "If I want to avoid consequences, I just need to go take care of it myself." This LIE - this fear - kept me in a cycle of performance and control. Interestingly enough, the very ways that would make me cringe, were somehow sprouting up in my life and showing up in my relationships.

One day, an honorable leader in our life asked to meet with us. He recognized the hurt in our marriage and the symptoms of Jezebel in me. We were in the middle of such a hard time in our life. I wouldn't disrespect my husband publicly, but privately, in frustration, I would criticize him right along with myself. You could literally see the weight of my words on him. I knew the truth of who my husband really was, a source of such wisdom and strength for so many. But there was something brewing on the inside of me that just wouldn't settle, especially when the pressures of life were intensified. Danny shared the revelation of Jezebel and Ahab with us. I've known of this story but had never heard it in this way. It completely made sense. He asked if we wanted to be free and offered to pray with us. I could see how the Jezebel spirit had been in my family, in both males and females, for many generations. It was allowed to rob so many of us of peace, joy and healthy relationships. I renounced all ties and lies connected to that entity. There was such an intense heat that burned through me as I felt the release of this bondage. Soon after, a peace rushed into a deep place in my soul, a river of relief that I hadn't felt in such a long time. It has been a true joy to continue to walk in and witness this ongoing freedom. Many situations have come my way that would have "brewed" inside of me but now they filter through a true trust in the Lord and an uncompromising unity with my husband. No matter what we face, we know that God is in control and we don't have to bow in fear, or lose our peace over anything. Praise God!

— Christine, California

Ahab and Jezebel, The Dynamic Duo

"So pervasively has Enlightenment culture's anti-supernaturalism affected the Western church, especially educated European and North American Christians, that most of us are suspicious of anything supernatural."
— Craig S. Keener[1]

After my wife and I went through spiritual freedom in January of 2001, our lives were dramatically changed. There were significant differences in our behaviors, reactions, responses, and increased spiritual hunger. We were more hungry for God than ever. We began hosting ministry nights in our home regularly. We started to pray for the sick and witnessed significant miracles every week. We saw people healed from all kinds of diseases and physical ailments. It seemed like the Bible was coming alive in our lives. Nothing is impossible for him who believes! God began to show us how the impossible becomes possible in people's lives.

We rode that spiritual high for about three months before we began to hit a brick wall in the spirit. Day by day, Diane and I began to grow more and more frustrated with each other. It got to the point where everything that came out of my mouth repulsed her, and everything that came out of her mouth frustrated me. She even admitted to having thoughts of not wanting to be married to me anymore. She never used the word divorce, but her thoughts were entertaining the subject. She left town for three days on a business trip, and I was extremely glad about it because I was just as frustrated with her, yet neither of us could put our finger on the problem. We each thought the other person was the problem! The mystery to both of us was the fact that we had gotten delivered from so much demonic oppression just a few months earlier, and now our marriage was in the worst shape it had ever been. Diane's trip was a setup by God for a huge comeback in our marriage.

A Setup for a Comeback

While she was gone, two of our dear friends came by the house to share some good news with me. This couple had also gotten set free at the same time as we had, and they were on fire for God. They had just returned from El Paso where they had attended a ministry conference about spiritual warfare. It was held by Pastor Joe Salcido, who had introduced all four of us to a book about deliverance. Pastor Joe has since passed, but he was an amazing man of God. He was so full of life, peace, joy, and righteousness. We are forever grateful for this man's life and his impact upon our lives. It shows you how the power of one man's action can change the lives of thousands upon thousands of lives to come. You can have that same effect. That's why God has such a great plan for you!

During this conference, our friends had learned about ruling spirits that wreak major havoc on marriages and families, as well as the church. None of us had ever heard of these two spirits before. Their names were Jezebel and Ahab. Our friends sat at the table with me, glowing with joy, as they told me all that they had learned about Jezebel and Ahab. They wanted me to get all of the revelation they had received from the conference because they knew how vital it would be for all of us as we ministered to more people. As they were filling me in on the characteristics and assignments of Jezebel and Ahab, I quickly realized that this was the problem with Diane and me. We were under the influence of these two spirits, and they had both turned up the heat in their activities to destroy our marriage before they could ever be exposed. This is where we have to stop and recognize that God truly hears our prayers. When we cry out for answers, God will bring them. The question will always be, "Are you listening, and are your eyes wide open for the answer to your prayers?"

Unmasking The Enemy

Before I tell you "the rest of the story," let's take a look at these two spirits and what they are all about. I believe it is essential that you learn about these two demonic spirits because they play a significant role in the destruction of marriages and churches throughout the United States. I'm not saying that these spirits are strictly spirits that operate within our borders. I mean that these two spirits named Ahab and Jezebel have completely invaded our culture. I do not know what their ranking is, but I know they are high-ranking spirits and carry a lot of authority over many types of demons. They are wicked and cruel, and they want to destroy your family. They want to cause division in the church. There is an all-out assault of the Jezebel spirit on our culture in America, and it usually works in and through people with authority.

Ahab and Jezebel are spirits, but their characteristics come from real Biblical figures. Ahab ruled over Israel somewhere in the area of 873 BC for 22 years. He was a very wicked king as the Bible describes in 1 Kings 16:29-32, "In the thirty-eighth year of Asa king of Judah, Ahab the son of Omri became king over Israel; and Ahab the son of Omri reigned over Israel in Samaria twenty-two years. Now Ahab, the son of Omri, did evil in the sight of the Lord, more than all who were before him. And it came to pass, as though it had been a trivial thing for him to walk in the sins of Jeroboam the son of Nebat, that he took as wife Jezebel the daughter of Ethbaal, king of the Sidonians; and he went and served Baal and worshiped him. Then he set up an altar for Baal in the temple of Baal, which he had built in Samaria. And Ahab made a wooden image. Ahab did more to provoke the Lord God of Israel to anger than all the kings of Israel who were before him."

Defying God Brings Destruction

Ahab, King Omri's son, married a Phoenician princess named Jezebel who became his queen. This was probably to maintain healthy alliances between the Northern Kingdom of Israel and Phoenicia. Ahab was a conqueror and was second only to King Solomon in conquering the most lands by an Israelite king. However, Jezebel came into the picture and demanded that her idols be worshiped, which led to further defilement in Ahab's life. Not only did Ahab turn to Baal, along with Jezebel, but he abdicated his authority to her as well. Jezebel was a controlling, manipulative queen who defied God and His prophets. She slaughtered many of God's prophets and tried to do the same to the prophet Elijah. She created horrible atrocities on behalf of her husband, which caused the Lord's wrath to catch up to her finally. Ahab died in battle, and Jezebel died a catastrophic death by getting thrown out of her window by her two eunuchs. This was the fulfillment of a prophetic declaration Elijah made to Ahab concerning his death and the death of his wife. Elijah informed Ahab that the dogs would lick his blood from the ground where he lay and that the dogs would eat his wife by the wall at Jezreel. This account is worth opening your Bible and studying this story beginning in 1 Kings 21:17 when the Lord condemns Ahab and his wife, Jezebel. There are quite a few details that can give you great insight into the teaching notes that will follow.

The other major account of Jezebel in the Bible addresses the spirit of Jezebel specifically. This is found in Revelation 2:18-23, "And to the angel of the church in Thyatira write, 'These things says the Son of God, who has eyes like a flame of fire, and His feet like fine brass: 'I know your works, love, service, faith, and your patience; and as for your works, the last are more than the first. Nevertheless, I have a few things against you because you allow that woman Jezebel, who calls herself a prophetess, to teach and seduce My servants to commit sexual immorality and eat things sacrificed to idols. And I gave her time to repent of her sexual immorality, and she did not repent. Indeed I will cast her into a sickbed, and those who commit adultery with her into great tribulation unless they repent of their deeds. I will kill her children with death, and all the churches shall know that I am He who searches the minds and hearts. And I will give to each one of you according to your works'.'"

The Subtlety of Ahab and Jezebel Spirits

Now that you have a very brief and general synopsis of Ahab and Jezebel, let's examine what the spirits of these two entities are up to. First of all, Ahab and Jezebel usually work together. If there is a strong Jezebel spirit present, there will be an Ahab spirit as well. Jezebel is a controlling and manipulative spirit of witchcraft. It is not exclusive to women, and the spirit itself does not have a gender. I had a Jezebel spirit inside of me, which I will explain in the pages ahead. The root of Jezebel is witchcraft, but it can be identified primarily by a lack of Godly authority in the home. In the case of a married couple, if the man does not assume his role as head of the household and lead his family according to scriptural principles, a Jezebel spirit can enter the picture. Have you ever seen a home where the woman "wears the pants" in the marriage? When you see a home where the wife calls most of the shots and provides most of the family's direction, you are staring right at a Jezebel spirit. The Jezebel spirit wants to retain control. It will use any tool to gain control of a situation, a family, or a church.

Flattering Lips

Flattery is one of Jezebel's greatest weapons and is usually one of the most vivid ways that Jezebel exposes herself in working through people. This spirit is the queen of flattery because the flattery can cause Jezebel to get her foot in the door to influence someone. Be careful to observe one's motives when he or she flatters too much. Sometimes, the flattery is used indirectly to "name drop" so that the person can use the leader's credibility to sway others into their way of thinking. I have seen that Jezebel spirit flatter me in the business world to the point that I almost wanted to cringe. It is usually from an influential leader who doesn't even recognize how much they flatter me to gain influence with others by using my name. The sad part is that my name gets attached to all the people that the leader hurts, wounds, or drives away. When using my name so much, they are trying to get their followers to believe that I approve of their methods. In turn, the disgruntled followers will not only blame that particular leader, but they will also assume that I lead in the same hurtful way.

Intimidation

Intimidation is another key weapon of the spirit of Jezebel. A person who uses intimidation, control, dominance, and manipulation will always host a Jezebel spirit. These are tactics that Jezebel uses to get her way. Guilt trips are a form of manipulation. When you experience heavy guilt trips by someone, it is usually a sign that a Jezebel spirit is present.

Control

Control is one of the most prominent weapons of Jezebel. The Jezebel spirit will try to control every decision for the family, and if the family doesn't respond accordingly, there will be a backlash. When Jezebel is confronted, she usually will retaliate because Jezebel does not like advice. Jezebel tends always to be right, and if her authority is questioned, you could face retaliation. Jezebel will completely withdraw from the confrontation and begin to devise a manipulative plan to bring down her attacker. She does this by gossiping, lying, and defending herself to others to build a case for herself. She would rather see her attacker go down than give up her ability to control the people around her and control every situation.

A Critical Spirit

A Jezebel spirit is critical. It is critical of other people and their methods of doing things. It is critical of her husband. She is also disrespectful to her husband in front of her children, or vice versa. If in a man, this spirit is disrespectful and rude to the wife in front of the children. The Jezebel spirit talks about her husband negatively to other women, bringing dishonor to her household. The Jezebel spirit is sharp with her children. She is overprotective in many cases, instilling fear in her children. She is overly corrective with her children, turning them into basket cases where they learn to walk on eggshells. Jezebel tends to be a constant nagger.

A Seductive, Seducing Spirit

The Jezebel spirit is also a contributor to sexual immorality. It is a very seductive spirit and uses this seduction to entrap its prey. There will always be a Jezebel spirit present when there is infidelity in the marriage. Jezebel is not an excuse to commit adultery; however, it is one of the main instigators. When you battle with constant thoughts of sexual immorality, this is the influence of the Jezebel spirit. It can indeed be suppressed by prayer, reading the word, and obeying God, but that doesn't mean that "Jack doesn't want to pop out of the box." We don't just want to put lids on our "Jack in the box." We want to rip the root of "Jack" out of the box so it doesn't spring up from within us anymore.

Manipulation and Compromise

It is also a spirit that will compromise the things of God. Jezebel will use God and use the Bible in a twisted way to manipulate its victims. It has a sly way of compromising the things of God to manipulate.

The Jezebel spirit manipulates prayer and will try to control people's lives through prayer. It will always try to creep in close to the pastor and other church leaders to control them. One of the most effective ways is to pray manipulative prayers in private that try to control the direction of the church based upon their soulish desires, not what God necessarily wants for the church. The Jezebel spirit always knows what's best for the church instead of the pastor. The Jezebel spirit gets extremely frustrated when the pastor does not bow down and succumb to all of her wisdom and advice. She will begin to talk to her friends and other faithful prayer warriors about how the pastor does not listen to her.

Ahab, who partners in crime with Jezebel, is also a very wicked spirit of witchcraft. Idolatry is a prominent trait of Ahab. A man with an Ahab spirit will sink all of his efforts into his career and neglect taking care of the family unit. He will fail to raise his children under the fear and admonition of the Lord and fail to teach them the love of God and the wisdom of

God. He will abdicate his authority to his wife and let her run the home completely. If his wife carries a strong Jezebel spirit, he will usually just lay down in weakness when he arrives home. A man with an Ahab spirit is the kind of guy who comes home, grabs a beer and the remote control, and watches television for the rest of the evening. He is so used to his wife's criticism, nagging, and complaining that he avoids all confrontation. He takes a deaf ear to problems in the home. He is weak and compromising.

Idolatry

The Ahab spirit thrives on idolatry as well. It could be idolatry of sports, money, women, or career. The idolatry is a replacement for lack of zeal for God and all that God has for his life.

The Ahab spirit can also reflect somewhat of a "macho" attitude or "cocky" attitude to cover up for his insecurities and wounds that may run deep in his soul. The person carrying an Ahab spirit might not have had a proper father figure. Therefore, he or she only knows how to react to how Ahab guides him from within, from the soul realm. The soul realm affects the choices of the flesh, which can be detrimental. Ahab displays a powerful front in public; however, he is weak-minded and compromising on the inside.

No Conflict, Please!

Ahab fears confrontation. He is insecure about his decisions, and he avoids conflict. He would rather the problem just go away. Ahab has a hard time making decisions. The Ahab spirit refuses to assume his leadership role, whether in the home, church, or work. That doesn't mean that he won't work, but it does mean that he will not rise to the leadership level to which he has been called. An Ahab may have a "position" of leadership, but he will allow other people to push him around and become flaky in all of his decision-making. Deep down, he is not confident enough to cast a vision and lead people to fulfill the vision.

Recognizing Who You're Dealing With

The Jezebel spirit is much more threatening than the Ahab spirit, but both are equally evil. It is important to know when you are being influenced or affected by a Jezebel spirit. If you are dealing with a relationship in your life where a Jezebel spirit affects you, the desire to retreat from that relationship becomes prominent. It may even come to the point where you want to completely isolate yourself from the world.

Toward the end of 2017, I had completely given up on life on the inside. I wasn't depressed; however, I did not want to go to church, pastor a church, be around anyone in our business, nor be around anyone in general. All I could think about was moving to a remote island and living out the next few years eating pineapples, coconuts, and fishing. Now I realize a Jezebel spirit had launched an all-out attack on our family, our church, and our business. Being in the middle of it, I could not pinpoint the root of the problem. So, I committed to a twenty-one-day water fast and began to seek God from January 1, 2018. Within the first three days of the year, all of the heaviness on me broke off. The Lord had begun to push back the Jezebel spirit on my behalf and give me room to breathe and get back to productivity in all areas of my life. Since then, I am still identifying the root causes of that attack and dealing with them with God's help. The lesson here is you have to recognize Jezebel and remove yourself from its influence. You may also need to fast and pray to loosen the bands of wickedness with which Jezebel may be influencing you.

Fear of Retaliation

Fear of retaliation is another indicator you may be under the influence of a Jezebel spirit. If you are regularly intimidated by a controlling and manipulative person, it could be that a Jezebel spirit is unduly influencing you.

Dealing With The Jezebel Spirit

The influence of a Jezebel spirit is utterly exhausting. Whether it is at home, at church, or work, consistent exhaustion due to being around a person who is draining all of your energy is not fun. From personal experience as a pastor, I can tell you the Jezebel spirit is the one spirit that works through people to try to get right in front of me and start talking for 20-25 minutes straight. I don't have a problem listening to people. I enjoy interacting with people and listening to them. However, I am referring to listening to 20-25 minutes of rambling about victimization, life's setbacks, or family drama that simply drains every ounce of energy out of my body. That is because the Jezebel spirit prides itself in sucking the anointing out of a pastor, just like a mosquito sucks the blood out of your body. The sad part is, most of the time, the person doing this is not even aware of what kind of influence they are really under.

Now, getting back to the story about Diane and me. As you will recall, Diane was away, and I was home by myself. Sitting at the table, I listened as our friends who had returned from attending a ministry conference about spiritual warfare, shared what they had learned about Ahab and Jezebel. When they finished, it was like a light bulb came on. I said, "This is it! I've got it. Now I know why Diane and I are at odds with each other. It is the Jezebel spirit." Based upon what our friends had shared with me, I could instantly see my life and Diane's life flash before my eyes, and what I saw brought understanding to me like I had never seen before.

206 • FREEDOM: Winning the Battle Within

My Heritage

I was raised in a classic Jezebel household. My dad was a great father, and I love my mother. Unfortunately, our family was in total disarray. My mom was extremely controlling, nagging, and a master instigator of guilt trips. Looking back at the number of guilt trips that were leveled on my father would have been enough to cause me to have packed up in the middle of the night and disappeared. He only stayed because he didn't want to break up the family unit. I loved my grandmother dearly (on my mom's side), but she was a very dominant woman. Her nickname was "Sargent." She married and divorced three times. She was an excellent leader on the one hand but very authoritarian on the other. She was one of the first female superintendents of public schools in Texas history. She knew how to lead, but Nana always got her way. She dictated every move that anyone would ever make in our family, including my dad. In other words, Nana had a very strong Jezebel spirit. My mom was so controlling that my dad devoted all of his time to being a great football coach and tried to be the best dad he could amidst the chaos in our family life.

Dad was a great leader outside of the house and away from my mom, but when he was at home, all I can remember is that he tried to avoid all of her constant bickering and complaining. I was the youngest of three kids, and when I graduated from college, my mom immediately ran off and married a very bad man, which caused our family years of misery and grief. Mental and emotional breakdown and destruction of the family unit ran strong in my lineage; therefore, I had been carrying a Jezebel spirit and Ahab spirit throughout my life and didn't even know it. During all the years of my boyhood where I backed down from every fight and feared confrontation, little did I know that a ruling spirit named Ahab was controlling me.

A Life-Changing Revelation

As I got this new revelation, I knew I would break the cycle of dysfunction in our family, and I was going to go straight after that spirit that was trying to destroy my marriage and family. After my friends left, I went into my closet and began to cry out to God. I then began to try to cast those two spirits out of my body, but nothing happened. I asked the Holy Spirit what was wrong, and He told me that I needed to fast and pray for twenty-four hours. So, I did just that. Afterward, I went back into my closet and cast both of those spirits out of my body.

A Transformed Family

As soon as I was free from those two spirits, I went and got my nine-year-old son and I took him into the closet. By the way, he already knew all about demonic spirits and freedom from oppression, which I will tell more about at the end of the book. I sat down with him on the floor of the closet and began to explain to him that there were a couple of wicked spirits that had been passed down to him from his mom and me, and we were going to kick them out of our house. He understood completely, so I went after those spirits. I still remember the look in my son's eyes when Jezebel rose up and came out of his throat. His eyes made a dramatic change.

Later that day, I was driving him home from a dental appointment, and he asked me, "Dad, you know that woman (no gender) that you cast out of me this morning?" I said, "Sure, son." Then he said, "Well, when you started calling her name and telling her to get out of me, all of a sudden, I saw a witch, and she was old and wrinkly. She had a green face and long black claws, and she also had a sword in her right hand. She was screaming at you as she was falling backward into blackness. Right before she came out, I saw a flash of light, and it grabbed the sword out her right hand. She fell into the darkness." Only God! Only God can be so merciful that He would show my nine year old boy the reality of what his dad was ministering to him, along with the value of it. God was showing my son that he could trust his father's wisdom. God was also showing my son that spiritual warfare is very real. It is nothing to be scared of, and it is necessary.

Next in line was my six-year-old son. I took him through the same process that I had done with his older brother. I cast Ahab and Jezebel out of him. The day after I had ministered to him, he also had a story to tell me. "You know, dad, when you started casting that Ahab spirit out of me, I saw a man. He was a very old and ugly, wrinkly old man. He was in a pit, like a muddy pit. You kept telling him to get out, but he kept clawing his way back up through the mud, trying to get out of the pit. He had long claws, but when he finally came out of me, he fell into the pit and disappeared." Only God can bring this kind of understanding to a child so young! Do I need to say more?

At some point, my wife returned home, and I could not wait to tell her the good news. The problem was that she was not looking for a new revelation or good news. She had it fixed in her mind that I was a jerk and nothing I could say or do would improve our situation. We were lying in bed the night she got home, and I began to tell her that I had the answer for our frustrations with each other. She wanted to just go to sleep, but I would not let her. I began to tell her the whole story about what you just read. She wasn't buying it. As I told her the story, she kept seeing this look of evil on me. What she was seeing with her eyes as I was talking to her were horns on top of my head and a mustache that made me look like some kind of "devilish character." We all know that the devil doesn't look like a cartoon devil or a Halloween costume, but what my wife saw when she looked at me that night was infuriating her. She actually saw horns on my head, as well as a mustache and goatee!

I kept persisting and telling her this was the answer, and it had to be taken care of. She reluctantly relented and allowed me to take her into our closet and go to work. We sat down on the floor, and I began to command the Jezebel spirit to come out of her. As soon as I called out that name, my wife started laughing at me and mocking me. Her eyes were looking at me so disrespectfully and so sarcastically that this is the only way I can describe it to you. She continued to laugh and sneer as I continued to command that wicked spirit of Jezebel to come out of her. Finally it came out, and the rest is history. Our marriage was instantly at peace. My wife was completely blown away that she had felt so much resentment toward me, and, in an instant, she realized that she was under the influence of an evil spirit that had been lurking in the shadows for decades. That night brought freedom and a miraculous turn of events, and we are currently celebrating thirty years of marriage. Jesus can change things in an instant!

Dealing With The Rats in The Attic

The thing you must know about unclean spirits is they hide like rats do in the attic. They operate covertly and inconspicuously, that is, until they have been exposed. When demons know they have been exposed, they will sound every alarm they have to turn up the heat on your life to accomplish their goal: steal, kill, and destroy. They know, if they don't pull out all of the stops, their time is short, and they will be cast out. They have an assignment to fulfill, and they do not want to be cast out until they have completed their mission and worked through a person's body to steal, kill, and destroy. You may be thinking, "What do you mean by steal, kill, and destroy?" Jesus said, "...the thief comes not, but to steal, kill, and destroy..." (John 10:10). That means destruction on any level is their mission. Demons may not want to physically kill someone because they use that person so brilliantly to steal from so many other people's lives and destroy so many lives. Ultimately, demons want to kill you, but they sometimes would rather keep you alive and use you for destruction first if they can.

When you read a book like this or have conversations leading towards deliverance, every demon is on high alert. Many voices can speak to us besides the Holy Spirit. Sometimes we can hear, "Get away from this guy. He's weird. This stuff is freaking me out." Many voices try to keep people from seeking freedom from demonic oppression, but there is nothing like having the courage to step up to the plate and go for all that God has for your life. It takes courage to fight for your destiny and your family. It takes fortitude and determination to shut out the voices that want to convince you that deliverance is a fraud, or deliverance is weird, or deliverance is just for "crazy" people. It takes courage to fight against the enemy.

In 2001, I decided that I would not let a bunch of unclean spirits whip me for the rest of my life. They had whipped me around enough for the first thirty-five years of my life, and now that I knew with whom and what I was dealing, I was going to cast the devil out! The freedom I have had since that moment has transformed my life, my family, and our futures.

How about you? Are you going to let a little spirit whip you for the rest of your life? Are you more tolerant of rats (demons) in your spiritual attic (soul and flesh) than you are of rats in your physical attic? After you find out that you have roaches in your home, would you just let roaches crawl all over your toothbrush at night? I would hope you would devise a plan and take action to kill all the roaches trying to invade your home and multiply? The same principle holds true with freedom. Are you ready to get rid of the rats and the roaches that are trying to multiply around you?

Key Points
- Even after gaining freedom, you may find other spirits attached to you that you didn't see before.

- The Jezebel spirit uses flattery, intimidation, and control, and the Jezebel spirit is critical, seductive, compromising, and manipulative.

- The Ahab spirit idolizes, hides insecurities, and fears confrontation.

Ask Yourself
- When have you seen the spirit of Jezebel at work in your life or the lives of others?

- How about the spirit of Ahab?

- What did you gain from my real-life example of how to deal with unclean spirits?

For Further Study
- *Unmasking the Jezebel Spirit* by John Paul Jackson

- *Jezebel: The Witch Is Back* by Landon Schott

TESTIMONY

Transformed By God's Love

When I think of my freedom, I recall how lost I was ... so lost I didn't know I was lost! My life changed in 2001, when I truly gave my life over to God. Over the next ten to fifteen years, I met people who walked in a place I didn't. I had shame, doubt, guilt, lack of self-confidence, unworthiness, rejection, and hurt. I wanted to be as they were ... full of faith, peace, joy, and love. As I inquired, they shared how they were able to walk in freedom. They helped me discover how to receive that freedom.

The next several years I found I could surrender, forgive, release, repent, rebuke my past and become free of the bondages that were holding me down. I felt at times like I was being peeled like an artichoke. On the outside, there were thorns and tough layers. As I searched for God and freedom, the layers began to soften and fall off. Digging deeper, I still felt feelings of insecurity and had feelings of rejection and unworthiness.

Backtrack with me for a moment. I was told as a child I was an unwanted pregnancy. Little did I know, the spirit of rejection and unworthiness had started in my mother's womb. Four years ago, I was able to break through that place in my freedom walk. Even though I felt rejected and unwanted in the flesh, God was with me. I saw Him holding me in my mother's womb, and I was wanted. I was worthy because He created me. Realizing that He wanted and loved me brought me to the place where I am now: walking in true freedom!

— Mary Kay, Texas

CHAPTER FIFTEEN

Preparing For Deliverance

"The secret of spiritual success is a hunger that persists...
It is an awful condition to be satisfied with one's spiritual
attainments...God was and is looking for
hungry, thirsty people."
— Smith Wigglesworth

There is no greater factor in answering the question of how to be delivered than spiritual hunger. Jesus said, "Blessed are those who hunger and thirst for righteousness, for they shall be filled." Hunger or desire is the key issue regarding freedom. I have seen thousands of people introduced to the authentic ministry of Jesus since 2001, and I have witnessed a myriad of reactions and responses. I can safely say that most people who reject these Biblical truths are simply not hungry. Often, they are self-righteous and full of pride. They have been convinced that they know everything there is to know about scripture, or

their theological upbringing has taught them everything they
need to know about the scriptures. Therefore, there is no need
for more of Jesus. They have just enough Jesus to satisfy their
spiritual arrogance and to justify their false doctrines, so they
stay bound up with religious spirits in the same way the Pharisees did.

If you are ready to be free from any sort of demonic oppression, here is where to begin. You will need to begin to prepare
your mind and your heart by getting a grasp on all of the things
that follow:

Hunger and Humility ... A Partnership For Freedom

Needless to say, hunger is the essential component. Therefore, we must humble ourselves. The Bible says, "If we humble
ourselves before the Lord, He will exalt us in due time" (1 Peter
5:6). It takes humility to be set free. God will allow us to remain
in bondage if we choose to keep our pride, but humility is a
small price to pray for freedom.

Honesty and Confession

Honesty is another key factor involving the freedom process.
The Bible says, "Everything hidden will be uncovered" (Luke
12:2). It also says, "Confess your sins to one another" (James
5:16). It is important to come clean and confess all past sins.
God already knows your sins; however, His word does instruct
us to confess our sins to one another. Confession brings the
mercy of God into our lives.

Repentance

Repenting of all sins is of the utmost importance. It is one
thing to confess your sins, and it is another thing to repent as
well. There are few things as healthy as repentance. Repentance
also brings the mercy of God into your life. In addition, it frees
your mind and your soul of things that might weigh heavily on

you. Repentance cultivates the soil of your heart, so to speak, and it prepares your flesh and your soul to be set free with ease. Demons hate for you to confess your sins, and they hate for you to repent to God and others. It weakens their power and tears down their strongholds. Remember that the Bible says, "The weapons of warfare are not carnal but mighty in God for the pulling down of strongholds" (2 Corinthians 10:4).

I know a Godly man who cheated on his wife once prior to his salvation. Actually, I know several to whom this has happened, but this is one man's story. When he got saved, he rightly assumed that he was forgiven for his sin against his wife and knew he would have eternal life. However, he did not realize that he had sinned against his own body when he committed this act. He and his wife were one flesh, and the other part of his flesh did not know about this sin. When he found new revelation that leads to deliverance, the Holy Spirit reminded him that he was forgiven. The Holy Spirit reminded him that he was going to Heaven; however, he needed to confess his prior sin to his wife if he wanted to live in consistent victory on this side of Heaven. Because of his hidden sin, the enemy still had a stronghold in this man's life. Demons of sexual perversion, lies, and rebellion were operating in the background of their marriage because this man had not confessed his sin to his wife. So, the Holy Spirit told him that he could keep his secret and be somewhat tormented all the days of his life, and he would still go to Heaven. Or, he could confess the sin to his wife and get set free from the unclean spirits that had a legal right to haunt him. In addition, the Holy Spirit told him that he would have to deal with any of the possible consequences and trust Him in the process.

A Word of Caution
Now, if you are reading this and have committed a sin against your spouse, don't act too quickly. This is not a license

to run out and tell your spouse all of the baggage you are carrying. You may need to fast and pray, seek God, and ask Him for the right timing to reveal these things to your spouse. You may need to seek counsel first from your Christian accountability partners who understand these things. Will you need to confess? In order to be set free, the answer is yes, but the timing of any confession is crucial. Don't get mad at me. I didn't write the Bible, and I am not God. Furthermore, don't blame me because I am not the one that got you into this situation if you happen to be in it. It is important that you seek godly counsel before making life-altering and family-altering decisions. I repeat, I am not God, and I am not accountable for your mistakes or your future decisions. You are an adult. Seek God's direction, and seek wise counsel!

In the case of this man, God healed his marriage. His wife forgave him, but it took time for their marriage to heal. He had to be patient with her through the process of regaining trust and affection. You have to understand that the sinner is instantly relieved! However, the person who was sinned against needs time to completely heal from such a tragic betrayal. From my experience, it can take up to three years for one to completely heal emotionally. This forces the one who sinned to grow in wisdom more than ever and to learn how to be compassionate more than they have ever been before. Therefore, the one who sinned against the other spouse must take note of the journey to healing that this will entail.

Renouncing False Religions and Cultish Connections

Breaking free from any false religions, the occult, and/or secret societies is a must to be set free. If you have had prior involvement with false religions such as the Mormons, Jehovah Witnesses, Buddhism, Hinduism, cults and/or secret societies like the Masonic Lodge, Shriners, Eastern Stars, Yoga, New Age, or Satanism, please remember: freedom will come as you repent for your involvement or your family's involvement in these things. You will also need to renounce these things and ask God to forgive you for your involvement, whether knowingly or unknowingly. To refrain from writing a book within a book about all these cultish connections, I recommend that you study other books, writings, and videos on these subjects. I don't need to write a book on all of the reasons why Mormonism or any of these other things are not Christianity. I also don't need to expound on them in detail because many well-versed scholars have done extensive and thorough studies that can help shed light on that subject. A number of suggested resources that I respect on these topics are included at the end of this book.

What About Yoga?

Many people get involved with yoga without ever studying its history or the practice of yoga. In most cases, they start with an interest in its physical and emotional benefits, giving little or no thought to anything beyond what they perceive to be the physical benefits they are seeking. According to Merriam-Webster's online dictionary, yoga is "a Hindu theistic philosophy teaching the suppression of all activity of body, mind, and will, in order that the self may realize its distinction from them and attain liberation."[1] When an individual fails to look beyond the perception of only the physical benefits, he or she risks the possibility of being progressively drawn into the occult practice without realizing it. Yoga is essentially a spiritual experience that combines a style of stretching or exercise with it. I have read numerous books about yoga, both pro-yoga and anti-yoga books. I haven't seen a shred of truth in a "pro-yoga" book, and I've seen nothing but Biblical truth within "anti-yoga" books. The enemy's ultimate goal is for you to feel peace and tranquility through your experience with yoga. That's his trap. If you are so much more peaceful, calm, and tranquil, it is easy to think that it must be God, but this is not true. Similarly, sexual sin is pretty peaceful and euphoric initially, but the consequences of that sin are pretty dangerous. I believe the same holds true for yoga.

Do Your Homework

I encourage you to read books, writings, and watch videos from both perspectives of yoga, including those found in the Resource Section at the end of this book so that you can make an educated decision based upon truth. I carry a life philosophy that basically states, "Eat the meat and spit out the bones." Knowledge is power, so don't be afraid to explore and study why something may or may not be good for you. By studying topics like yoga and others that have been mentioned, you might ascertain the truth. Do the homework for yourself. Don't just accept that certain religious sects are going to lead to eternal life with God because the individuals you know who are involved are nice people with good morals. Don't assume that yoga is harmless because you have friends that do it, and you haven't seen any "evil" in them. Paul, the apostle, warned the early church to stay away from false teachers when he said, "For such are false apostles, deceitful workers, transforming themselves into apostles of Christ. And no wonder! For Satan himself transforms himself into an angel of light. Therefore it is no great thing if his ministers also transform themselves into ministers of righteousness, whose end will be according to their works" (2 Corinthians 11:13-15).

The Heart of The Matter

In her book, *The Heart of Yoga Revealed*, Judy White states, "Many people are under the false impression that yoga's primary objective is to bring unity to their spirit, soul, and body. Yet, nothing could be further from the truth. Yoga's primary objective is to bring their spirit, soul, and body into unity with Hindu gods." The word "yoga" carries a strong meaning because it refers to being "yoked" to a supreme being. Judy White explains, "Yoga is, by definition, the act of yoking the practitioner to Brahman, the 'Divine' higher self, who is said to enlighten the soul. According to the Hindu text, enlightenment of mankind comes from union with Brahman. Brahman not only brings enlightenment, but he also claims to be the "Universal World Soul." Through intense concentration, controlled breathing techniques, and prescribed yoga postures, Brahman and yoga practitioners are united as one." By the way, Brahman is a demonic spirit, and it will cordially waltz into your life if you allow it through the practice of yoga.

White goes on to document and explain the very roots and origins of the practice of yoga. It is too much information to cover in this book, yet my hope is that you don't get frustrated about what I am writing if your current beliefs lean towards the practice of yoga, or even if they are neutral. If this is the case, you owe it to yourself and your future generations to study this subject.

Derek Prince and Freedom

An example from the life of a man named Derek Prince (1915-2003) demonstrates the subtlety and power of yoga. Those who are acquainted with Derek Prince recognize him as a Bible expositor with a global ministry who published a number of books, including several about freedom and deliverance. Prior to that time in his life, his Indian parents introduced him to Hinduism and the influence of yoga. As a young adult, he was a Cambridge University scholar who became a medic in the British Army during WWII. While serving in the military, he began to study the Bible and experienced a life-changing encounter with Jesus Christ. However, after he accepted Christ as his Savior, he shared that he still struggled with many things. His struggles included cursing, a daily habit of self-medicating with whiskey, and a "power from below" that he later identified as a demon of yoga, as well as a "dark cloud" of depression that hung over him. It was not until he had a supernatural experience in the Holy Spirit, which he described as being "flooded by power from on high," that he was instantly freed from the profanity, whiskey, and the yoga demon. His deliverance from depression came some years later as he grew spiritually and finally had a revelation that was a generational pattern caused by a "spirit of heaviness" that plagued the male members of his family (Isa. 61:3).[2]

The Power of Yoga

I believe there is a "power" connected with yoga, and when a person practices yoga, it opens the spiritual doorway for unclean spirits to enter one's body. The kundalini spirit, connected to Hinduism, can be invited (knowingly or unknowingly) to enter one's body through the meditative experience connected with yoga. When this happens, this demon wraps itself around the base of the person's spine who is practicing yoga. This may be true, but it is just the first of many spirits that will invade one's body while practicing yoga. It certainly could masquerade itself as the Holy Spirit because every spirit that is not of God disguises itself in order to be the "voice" in someone's life. This is exactly why John instructs us to "test the spirits" and know whether they are from God or not (1 John 4:1). There are many voices that we are exposed to, externally and internally, but Jesus said, "My sheep hear My voice, and I know them, and they follow Me" (John 10:27).

Many valuable resources, including books and YouTube videos, clearly lay out the facts about yoga and the dangers associated with it. Whether you call yourself a Christian or have just begun to investigate this topic, I urge you to research various topics via the internet or other sources. However, in your yoga searches, be careful to discern what is written by those who take an extremely negative stance on things related to "the things of the Spirit" so your heart can discern the truth. There are mean Christians who do not believe in the baptism of the Holy Spirit, nor do they believe that the manifestations of the Holy Spirit like prophecy, speaking in tongues, deliverance, and supernatural healings are real and for today. In my opinion, those people might as well tear out half of the pages of their New Testament Bible and quit reading them because they don't believe what the Bible says about such things. Too many powerless Christians talk about what God doesn't do anymore or what God can't do today, rather than believing what the living Bible says. On the other hand, they might offer some valid points as to why yoga is an occult practice or why a kundalini spirit is a false holy spirit. That, in and of itself, is good. However, they are often resistant to the real things of God and fail to recognize the work of the Holy Spirit today. Many of these critics of yoga also take their liberty to criticize anointed men and women of God's army. Whenever we're talking about the natural realm or the spirit realm, it is important to remember that a counterfeit can only exist if there is first a genuine original. That's why it is important to discern what spirit is in operation. In the end, it's not about someone's opinion but about what the Word of God says regarding the things of the Spirit. That is why I always say we must eat the meat and spit out the bones when dealing with someone's writings and opinions.

Is "Holy Yoga" Holy?

There has been a popular movement within Christian circles of the practice of holy yoga. The basis for this suggests that God can sanctify an eastern practice such as yoga, and Christians should be able to take advantage of it. Sometimes these groups use Chapter 1 in the book of John to justify the fact that God created all things, and therefore, yoga is included. Well, that's a pretty tough one for me to swallow. Anyone who believes in creation acknowledges that God created the king cobra, but no one, including me, is going to let one come slithering into their house and bite everybody. God also created the crocodile, but I am not going to go wading in crocodile-infested waters. In the

222 • FREEDOM: Winning the Battle Within

same vein, I don't have any problem with stretching, exercising, or meditating on God's Word while doing so. The issue is when yoga terms, poses, and practices are incorporated into exercise.

I do not believe that God desires to sanctify yoga anymore than He wishes to sanctify a dream catcher. In my opinion, Christians should use common sense and avoid anything that is based on pagan worship or includes any type of demonic practices. Also, there is only One that is holy, and that is God the Father, Jesus the Son, and the Holy Spirit — the Godhead operating as a trinity in perfect harmony. We have attached the word "holy" to the Holy Bible, which is God's Word revealed, and other than that, there is none holy. Toledo is not holy. Buckets are not holy. Cr*p is not holy. Sh* t is not holy. Cows are not holy. Moly is not holy. And yoga is not holy! Why in the world would you want to take the risk of calling some exercise that you do "holy?" This is a word that carries significantly strong meaning. My advice to you is to be careful as to what you assign the word "holy."

When it comes to the power of words, we give the enemy so much power by attaching the word "yoga" to clothes and exercise equipment. I use an exercise mat, not a yoga mat. I use the same approach to anything I wear while I exercise. I don't wear yoga pants, yoga shorts, or anything of the sort. I believe that when you claim that you are using a "yoga mat," you are literally claiming that you are going to put down an altar of worship as a foundation for the exercises you are about to embark upon. I have found, in my studies, that the mat is literally considered an altar for the ritual practice of yoga. This is not a joke. It is very real, and I encourage you to study it thoroughly.

I do believe that God can sanctify exercise equipment and clothes. If they have been temporarily labeled in the store as yoga pants or a yoga mat, I believe that one can purchase the product and bless the product. I would probably go as far as breaking any curses that might have been put on those items in the name of Jesus and ask God to cleanse those items from any defilement. I would then ask God to bless those items in Jesus' name. You can do as your beliefs direct you in this matter. Believe it or not, there are companies that pray curses over clothing items and other marketable goods before they ever leave their manufacturing facility and the demons attached to those items can be transferred to naïve consumers worldwide. This really does happen. If you don't believe that, it is perfectly okay because you don't have to believe it. It's your choice. I strive to be vigilant in protecting my family and my future generations from the wiles of the devil. I'm not saying all companies follow these practices, but I do know that there are those who serve the devil. They are adamant about affecting and infecting you and me with as much defilement as they can.

Real Peace

Almost all false religion is disguised in terms of peace, joy, and the appearance of righteousness. The members of false religions can be some of the nicest people you will ever meet. They study God's Word, practice strong morals based upon God's Word, but they have twisted views about Jesus and eternity that do not match up with scripture. They have additional books they depend upon to determine their ultimate beliefs about Jesus and about Heaven, which causes them to stray away from the truth of God's Word and from the sacrifice that Jesus paid on the cross. If you base all of your beliefs on whether something gives you peace or not, there are plenty of drugs, cults, societies, and human acts that will give you the appearance of peace. Seek truth first. Jesus said, "I am the Way, the Truth, and the Life. No one comes to the Father except through Me" (John 14:5). Real peace is a by-product of knowing the truth and the truth setting you free.

The Masonic Lodge

The Masons are a straight-up cult. I have met so many people who were Masons, or their fathers were Masons. My dad joined the Masons when I was entering junior high school. I think he did it just to get away from the house more, away from the dysfunction. Either way, it wasn't a healthy choice for his family. I don't have to go into too much explanation about the Masons except for exposing the very first vow that a man has to take to become a member. Here is an excerpt from Truth Magazine XXIV: 45, pp. 727-728

November 13, 1980:

Before entering the lodge as an Entered Apprentice (First degree) and before advancing to each of the following degrees, the candidate must agree to take certain oaths binding him to secrecy and loyalty. These oaths can be found in several Masonic publications, including "Duncan's Masonic Ritual and Monitor" and "Look To The East," a ritual of the first three degrees of Masonry.

The oath taken by the candidate for Entered Apprentice is:

I, _____, of my own free will and accord, in the presence of Almighty God, and this Worshipful Lodge erected to him and dedicated to the Holy Saint John, do hereby and hereon (Master presses his gavel on candidate's knuckles) most hail, forever conceal, never reveal any of the secret arts, parts or points of the hidden mysteries of Masonry which may have been heretofore, or shall be, at this time, or at any future period, communicated to me as such, to any person or persons whomsoever, except it be a true and lawful brother Mason, or within the body of a just and lawfully constituted Lodge of Masons; nor unto him or them until, by strict trial, due examination, or lawful information, I shall have found him, or them, as lawfully entitled to them as I am myself. I furthermore promise and swear that I will not write, print, paint, stamp, stain, cut, carve, hew, mark, or engrave them on any thing movable or immovable capable of receiving the least impression of a sign, word, syllable, letter or character, whereby they may become legible or intelligible to any person under the canopy of Heaven, and the secrets of Masonry be thereby unlawfully obtained by my unworthiness.

All this I most solemnly and sincerely promise and swear, with a firm and steadfast resolution to keep and perform the same, without the least equivocation, mental reservation or secret evasion whatsoever; binding myself under no less penalty than that of having my throat cut from ear to ear, my tongue torn out by its roots, and buried in the sands of the sea, at low-water mark, where the tide ebbs and flows twice in twenty-four hours, should 1, in the least, knowingly or wittingly violate or transgress this my Entered Apprentice obligation. So help me God, and keep me steadfast.[3]

This is just the beginning for a young Mason. It doesn't take a rocket scientist to discern the evil in this particular oath. No Godly organization would ever require a man to proclaim such a thing over his life. This creates a breeding ground for demonic activity to encircle one's life.

A Note to The Reader

At the end of this book, I will include the titles of a few suggested books to read on the subjects mentioned previously, which are related to occult activity. It won't be an exhaustive list; however, it may point you in the right direction to acquire more knowledge on these subjects if they have been a part of your life in any way. It is important for the reader to know that I am not trying to condemn people who are or who have been involved in these cults or these activities. My role is to make the reader aware of these things that are in no way approved by

God, Jesus, or the Holy Spirit. Let's look at what the Bible says about condemnation, which does not come from me: "For God did not send His Son into the world to condemn the world, but that the world through Him might be saved. He who believes in Him is not condemned; but he who does not believe is condemned already, because he has not believed in the name of the only begotten Son of God. And this is the condemnation, that the light has come into the world, and men loved darkness rather than light, because their deeds were evil. For everyone practicing evil hates the light and does not come to the light, lest his deeds should be exposed. But he who does the truth comes to the light, that his deeds may be clearly seen, that they have been done in God" (John 3:17-21).

Trapped in The Darkness

What happens to many people who are a part of these groups, such as the Masons, is they are instructed by their parents, leaders, or teachers to never read any materials outside of what they have been given. They are taught to stay away from any of the writings that might expose the dark side of these organizations. Many who fall into these traps have grown up in it, so they are so entrenched in the beliefs they can't imagine that their whole life, up to this point, has been a lie. Even the thought of it scares them enough to not search for the real truth.

Personally, I know how this feels. I've been told straight to my face that I was involved in occult activity and did not have any clue what I was getting involved in. That hurt. More importantly, what it did was force me into God's Word like never before. I read and highlighted the New Testament over and over. I prayed for several hours per day, begging God to reveal truth to me so that I would not walk in deception and do anything that would displease Him. I devoured books about what I was being accused of and read all points of view on the subject. That "accusation" was one of the best things that ever happened to me because it forced me to grow. It forced me to study, not only just to reinforce my current stance, but also to weigh both sides of the argument. One of my mentors always told me, "Danny, always listen to your critics because there's probably an element of truth in what they are saying."

A Quest for Truth

Therefore, if you are reading things in this book that are challenging to you, especially if it relates to yoga or other forms of the occult, please make it your personal mission to dive in and seek God. Study His Word. Read books on the subject of controversy before you in order to gain a healthier perspective of what you may be engaged in. One day, when we get to the judgment seat of God, neither you nor I will be able to say, "But God...," followed by any of the following statements:

"My dad always taught me..."
"My grandmother said.."
"My pastor always told me..."
"I was raised in this religion, and they always told me..."
"My whole family is..."
"I just didn't know..."

God's Word says in Romans we are without excuse.

Roadblocks to Deliverance

There can be some real obstacles to deliverance for some people; therefore, it is important to educate you in this area. The most glaring obstacle to getting set free from demonic oppression is holding on to unforgiveness. I have never seen anyone get set free who refused to let go of the unforgiveness in his or her heart toward somebody else. Throughout scripture, Jesus clearly explains to us that we are to forgive those who sin against us. The entire chapter of Matthew 18 is worth reading if you are harboring any bitterness, judgment, or unforgiveness toward another human being. Jesus tells the story of the servant who owed a whole lot of money to his master, and his master was about to throw the man into prison because he would not pay his debt. The man begged his master to forgive his debt, which he did, and he let the man go free. The man who was forgiven his debt went about his day and ran into one of his friends who owed him just a little bit of money. He began to choke the guy and demand payment of his friend's debt. In the meantime, the master who had forgiven this man so much money had servants in the area that witnessed this travesty. These servants, appalled by what they had seen, grabbed the man, took him back to the master, and told the story of how he treated the other man who owed him so little. The master declared him to be wicked and turned him over to be put in prison and released to the tormentors. Jesus said the same thing would happen to you and me if we do not forgive our brother. God represents the master, and the point is, He forgave you of a debt that you could not possibly pay because your sins cost way too much. Because He did so for you, He expects us to forgive others for the little sin that they might have inflicted upon us.

The Lord's prayer says, "...forgive us our sins, as we forgive those who sin against us..." In other words, we are really saying to God, "If I don't forgive those who sin against me, then You don't have to forgive me." When we speak the words of the Lord's prayer, we are actually telling God to only release us from our debts AS we release other people from their debts.

The Path of Forgiveness

We don't forgive people because they deserve it. We forgive those who have wronged us because God forgave us of all of our horrible actions throughout our lives. We forgive so that we can be in right relationship with God. It is a choice. By forgiving others, it doesn't make what they did to us right. It doesn't make the traumatic experience disappear from our minds. It merely gives God the power to work in that situation. As long as we hold on to bitterness in a situation, God will withhold working on our behalf in that situation. He only works His plan when we have let go of our own vengeance.

The Price of Forgiveness

I have ministered to people who have experienced all kinds of painful and life-altering situations. I've ministered to those who have lost loved ones in gruesome deaths and to those who have been brutally raped. I have ministered to people that have been severely tortured physically, and I have ministered to people who have been horribly betrayed. In every case, it is not fun dealing with the pain of the memories, especially as I try to help bring people to the point of forgiving their perpetrators. The circumstances these individuals have faced are different in a myriad of ways, but in every case, it is essential that the person be reminded that God gave His only begotten Son, Jesus, to die on the cross. Why? So that we may be forgiven for our sin, our blasphemy, our murderous thoughts and words, and our betrayals. It is important to remember the lengths God went to by giving up His only begotten Son, Jesus, on Calvary's cross so that we are forgiven for the pain we have caused others, knowingly or unknowingly. Can you imagine what kind of pain you might have caused other people throughout your life with your words or actions? Many times, you're not even aware of the pain you have caused in someone's life or in a situation. I can think of all the guys I would want to go back and beat up if I were not a Christian. I would like to go back and throw my life successes in their face. I would want to show them that I'm not that little scrawny kid they abused when I was younger. These guys don't have a clue what kind of agony they caused me emotionally! So what about you? Think about how you and I both have hurt others in our lifetime.

230 • FREEDOM: Winning the Battle Within

Jesus died so that we can be forgiven. Jesus also died and rose again so that we can forgive. The only right choice is for us to forgive so that we can be set free. The Bible doesn't say that we have to understand why things happen. That's where faith comes in. Because of Jesus' death on the cross and His resurrection, we choose to forgive and live in faith that God will take over for us. If it is still too difficult for you, try wrapping your brain around understanding why and how God gave His only Son to die on the cross for you. He did something that neither you nor I could ever do or understand. That alone requires us to be grateful and have mercy on those who have hurt us.

Forgiving Yourself

Sometimes, before becoming set free, one has to forgive himself or herself. I have ministered to multitudes of people who were trapped in demonic oppression because they hadn't forgiven themselves for some sin they had committed. For example, my wife and I have ministered to many women who had a hard time forgiving themselves for an abortion. The guilt, shame, and self-condemnation accompanying abortions are very real. Deep down, every woman knows that they made a choice to kill their child during a moment of extreme confusion. They usually allowed it to happen because they were scared, overwhelmed, ashamed of how it happened, confused, financially distressed, angry, or for other tough-to-handle reasons. The aftermath brings inner turmoil which stays with that person until they realize that when they repent to God for the abortion, He forgives them. Not only does He forgive them, but He heals them. A woman must forgive herself and let God cleanse her and heal her. God is big enough for every situation. He is a big enough God to take the pain away and restore His precious daughter. This same principle applies to males who have participated in the abortion process.

Some people have a hard time forgiving themselves for failed relationships or failed parenting. It may be that someone has done something so wrong that they don't feel like God would ever forgive them for that particular act of sin. Just as in any case, one must realize that once we repent and turn to God, He forgives us. So, if God forgives us, we must surely forgive ourselves and be set free.

Be sure and refer to the steps in preparing for your deliverance located in the back of this book. Your deliverance and freedom are closer than you think.

Key Points
- Prepare your heart by being hungry for righteousness, affirming your faith in Christ, confessing your sins, forgiving others, renouncing false religions, cults and cultish practices, breaking any curses over your life, breaking unhealthy soul ties, and fasting.

- Repent of all sins.

- The two biggest hindrances to freedom: Unconfessed Adultery and Unforgiveness

Ask Yourself
- What does it mean to hunger and thirst for righteousness?

- Do you find it easy to practice the act of repenting to God?

- Is the practice of yoga important to me? Why?

- Are you willing to research in-depth the subjects that challenge your current beliefs?

For Further Study
- *The Mormonizing of America* by Stephen Mansfield

- *The Heart of Yoga Revealed* by Judy L. White
- *Masonry: Beyond the Light* by William Schnoebelen

TESTIMONY

The Joy of Freedom

My journey to FREEDOM was a wonderful experience. I just closed my eyes, and I prayed to reveal the spirit ... and I felt something come out from my body (a spirit of pride), and it has also helped me break soul ties and help me come out from many other things. That was really a great experience for me.

— Milan, Nepal

Help for The Hopeless

Exposed to pornography at the age of five, touched by a female cousin at seven years of age, sexually active at thirteen, I spent all of my time getting others to notice me. I desired my dad to tell me he loved me and that he was proud of me. Girls and coaches filled that void. In college, I became completely addicted. I abused alcohol, drugs, anything that kept me 'liked" by others. I spent my twenties with sin eating me alive on the inside. I became unfaithful, convinced I was beyond repair ... and eventually became suicidal.

I met Jesus when I was thirty-one years old. He accepted me, gave me the strength to forgive and delivered me from an orphan spirit. I received adoption into the Kingdom of God! As a result, I have access to all that I need. In Him, I can do all things! The days of believing the lie that I have to do something, so that I can have something, so that I can be somebody are over. I am no longer an addict. I AM A SON.

— Zach, Texas

The Reality of Soul Ties

"There are many streams of cleansing-beginning with the
blood of Jesus! I want us to study and experience them all, as
God works among us to free, heal, and mature His people!"
— Jack W. Hayford[1]

What is a soul tie? A soul tie is an unhealthy spiritual connection that you have formed with another individual in the
realm of the soul. These ties can come from an emotional
attachment we have had with an individual or a physical attachment that we have had with someone. For example, you
might have made an oath or a pact with a friend while growing
up that you have not been able to uphold. This can lead to an
unhealthy soul tie. You might have sworn an oath in a frater-
nity or sorority, which created an unhealthy soul tie to certain
people or organizations. Anyone you have had pre-marital
sexual relations with creates an unhealthy soul tie that must be

broken. It is important that you pray to God and ask the Holy Spirit to reveal any unhealthy soul ties that exist in your life. He will reveal those things to you.

I can tell you from personal experience that soul ties are real, and it will be to your advantage to learn the basics related to the topic. I knew nothing about soul ties until a few months after I got delivered and set free for the first time. I say "for the first time" because I had numerous demons that did not all come out at once. I had numerous demons inside of me due to all of the rebellion I had walked in. When you add up sexual addiction, recreational drug use, alcoholism, stealing, lying, cheating, manipulating, and all of the ancestral things that I had inherited from my family lineage, there was a lot to uncover. For example, multiple sexual encounters mean that you open your flesh and your soul to other people's demons as well, so the numbers can multiply very rapidly. Don't let this alarm you. Whether you are dealing with three demons or 300 demons, God is God. Jesus is the name above all names, and every knee must bow to Him and Him alone. James 4:7 says, "Submit yourself, then, to God; Resist the devil, and he will flee from you." Therefore, don't worry about how much baggage you are carrying. Just focus on the beauty of cleaning out the closet.

Here are three, out of many, examples of soul ties from God's Word:

"If your brother, the son of your mother, or your son or your daughter or the wife you embrace or your friend who is as your own soul entices you secretly, saying, 'Let us go and serve other gods,' which neither you nor your fathers have known" (Deuteronomy 13:6 ESV).

"As soon as he had finished speaking to Saul, the soul of Jonathan was knit to the soul of David, and Jonathan loved him as his own soul" (1 Samuel 18:1 ESV).

"Now Dinah the daughter of Leah, whom she had born to Jacob, went out to see the women of the land. And when Shechem the son of Hamor the Hivite, the prince of the land, saw her, he seized her and lay with her and humiliated her. And his soul was drawn to Dinah, the daughter of Jacob. He loved the young woman and spoke tenderly to her" (Genesis 34:1-3 ESV).

Basics About Soul Ties

Some of my understanding about the subject of soul ties came about by listening to a cassette tape I had ordered. I remember driving to Houston, Texas for business and listening to this tape. Here are some of the basics that I learned. Soul ties are actually strong ties that exist between the souls of two particular people based upon a number of factors. Soul ties exist between parents and children, brothers and sisters, best friends, lovers, and even work relationships. Soul ties can be Godly or ungodly, meaning that they can be healthy soul ties or unhealthy soul ties.

We have three boys, and we have strong, healthy soul ties between Diane, me, and our boys. On the other hand, I had to break all of the unhealthy soul ties that existed between my mom and me. I do love my mom dearly. I take care of my mom, and I honor her. However, there were decades of emotional turmoil which I was exposed to, creating an unhealthy soul tie with her. Her guilt trips, her over protectiveness, her fits of rage, and so on, left a tie in the soul realm that would pull on me, much like a fisherman reeling in a fish on the line. The fish is fighting as hard as it can to get off the hook, but it can't seem to break away from what might be another suffocating experience or even death. Today, I can visit my mom in her assisted living residence and not feel the energy drain, because I broke the unhealthy soul ties that existed between us. We now have a healthy soul tie, because she is my mother, and I love her.

Recognizing and Dealing With Soul Ties

When a person has subjected himself to ungodly authority, and that authority is abusive to them, it can create a soul tie. For example, suppose you served in a ministry where your authority figure, such as a pastor was very controlling, manipulative, or abusive. In that case, there could be a tie in the soul realm that you need to break in order not to feel an emotional drain when it comes to going to church. You may never want to work at a church again because the soul tie causes you to feel drained when you think about working for another ministry. The same principle holds true with any position of authority with which we have allowed ourselves to be in a close relationship. This can mean working close together, with or without strong personal feelings toward them. It could be a boss that you have looked up to and admired, and they severely disappointed you. It could be a boss that you have never really liked, but that boss has been abusive to you. These could be situations where unhealthy soul ties may have formed.

As I stated earlier in these writings, when you have had sexual intimacy with someone other than your spouse, there is an ungodly soul tie immediately formed. Not only do you trade each other's baggage, but there is a tie in the soul realm that could one day draw you back together. That tie could draw you to social media to keep up with them. That tie could continually cause you to think about them when you really don't want to think about them, nor do you need to. That soul tie linked your lives together intimately, and it is best to sever it. If you are divorced, you would want to break any ungodly soul ties with your ex-spouse.

Getting Started

As I learned about soul ties in my car that day as I listened to that tape, I began to go down the list of people with whom I needed to break ties. As I prayed each prayer and renounced each tie, I would start to burp constantly. Something was leaving my body, and I knew it. I do not know how to fake a burp, and I cannot make myself burp. It was God working through me to get rid of familiar spirits that I had inherited from ungodly encounters. In other words, I had acquired some extra baggage as a result of my acts of unrighteousness and disobedience towards God. My repentance to my Lord brought His mercy and grace into my life to continue to sanctify me.

A prayer for breaking soul ties is found in the Resource Section at the back of this book for you to utilize. It is not some formula or "patented" prayer. It is a guide to help walk you through the basics of breaking soul ties with those in whom it needs to happen. I feel that it is important to remind you that I did not know about soul ties prior to my initial deliverance. I received so much freedom before I ever knew about soul ties. It is my prayer that, by reading this book, you will gain the understanding you need to deal with the areas of bondage in your life and deal with a lot of these things all at once. This should, in turn, help reduce your learning curve to many of the things regarding spiritual warfare and freedom from oppression, which are part of your journey to freedom.

Key Points

- Our souls can be connected to other people's souls in the spiritual realm.

- Soul ties can be healthy (Godly), and they can also be harmful (ungodly).

- Sexual intimacy, oaths, vows, manipulation, and domination are the most common creators of a soul tie.

Ask Yourself

- What vows or oaths have you made that could have created a soul tie in your life?

- Have you felt dominated or manipulated by someone in such a way that it created an unhealthy pull on your life?

- With whom do you have unhealthy "soul ties?"

For Further Study

- *Breaking Unhealthy Soul Ties* by Bill and Susan Banks

TESTIMONY

Walking In Freedom

The eyes of my heart were enlightened to the supernatural power of walking in the freedom of Jesus Christ in 2013. At the time, my wife and I were on the verge of divorce. I was unfaithful in our marriage, addicted to pornography, and tormented by a spirit of jealousy. After reading a book similar to this one, my faith began to increase about walking in true freedom. Before this knowledge, I had never acknowledged that demons and the devil were the sources of my addictions and torment. "The thief comes to steal, kill and destroy, but I have come to give life and life abundantly" (John 10:10).

I was not walking under the Lordship of Jesus Christ at that time. Upon having this revelation, I began to get desperate for Jesus ... to be seated in Heavenly places with Christ Jesus ... to be like the prodigal son, who came home to his Father ... to experience a place of protection, forgiveness, freedom, love, joy, and the glory of our Lord Jesus Christ. To begin the process of freedom, I humbled myself before the Lord, repented of all my sins, and confessed everything to my wife. She forgave me and also shared some things with me. There's nothing between us now, except the love and glory of our Lord Jesus. Today, we are pastors, have four beautiful daughters, and continue to walk in freedom. We believe what the enemy meant for evil, God uses for good. I no longer struggle with jealousy and have been completely delivered from pornography. We have a marriage ministry that helps to set the captives free because of the mercy of Jesus. If He can do it for my family, He can also do it for you!

— Joe, Texas

Deliverance:
The Road to Freedom

"For the sake of a dying, suffering world, count the cost, pay
the price and set the captives free."
— John G. Lake

Once someone has taken care of issues that require coming to God and repenting, they can now be set free. But how
does deliverance happen? First of all, there is nothing to fear
about the process of deliverance because God's anointing has
the power to break every yoke of destruction, regardless of the
processes. We read in scripture about examples of people being
set free and healed without a long list of ministry "to do's"
prior to their supernatural encounter. I don't ever want anyone
to presume that I have a philosophy tied to only systems and
processes and not to Jesus Christ and the power of His blood.
Through Jesus and the power of His blood, our victory comes.

244 • FREEDOM: Winning the Battle Within

Rules of Engagement

Therefore, before I begin to expand on some ministry basics related to deliverance, it is important that I remind you that there is no "formula" for deliverance. Jesus, God's Word, and the Holy Spirit are completely in charge of establishing the rules of engagement for setting captives free. If we continue to read the New Testament and adhere to the New Testament, we will find that getting set free from demonic oppression is quite simple. It is sometimes ministers who make it hard. I have read an array of books on deliverance, and I have been exposed to a host of seminars and/or programs geared toward taking people through the process of spiritual freedom. Most of them have tremendous merit; however, I am going to stick as closely as possible to the simplicity of the New Testament teachings of God's Holy Book. I like to keep things simple. Most people that you or I will ever minister to do not need months of preparation before getting set free by the power of Jesus Christ. They just need understand that they have demonic oppression in their lives, how it may have gotten there, how Jesus can set them free, and how to maintain their freedom.

On the other hand, there are exceptions. Because of the broad spectrum of things people have dealt with in their lives, we always have to consider what processes we use or even how we take people through them. For instance, I have ministered to people who have been deeply involved in Satanism. Ministering to someone with this kind of background versus someone who lived a pretty "average" American lifestyle, who engaged in some rebellious partying in college, are two different things. Jesus even said to His disciples, "Some of these come out only with prayer and fasting." Therefore, someone who comes from a really dark background may need layers of ministry throughout the course of a year in order to get completely set free from their past.

I have ministered to people who have been subjected to Satanic ritual abuse as a child, which is nothing they asked for as a kid! It wasn't their choice. This takes a tremendous amount of time and ministry skillset to help someone unwrap all of those particular layers of trauma. Anyone who has walked through this process would tell you the same thing. However, if someone has never been subjected to these kinds of horrors, and I do mean horrors, it would be hard to understand that it takes a process for all of that to be healed.

Don't Rush The Process

Sometimes, people have come from backgrounds where there were a number of mental and emotional curse spirits working in the family lines, and this type of ministry can take much more time to unravel all of the enemy's doings. When there is a history of bipolar tendencies, obsessive-compulsive disorder, or severe depression, I have found it to take a few months or even a year to unravel all of the layers of demonic oppression and see someone get completely set free. It doesn't mean that God can't supernaturally do it all in an instant because He can! Some people may have been entirely delivered supernaturally at the moment of their salvation, and I would not argue that point with anyone who bears the fruit of that freedom. However, from over twenty years of ministering to people, some need ministry in layers.

A Transformed Life

On the other hand, the average person will experience a 180-degree, life-transformation immediately after a time of deliverance ministry. This is why I am so passionate about teaching you about freedom. I want you to receive ministry, if necessary, and also minister to others like Jesus modeled and commanded us to do.

I am setting all of this up because the Bible clearly states that we are to "cast out demons." However, you don't necessarily read where Jesus or one of His followers told someone to "sit down right here," and we will minister to you. You don't necessarily read where Jesus or one of His followers told someone to "repent for this or that" before they commanded demons to come out of them. However, that certainly doesn't mean that it did not take place. The Bible doesn't give a detail-by-detail account for every sentence that Jesus or one of His followers spoke while ministering to people. We get from the Bible the necessary details that provide us with insight into what we should do and how we should go about doing it. We are given testimonies of powerful deliverances and healings done by Jesus and His followers. Still, there are not enough books in the world that could contain all of the details of every ministry setting in which Jesus or one of His early followers took people through before they got set free or healed.

Ministering Freedom

When we give powerful testimonies in church, those testimonies are short and impactful. At the same time, it is understood that all of the events leading up to the testimony and all the details surrounding what took place are usually much too detailed to tell in a public testimony. So, when we hear a testimony in church, we know there were probably a few more steps or situations in there that were not mentioned for the sake of telling the "meat" of the testimony. This principle holds true in biblical accounts concerning freedom. In some of these Biblical instances, do you think that Jesus might have gone into a few homes and told people to sit down? As he was sitting down next to them, do you think it's possible that He might have actually had a conversation with them and listened to their story? I think Jesus was probably quite relational, and I believe He was a fantastic listener. It is quite possible that Jesus had several intimate conversations with various people before ministering to them.

Partnership

I have ministered freedom to people by myself, in pairs, in small groups, and large group settings. When we do the ministry of Jesus, we must always be prepared to do what the Father asks of us. There are times when I have just been caught alone, and I must minister to that person individually, although I would rather minister with a partner. When I was ministered to for the first time in 2001, there were five people in the room; three men and two women. One man was leading me through freedom while the other four were praying and asking the Holy Spirit for words of knowledge for me. They were simply interceding for me in prayer so that my freedom was happening with more ease. Prayers of the saints, in unity, bring power. God moves with our prayers. He is sovereign, but He wants us to pray so that He can partner with us and move with us in prayer.

Do You Want to Be Free?

Let's use the example of ministering freedom to someone in pairs or in a small group. If I am the ministry leader in this particular situation, my partner will be praying and agreeing with me, as well as interceding on the person's behalf. I will sit down with that person and ask if he or she really knows why we are sitting there. I need to know that they are hungry for God, and I want to know that they genuinely want to be set free. I can want freedom for people all day long, but they must also genuinely want to walk in freedom.

Stay on The Path

Jesus has some teaching about the aftermath of wrong motives. He said, "When an unclean spirit goes out of a man, he goes through dry places, seeking rest; and finding none, he says,

248 of FREEDOM: Winning the Battle Within

'I will return to my house from which I came.' And when he comes, he finds it swept and put in order. Then he goes and takes with him seven other spirits more wicked than himself, and they enter and dwell there; and the last state of that man is worse than the first" (Luke 11:24-26).

This is nothing to be scared or fearful of. If you are a Christian and want to walk in freedom, this is usually nothing to have any major concern. Some people want freedom from oppression, yet they don't want to give up their sin. They may want to repent and have a moment with God temporarily, but they can't abstain from walking right back into those fleshly desires that got them in that situation in the first place. That's why Jesus said, "Go and sin no more lest a worse thing come upon you" (John 5:14). Jesus is warning us to remain on the path. It's like walking on a road with ditches on both sides. Jesus shows us the way and even warns us that there are consequences that await us by veering off into the ditch. With every step that we take off the path of following Jesus, a demonic force is waiting to shoot an arrow at us that can possibly penetrate our flesh and our soul. As Christians, we are called to stay on the path and follow Jesus and refrain from practicing sin. The moral of the story is, "Don't let yourself fall into a roadside ditch!"

Taking The Next Step

After I find out if the person is hungry for freedom, I will ask them if they know what to expect. They will often say that they do not know what to expect. It is important to give them some encouragement concerning what they might experience. Although there is no formula and none of us can put God in a systematic box, some tangible things usually happen when one goes through deliverance. First, I explain to the person that an unclean spirit is like air; therefore, it is going to come out painlessly. Although it is real warfare, the battle was already won at the cross, and the demons have been defeated in the name of Jesus. Because of this, the demons must obey God and come out when called upon. I instruct the person who is receiving ministry that these unclean spirits may have talons, claws, tentacles, or some other gruesome form of attachments that cause them to be able to hold on for dear life when they do not want to leave a person. Although they are just air from a spiritual perspective, their bodily members are just as real as our fingers or toes are to us. Because of this, they do not want to detach and exit the body without a fight. Let me give you a completely extreme and rare example so that this makes sense.

A Rare Occurrence

On one occasion, I ministered to a man who had sold his soul to the devil and joined a Satanic cult. I cast the first demon out of him, and he coughed up blood as the demon came out. I cast three more demons out of him, and all three times, he coughed up blood. After the fourth demon came out, he laid on the carpet, thoroughly exhausted. I don't remember how long he laid on the ground, but he was completely exhausted and needed some time to recuperate. He even had the appearance of being dead as he laid on the floor. I was perplexed as to where the blood came from because I had never experienced this in ministry before, but I got my answer the next day as I read a new book that I had ordered about the subject of deliverance. In this book, the author described what would sometimes happen when a person who has sold their soul to the devil gets delivered. The author said that certain demons that occupy a person's body who has served Satan would come out ripping the person's flesh with their claws as they are being cast out. The author went on to say that it was common to see people who have been in Satanism cough up blood when getting demons cast out of them because of this reason. Now, this is a rarity, but it is a clear example as to the fact that demons have claws, talons, tentacles, or other attachments that they use to establish a stronghold in a person's body and soul. The extreme example of coughing blood is not ordinary, so do not be alarmed! I don't recall ever seeing blood except in this case.

Rendering Demons Powerless

I will also let the person know that we have the authority to bind the power of demons, causing them to be powerless. In turn, we have the authority to instruct them to loosen their hold on any person's life and let him go, and they must obey God. Then, the spirit has to respond and come out in the name of Jesus. I tell the person that the demons are likely to manifest because they have been called out in the name of Jesus. This upsets the demonic spirits because they can't hide anymore. It's as if you turned on the light in the attic, and all of the rats scatter and run for cover.

As Christians, we have the power to bind and loose in the name of Jesus because of the authority He gave us: "And I also say to you that you are Peter, and on this rock, I will build My church, and the gates of Hades shall not prevail against it. And I will give you the keys of the kingdom of Heaven, and whatever you bind on earth will be bound in Heaven, and whatever you loose on earth will be loosed in Heaven" (Matthew 16:18-20).

How Do Unclean Spirits Exit?

There is scriptural support as to the fact that demons come out of people through an opening in the body. It is quite common for unclean spirits to come out through an opening such as the mouth, nose, eyes, and occasionally the ears. This does not mean that it has to happen this way, but I have found it quite common. Even in the Bible, you can read cases where a demon tried to talk back to Jesus, let out a scream, or threw someone down on the ground and caused them to convulse. Although I have not seen any real statistics on this, I have found that most demons will come up through a person's throat (as air) and exit the body through the mouth. I also let those to whom I minister know that there is no faking involved. Still, they may wind up burping repeatedly, coughing repeatedly, sighing repeatedly, or experience slight or deep yawns repeatedly. For example, when I had my first experience casting demons out of myself, I had these huge yawns that I could not fake. After each yawn, I could literally feel the release of oppression and the feeling of God's peace taking over my life. Since that time, I tend to burp repeatedly when I experience spiritual freedom. Over the course of my entire life, I have never been able to burp on purpose. In other words, I have never been able to manufacture a fake burp! I know that it is a spirit coming out of me in the name of Jesus, and I am very happy about whatever is leaving my life so that I can walk in new measures of freedom and sanctification.

Sometimes unclean spirits will manifest and exit through the nose in the form of congestion or a snotty nose. The person will have to use a tissue or a soft rag to wipe their nose during ministry time. Occasionally, a person will go through an entire ministry session, and most or all of the unclean spirits will exit through their eyes, which results in a lot of tears running down their face. Once again, a tissue or soft rag takes care of the tears.

I once ministered to one of my close friends that had been through a tremendous amount of heartbreaks and disappointments in his life. From the tragic death of a family member, family betrayal, to an unseen divorce, he had really begun to question whether God loved him or not. He wanted freedom so badly but didn't even think that he was loved enough by God to be free. During our ministry time, all he did was sob uncontrollably, and he shed tears like a river. After he got set free, he was a changed man instantaneously. The weight of the world had left him, and he was amazed that he had so many tears running out of his eyes. He explained that he wasn't crying at all, but he could not help the sobbing and tears rolling down his face. He knew it was God.

No Prescribed Patterns

One time, my wife and I were ministering to a married couple who were dear friends. They were strong and committed Christians, but they battled with issues that a lot of strong and committed Christians battle within their family life. They believed in all of Jesus' teachings, but they were not walking in all of the freedom that we read about in the Bible. We had given them a book to read and CDs to listen to, which prepared them for learning more about the real ministry of Jesus.

When they were ready, they drove three hours to come to see us and get set free from demonic oppression. They had two young children at the time, and a relative stayed at home to take care of the kids. Needless to say, our friends got delivered, and their lives were dramatically changed in an instant. The next day, my buddy called me and gave me a testimony. He told me that his relative had informed him of a situation that occurred with their son and told him the exact time that it had happened. The relative told the parents that their son (approximately six years old) had gone to the restroom and did not come out for an hour. The relative went on to say that she heard some of the loudest noises coming out of the child's bottom that she had ever heard. She told the parents that it carried on for an hour. The time that this was happening was the exact time that this boy's parents were getting set free at our house.

I want to bring up a couple of points to you here. One is that a demon can come out of any opening in the body. Secondly, adults don't have to worry about this issue. I have never seen an adult experience this in any setting. Also, it shows how much authority we have over our children's lives, and what we do matters in the lives of our children. Our righteousness affects our children, and our sins affect our children. What we carry, our children carry. It should not be hard to believe since the medical world continually bombards you with questionnaires and forms asking you about things that run in your family lines. Unclean spirits run in family lines until a righteous man has the courage to break the enemy's power over his lineage. As long as your children are under your roof, you are their spiritual covering. The fact that this young boy, who did not understand spiritual things like this yet, basically sat on a commode and made a lot of noises beyond his control shows the incredible mercy of God. I know this family well, and their two children are both adults who love God and do the ministry of Jesus. In fact, both of their children grew up loving God and doing the work of the ministry throughout their teen years also.

No Set Manner

Before we move on, it is extremely imperative that I mention that demons do not always have to come out through an opening in the body. They can simply leave the body without any kind of visible or tangible manifestation. This is possible, and it does happen. In 1997, prior to me becoming a Christian, I had a very strange run-in with a couple of really anointed men. At the time, I did not know they were anointed. I just thought they were a little crazy. I was coming out of a business meeting one night and was one of the last ones out of the room. Standing by the door were these two men. One was a pastor, and one was a prison minister. They stopped me and told me that they really felt like they were supposed to ask me if there was anything that I needed prayer for. Without hesitation, I told them, "Yeah, you can pray for me not to be so angry because tomorrow I am going to go to meet a man and invite him to my backyard for a fight. I am going to whip his _ _ _!" So, these guys put their hands on me and prayed. As they were praying, I felt this release coming through my shoulders as if all of that anger was leaving me, and it felt quite amazing. The next day, I did have a confrontation with this gentleman; however, I was all smiles! He was actually provoking me and saying things to me that were really disrespectful, but I just smiled and was very courteous to him the entire time we faced each other. When he left my presence, I was just as happy and had no regrets that I did not react to the situation. The night before, however, I had already premeditated that we would fight the next day, and I was determined to make it happen. Looking back, I realize that those guys were praying for those demons of anger to leave me that night, and they did! But they didn't come out of my mouth, my nose, my eyes, or any other opening. They came right out of my body through my shoulders. I remember something was coming through my shoulders. The lesson here is still this, "Do not put God in a box." There is no specific formula, but it is perfectly okay to let people know what to generally expect when a spirit comes out of a person. And they must know that it is only air, and it is not scary, weird, or crazy. It is the ministry of Jesus.

Deliverance and Prayer

At this point in ministry time, I will let the person being ministered to know their personal prayer time is essentially over. Through experience, I find the person getting ministered to is most at peace and rest when they are just meditating on Jesus and totally relaxing. There has been a lot of prayer and fasting that has led up to this moment. Deliverance itself occurs by command, which follows great prayer time. When I am commanding unclean spirits to manifest and come out of a person, I do not need the person to whom I am ministering to be praying at that time. We have been praying, and any partners that I have in the room are still praying. I would rather the person receiving ministry just sit back and receive ministry. I have found that this leads to a much more fruitful outcome. Since I have seen so many people get set free, and in most cases, tangible manifestations of unclean spirits come out of people through the mouth, nose, or eyes, I really don't think it is necessary for them to be praying out loud at that particular time. If spirits exit so easily from the throat, I prefer the person just to relax and let the minister, the prayer partners, and Jesus do the work. If we examine the scriptures, there are no unique stories where Jesus or one of His followers was casting demons out of a person, and the recipient was praying the whole time it was happening, or even praying at all. So, the point here is, if you are the one receiving ministry in the area of deliverance, just relax and let God move.

Now, there are times when I have discerned something while ministering, so I will stop and ask the person to renounce a particular spirit in the name of Jesus. For example, I might say to that person, "I would like for you to renounce all idolatry in the name of Jesus," and they will. After that, I will cast the spirit of idolatry out of that person. Remember, it is just air at that point, defeated by the blood of Jesus Christ.

Essentially, basic deliverance involves the casting out of demons from a person's body, just as the Bible describes. One must ask the question, "If casting out demons was so common when the Bible was recorded, why did the teaching of it suddenly quit?" There's a very easy and straightforward answer. It is not widespread teaching among the church because Satan has been slowly deceiving mankind over the past two thousand years to get the church to avoid the subject of casting out demons and healing the sick. If we, the church, are casting out demons and healing the sick, we deliver a significant blow to Satan and his plan to keep Christians weak, wounded, divided, and much less effective.

An appointment or ministry setting in which a person is going through deliverance can take anywhere from twenty minutes to two hours, depending on what kind of conversation and prayers take place prior to the actual ministry time of casting out demons.

Casting out demons does not always involve reading books, studying, and setting up appointments. I see people get set free all the time without them really knowing that I am literally casting a demon out of them. Because demons have names, ranks, and assignments just like any militaristic force, I just pray for people and address their situations by name. I have prayed for a significant amount of people at the altar who needed freedom from demonic oppression that did not know anything about deliverance or the fact that they might have a demon inside of them. When I lay my hand on their shoulder and pray, I just pray a normal prayer for them at first. But then I speak to their situation directly. For example, I might say as I am praying, "... and fear, you leave this person right now in the name of Jesus. I command all fear to leave this person's life right now in the name of Jesus. I command anxiety to go, worry to go, stress to go, in the mighty name of Jesus. The Bible says in 2 Timothy 1:7, 'I did not give you the spirit of fear, but of power, and love, and of sound mind.' Therefore, all fear must leave in Jesus' name. Thank you, Lord."

As I am praying like this, they have no earthly idea (or spiritual idea) that I am casting spirits out of them. But the whole time I'm doing this, they begin to cough, burp, sigh, yawn, or start sobbing, and they don't even know why it is happening. It brings no alarm to them. They walk away with joy that a real prayer got answered. We get testimonies all the time from people who come up to the altar for prayer that have had supernatural encounters like this. When I am pastoring or leading, our prayer team is taught to pray over people and even take them through measures of freedom by casting out demons without alarming them.

Godly Wisdom and Deliverance

We need the wisdom of God when we minister. Deliverance is not a freak show, nor is it some carnival act. These are human lives that we are talking about, and we will be judged on how we handle people in ministry. In Matthew 9, the bible tells us that Jesus moved with compassion on all of those who were harassed and afflicted. Compassion is essential! We are to be wise as serpents and gentle as doves, when dealing with God's people. You can be sitting in our church where ten people are getting set free from demons, and you might not even know it is happening at the time. That is because we train ministers to be wise with their words. It is amazing what you can accomplish when the spirit of the Lord is present. When you understand that so many of the terms we use in the English language are names of demons, we can address those issues directly without causing someone to be overwhelmed or confused. "For the Lord is the Spirit, and wherever the Spirit of the Lord is, there is freedom" (2 Corinthians 3:17 NLT).

Key Points

- There is nothing to fear about the process of deliverance.

- There is no formula. The Bible makes it simple.

- Demons are just air. They must obey Jesus.

- There are no prescribed patterns, but there are common ways that demons come out of people.

Ask Yourself

- Does any part of the process of deliverance make you uncomfortable? Why? What does the Bible say about it?

- Why is it important that a person understands their need for freedom?

- Did it help to read about the various ways that demons exit people's bodies?

For Further Study
- *Born to Be Free* by Tom Vermillion

TESTIMONY

The Doorway to A New Life of Freedom

In 2018, I was handed a book that opened the floodgates to freedom in my life. The Lord began speaking to me in ways that I had never experienced before. For example, it was the first time I learned that demons were put on assignments, and there was an immediate stirring in my soul that I absolutely knew had to go. Before I even finished reading the book, I had been delivered from dozens of unclean spirits right in my living room. Generational curses were being broken, and a new awakening had taken place.

As I became free from bondage, the Lord gave me a new identity. It was the beginning of a two-year (and counting) radical transformation. Jesus became tangible. My eyes were opened to an entirely new realm that I never knew existed but had silently held me in death's grip. Jesus so lovingly took me by the hand and walked me into complete healing of my mind, body, and soul. I was then led into a three-day radical deliverance on the same exact day that death had stolen my mother's life sixteen years prior. On December 7th, 2019, I was fully delivered from the spirit of death, mental illness, and hundreds of other unclean spirits and generational curses. FREEDOM: Winning the Battle Within was the doorway to an entirely new life ... a life for which I am forever grateful!

— Kristi, Michigan

CHAPTER EIGHTEEN

Is Self-Deliverance Possible?

"Beloved, if any unholiness exists in the nature, it is not thereby the consent of the Spirit of God. If unholiness is in your life it is because your soul is giving consent to it, and you are retaining it. Let it go. Cast it out and let God have His way in your life."
—John G. Lake

I am grateful that the book I read on deliverance had a chapter about self-deliverance. It has been some time since I read the book, and although I may not recall everything, what I do remember was that the author warned the reader not to try deliverance on yourself for the first time! The author instructed the reader to find a minister who believed in the real ministry of Jesus and let them help you get set free from oppression. He also taught about how you could cast demons out of yourself to be free.

When I think about my own deliverance, I always reflect on what happened in December of 2000 in my hotel room in Atlanta, Georgia. I had just finished reading that book about deliverance. As you may remember from an earlier chapter, it was the amazing book with a very uninviting cover!

New Understanding

After reading that book, it is hard to describe the enthusiasm I had to get set free. There I was, in my hotel room all alone, knowing that I had thirty-five years of demonic oppression that needed to be broken. I wanted someone to minister to me right then! The first thing I did was call my wife and share the good news. I told her all about what I had read and what kind of authority we had to kick demons out of our lives in Jesus' name. She was taken back a bit because she was hearing about demons being inside of us for the first time. But she heard my excitement and knew something was going to happen.

Desperate To Be Free

After the phone call, I was lying on the bed at 1:00 a.m., wondering who in the world I was going to find to cast demons out of me when I got back home. We were going to a mega-church, so we didn't know anybody there, and they sure hadn't given us any indication that they cast demons out of people. I thought about my previous pastor of the wonderful Lutheran church where we had previously been members. Then I realized that he had never talked about demons, so he probably wasn't going to help me. Consequently, my only choice was to go back to the chapter on self-deliverance and do what the book said to do.

A Step Toward Freedom

The next morning, I woke up so excited about my newfound freedom. I wanted to tell the whole world how to get set free from demonic influences. However, I soon learned the whole world is not ready to hear such good news. Demons don't like that message, and Christians with demons especially don't like that message. They are usually the ones who get mean and nasty. It is a lot like the Pharisees and Sadducees. They knew so much about the Holy Scriptures, but they could not see the truth when it was right in front of them. So, what did they do? They got mad, mean, and nasty, and they killed those who had the good news. Hopefully, you are not one of those types of people, but you are one who can read your Bible and allow the Holy Spirit to teach you all things. I pray that you are not stuck in your religious ways just because you may have been conditioned your entire life to believe only what your "religious affiliation has taught you." The Bible is real; it is the Living Word of God. Jesus is the Word. Jesus is alive, and He is the same yesterday, today, and forever. Everything that is included in the Bible is for us today. We are fighting the same devil. We are fighting the same sins. We are fighting the same sicknesses and diseases, plus a whole lot more. We are also fighting the same religious mindsets. You just have to decide if you are going to believe God or man.

Regarding your freedom, you get to decide if you are ready to take steps to freedom. You are an adult. It is your choice what you do with your life. For anyone who is as desperate as I was, it is as simple as what follows. I also have to keep in mind that there are people who will read this book who will be completely isolated from a person who has any clue on how to minister in this area; hence, the need for listing these steps:

1. Repent for all sins, known or unknown

2. Call upon the name of the Lord

3. Ask the Holy Spirit to show you what demons need to be dealt with. Listen to Him because He will speak to you, give you impressions, or give you pictures of what you are dealing with in order to help you, for the Holy Spirit

is our Counselor and our Comforter. (You may want to make a list of them on paper first.)

4. Command the demons to manifest in Jesus' name

5. Bind their power, in Jesus' name

6. Command them to come out of your body and leave you in Jesus' name. Repeat if necessary, and continue to demand that they come out in the name of Jesus', by your command. Speak directly to demons, using your command, and using the name of Jesus. Be persistent!

7. After you are finished, praise God, spend time worshiping Him and ask Him to fill you with the Holy Spirit

With all of that said, for someone who has never been through deliverance, I would still strongly suggest you find a minister of the gospel of Jesus Christ to minister to you for the first time. Find believing believers who authentically believe what the Bible says. Find believers who believe what we are supposed to believe and are willing to do what believers have been commanded to do by Jesus Christ of Nazareth, the Son of the Living God. Soon after, it will be beneficial for you to clearly understand and utilize the concept of self-deliverance, which we will discuss further in the next chapter. I have successfully used self-deliverance many times to bring freedom to my life, not because of my knowledge and power, but because of the power and authority granted to me through the mighty name of Jesus. You can do the same when you understand the power that is available to you through His name! Jesus is alive!

Key Points

- Self-deliverance is normal.

- The name of Jesus really works, and demons must obey Him.

- You must command demons to come out in Jesus' name.

- Every believer should work toward a lifestyle of periodic self-deliverance, when necessary.

Ask Yourself

- Do you have the confidence to command demons to come out in Jesus' name?

- Why is self-deliverance a regular part of a Christian's life?

TESTIMONY

Healed And Made Whole

Many years ago, I was diagnosed with cancer. The doctors had X-rays of the tumors and many other test results. I was waiting on the next appointment to find out what the next steps were that we would take.

On the weekend before that doctor's appointment, our prayer warriors, Danny and Diane McDaniel drove to our house for a day of prayer. The prayer was intense with much love, tears, laughter, sadness, and praise to our Lord! That was on a Saturday. On Monday I went to my scheduled doctor's appointment. After many tests, the doctor came back to the room, a bit agitated (actually, he was angry) and holding up a new X-ray, said with much anger, "What has happened here?" He told me the new X-ray showed no signs of any tumors and said the original X-ray must have been the X-ray of someone else. I smiled and told him," Praise God! It is the power of prayer! I am healed! I accept this in the name of Jesus!"

That seemed to make him even angrier because he stormed out of the room and slammed the door behind him. He was gone quite a while and then came back in the room and de-manded that he take more tests because there was something wrong. I smiled and said, "You take all the tests you want but, it is the power of prayer and I am healed, thank you, Jesus." I also told him all tests would be at his cost. They never took any more tests or offered any more appointments. To date, I am still healed, whole and healthy in the name of Jesus!

— Soozi, Texas

Keeping Your Freedom After Deliverance

"Take care of your body as if you were going to live forever;
and take care of your soul as if you
were going to die tomorrow."
— St. Augustine

Two things happen when demons are cast out of people.
First of all, they experience a new-found freedom and peace
in their lives because what had previously inhabited an area of
their lives is now gone. However, when an evil spirit has been
cast out, a vacancy needs to be filled because your temple (your
body) has been swept clean. The Holy Spirit is the only choice
to fill that vacancy. As is evidenced by the words of Paul to
the believers in Ephesus, "And do not get drunk with wine, for
that is debauchery, but be filled with the Spirit, addressing one
another in psalms and hymns and spiritual songs, singing and
making melody to the Lord with your heart, giving thanks al-

ways and for everything to God the Father in the name of our Lord Jesus Christ, submitting to one another out of reverence for Christ" (Ephesians 5:18-21).

The Power of The Holy Spirit

After casting demons out of someone, the first thing we do is pray for him or her to get filled with the Holy Spirit. I did not know about this when I had my personal encounter with God in my hotel room in Atlanta. When I went to a minister's home in January of 2001 to get set free from the multitude of demons I had acquired throughout my first thirty-five years of life, the first thing they did for me after they ministered freedom to me was ask me if I was ready to get filled with the Spirit of God, and I responded with a "Yes!" He took a step toward me and reached out his hand to lay it on my chest and said, "Father, in the name of Jesus, baptize him with the Holy Spirit and fill him up." No sooner than he said that, I began to feel electrical surges through the middle of my two hands that traveled all the way up my arms and into my body. The power of the Holy Spirit overcame my body. I was trembling and laughing with a roaring laughter like a lion. Now that doesn't mean that I was making lion sounds. I mean that I was laughing from the depths of my soul with joy that was like a roar. I do remember repeatedly praising God as I was laughing. I felt as if I were going to Heaven. If this is new for you, I would suggest you read more about the Holy Spirit and learn all that you can so that you know what is available to you as a believer of Jesus Christ. There will be a few references for you at the end of the book. Being filled with the Holy Spirit is essential because the Holy Spirit fills any voids left by the number of trespassers that were evicted from your spiritual property.

A Prayer Life

Next, make sure that you develop a consistent prayer life. I recommend that you begin to journal with God. God loves it when we have a journal and pen handy as we spend time with Him. After all, the Holy Bible was written because God had faithful servants who were willing to write down the things that He was speaking to them. Now, those things have been passed down from generation to generation, and we are the wonderful recipients of God's revelations to His people. You, too, get revelations from God, but you will always want to write them down because you cannot trust your memory. Someday, your children and your grandchildren will need to have access to your journals and your time spent with God.

Fasting

Andrew Murray was a noted writer, teacher, and Christian pastor from South Africa. He made this observation about the correlation between prayer and fasting when he said, "Prayer is reaching out after the unseen; fasting is letting go of all that is seen and temporal. Fasting helps express, deepen, confirm the resolution that we are ready to sacrifice anything, even ourselves, to attain what we seek for the kingdom of God."[1]

Fasting is a term used at times related to health, but it also has a spiritual application. I believe most believers are familiar with the term, but for those who may be less informed, I want to offer this brief explanation to help you understand how it relates to keeping your deliverance. For the Christian, fasting is a time set apart to abstain from some or all foods for a set amount of time while the individual focuses on spending time with God. There are different kinds of fasts; some are as strict as water only, and others take a modified approach. I won't take time to get into the various types of fasts, but I only wish to explain the concept and purpose to those unfamiliar with fasting as something a believer does. Ultimately, fasting helps to sharpen our spiritual senses and draws us into a closer, more intimate fellowship with God, as we spend more time with Him because we are not eating as usual.

Jesus talked about fasting to His disciples, and when He spoke of it, He did not say, "If you fast..." He said, "And when you fast, do not look gloomy like the hypocrites, for they disfigure their faces that their fasting may be seen by others. Truly, I say to you, they have received their reward. But when you fast, anoint your head and wash your face, that your fasting may not be seen by others but by your Father who is in secret. And your Father who sees in secret will reward you" (Matthew 6:16-18).

A Lifestyle of Fasting

In my opinion, a lifestyle of fasting is the third basic requirement of a believing believer for keeping one's deliverance. Fasting takes development just like exercising or lifting weights. You have to work your way into the disciplines of fasting so that you can reap the rewards of the fasting lifestyle that causes God to move on your behalf. Reread the passage from Matthew 6. The Bible says your Father, who sees you fast in secret, will reward you. There are rewards involved with fasting that also break strongholds of Satan and his demons. Here is what the Bible says about fasting in Isaiah 58:6-9, "Is this not the fast that I have chosen: To loose the bonds of wickedness, To undo the heavy burdens, To let the oppressed go free, And that you break every yoke? Is it not to share your bread with the hungry, And that you bring to your house the poor who are cast out; When you see the naked, that you cover him, And not hide yourself from your own flesh? Then your light shall break forth like the morning, Your healing shall spring forth speedily, And your righteousness shall go before you; The glory of the Lord shall be your rear guard. Then you shall call, and the Lord will answer; You shall cry, and He will say, 'Here I am'."

Fasting does the following:

- Loosens the bonds of wickedness in and around our lives

- Undoes heavy burdens

- Frees us from demonic oppression

- Breaks every yoke of the enemy

- Compels us to be compassionate and generous

- Causes our light to shine

- Brings healing

- Causes us to be in right standing with God

- God will have our back

- God answers our prayers

Feed On God's Word

The next step is diving into the Word of God. Take time to study God's Word and strengthen your faith by discovering who you are in Christ. The Bible says, "So then faith comes by hearing, and hearing by the Word of God" (Romans 10:17). We develop our faith by getting the Word of God inside of us, but one must become hungry for the Word. Whatever we eat comes out. If we feast on the Word of God, righteousness, peace, and joy flow out of us. Jesus said, "Blessed are those who hunger and thirst for righteousness, for they shall be filled" (Matthew 5:6). The bottom line is that the Word of God fills our hearts and builds our faith. As we grow in faith and obedience to God's Word, the devil and his demons have a hard time finding a breach in the walls of our temple, and without a breach, they have no access.

Blessings Through Giving

It is important that you develop a lifestyle of obedience to God in the area of generosity, which I believe is the fifth area that helps us live a life of obedience to God and ultimately helps us keep our deliverance. It may not be what everyone wants to hear, but giving God back the tithe (10%) of what He minimally expects from us is paramount. It doesn't matter what your financial status is. Ten percent is ten percent, and it may not always seem easy. God sees everything. He sees when we are generous, and He sees when we rob Him. Robbing God can cause a breach in the walls of your temple, meaning your personal life and your family. Here's what God says about this issue in Malachi 3:8-12, "Will a man rob God? Yet you have robbed Me! But you say, 'In what way have we robbed You?' In tithes and offerings. You are cursed with a curse, For you have robbed Me, Even this whole nation. Bring all the tithes into the storehouse, That there may be food in My house, And try Me now in this," Says the Lord of hosts, 'If I will not open for you the windows of Heaven And pour out for you such blessing That there will not be room enough to receive it. And I will rebuke the devourer for your sakes, So that he will not destroy the fruit of your ground, Nor shall the vine fail to bear fruit for you in the field,' says the Lord of hosts; 'And all nations will call you blessed, For you will be a delightful land,' says the Lord of hosts."

Regarding the tithe that wasn't yours in the first place:

1. Bring your tithe/ten percent to the storehouse (to God)
2. So there will be provision in the body of Christ
3. God says, "Test Me," which is the only time He ever said, "Test Me."
4. God will open the windows of Heaven
5. Pour out so much blessing that you will not have room enough to contain
6. God will turn back Satan and his demons on your behalf
7. He will not allow Satan and his demons to destroy your productivity

8. People will call you blessed

9. You will be seen as delightful

The Road to Blessing and Freedom

The real question here is, "Who doesn't want to be a part of this plan?" This is God spelling it out for us. He wants to bless us. He wants to rebuke the enemy on our behalf. He wants to give us favor with Himself and with man. All He is asking is that we are obedient to His Word. It's a choice that goes way beyond just keeping your castle protected. By that, I mean protecting your life and your family, through obedience to God's Word. Tithing helps keep the walls strong and the gates shut on the enemy.

Be a Giver, Not a Taker

Beyond tithing is the area of offerings. Never forget the principle, "As we sow, so shall we reap." I have met a lot of "takers" in my life, and they never seem to wake up and capture the essence of the universal law of sowing and reaping that God established. They want a field of harvest without paying the price. The price is in the sowing, and it is the sower who reaps, not the field. Here is an example from God's Word that should encourage you about being generous towards others, "Give, and it will be given to you: good measure, pressed down, shaken together, and running over will be put into your bosom. For with the same measure that you use, it will be measured back to you" (Luke 6:38).

Absolute Faith and Trust in God

This is an essential part of walking in freedom. We don't want to be enslaved by Satan and his demonic forces. Stingy people play right into Satan's hand. Trusting God means trusting Him with everything we have, including our money. In turn, our God is a God of protection, provision, and power. I would rather be on His side; therefore, generosity is just part of

274 • FREEDOM: Winning the Battle Within

being a believing believer who desires to walk in freedom while God is our rear guard.

Build Healthy Relationships

The sixth thing that is necessary to keep your freedom is to develop healthy relationships with fellow believers, especially believing believers. This means believers who believe that all of God's Word is true and relevant for today. That doesn't mean that you aren't to engage the culture because God wants you to do that. God will put you around sinners so that you can love them and engage them with a life-saving message. However, you need healthy Christians to be around more often than just an hour or two on Sunday morning. Many church-goers are living these busy lives and don't have time for God except when the world shuts down on Sunday mornings. So, they meander their way to church, get motivated to live for Jesus for another week, and go right back into the world. It ought not to be this way for a Christian who wants to walk in freedom and help others do the same. Healthy relationships will be crucial. I encourage you to get in a small group or start a Bible study. Just get active and grow in Christ alongside other people who want to do the same.

Persevere Until Freedom Comes

The seventh thing you need to know about keeping your freedom is realizing you may not get every demon out the first time you go through freedom. Like I said before, God is God, and He can supernaturally deliver somebody at the point of salvation. That person may never have to go through some of the scriptural processes that I went through or have led countless others through. That's great news. I wish that all people would get a revelation of the power of "sozo," the Greek word for salvation, healing, and deliverance. If more people got supernaturally set free at the point in which they give their lives to Jesus, that would mean a whole lot less work for people like me.

But, not everybody has a story like that. A deliverance session takes a lot of physical energy out of both the minister and the person receiving the ministry of Jesus. It is painless, of course, and it doesn't seem to be energy-draining, but you will know that you were in a war after the fight is over. It is not coincidental that one can sit in a chair and get ministered to for 45 minutes, do nothing but maybe cough, yawn, burp, wipe their nose, or something similar to this, and feel like they just finished a fight after it's over. Most people want to go home and rest or take a nap after they have gone through a deliverance session. There is the incredible peace of God, but there is warfare. Virtue or power goes out of the minister, and the unseen battle for freedom causes some physical draining for the person getting rid of demons. I am stating all of this is to prepare you for the fact that there is a stopping point for everybody. If someone has a past similar to mine, it might take two solid sessions during the course of a week or two. There comes a point where the person who has been getting ministered to needs to rest and recuperate and celebrate the great victory that God has given them. After one or two deliverance sessions, a believer should have enough confidence and knowledge to simply cast demons out of themselves in the future, if necessary.

Walk It Out

If you come from a background of a lot of mental curse issues that seem to have run in your family lines, this could take several sessions of freedom over the course of a year or more. Paul was not joking when he wrote, "...walk out your salvation with fear and trembling." Now that you know what "sozo" really means, that statement also means to "walk out your deliverance with fear and trembling."

If you have a history of bipolar disorder, passive-aggressive issues, obsessive-compulsive issues, or any other type of what the world calls "mental disorders," it is advisable that you commit to the lifelong process of getting totally set free. Where the enemy has infiltrated some people's lives by destroying their confidence in the area of the mind, it takes a lot of work to rebuild what the enemy has wreaked havoc upon. It is also wise to consult and work with your physician if you consider weaning yourself off of medications related to these disorders.

Mind-Binding Spirits

In my earlier years of ministering to people who had a history of bipolar disorder or other mental issues, I found that we had great measures of success in the beginning. Because the transformation can be so profound and dramatic for someone who has been in that kind of mental warfare for many years, when they get set free of a lot of mind-blinding spirits, they are completely on fire. What I came to realize early on is that person really needed more freedom throughout the next few months in order to continue to walk it out. Their initial session was so dramatic that it was easy to rejoice with them about the mighty miracle that God had done in their life. However, I didn't realize that the vicious demons that had not yet been identified or cast out during the first session would often turn up the heat in those people's lives. All of a sudden, this person was hearing those crazy little voices feeding them all kinds of lies about how their deliverance was not real, and they were going to be worse off. Those vicious demons who were left behind literally began to sabotage those people who had gotten incredible early victories of freedom in their lives. So, I learned the hard way. When dealing with long-term mental issues, it is vital that you give the process at least a year. In addition, you have to commit to not listening to the other voices of evil spirits that try to steer you away from achieving total victory and healing. Once again, consult and work with your physician if medical or medication decisions are involved.

The Process of Deliverance

I have a friend who has a son that used to be severely autistic when he was a little boy. When we first met her and her husband, their little four-year-old boy would eat the rubber off the soles of shoes. He would put holes in the wall and eat sheetrock. His parents had to guard their room at night so that he didn't do anything like stab them and kill them in the middle of the night. The stories the mother shared with me about their son are still vividly etched in my memory. The mom had become a severe alcoholic just to cope with the stress and the pressure of this battle. On top of that, her husband left her, but she found deliverance! She went through spiritual freedom and knew, if it was good enough for her, it was good enough for her son. She was convinced that God would heal her son. Keep in mind that this was a young boy with severe autism.

With each session, the little boy would get a new measure of freedom. The mom would keep unraveling the demons who were oppressing her son. After a battle that took several years, the boy became a 100% fully functioning student-athlete at his local high school. He was completely healed from autism and is 100% normal today! This is an encouraging story about God's grace and mercy. It is also an incredible testimony of a mom who understood the process of recovery. She recognized the process it would take to unwind all of those mental issues that the boy had been hit with by Satan and his demons. If she would have given up after one session, can you imagine what she and her son's lives would look like today? She is a Christian minister, and she is successful and thriving in her career today. Not to mention, she has a healthy young man entering into his adult stage of life as a different person than when he was four. I used an extreme case to show you that it can take a while for someone who has had mental difficulties, and it goes to show that it will require commitment, patience, and process. Embrace the process of deliverance!

Deliverance ... A Lifelong Process

The eighth thing that you need to know to keep your freedom is that deliverance is, without a doubt, a lifelong process. If it weren't, we could get to the point where we didn't have to put on the full armor of God. We would arrive to the point where we did not have to take our thoughts captive unto the obedience of Christ. The facts are, the devil and his demons are always looking for a way to get a fiery dart in us. They are just looking for a crack in the door, but they have to have a legal right to enter. Practicing sin or consistent sin patterns re-open the doors for the enemy to infiltrate, and no one really wants that. But we are human, and we have the ability to mess up due to our sinful nature. For example, do you think you will go the rest of your life without gossiping about someone? Gossip is a sin against God. It is quite easy to engage in gossip and not even realize it until the Holy Spirit convicts you of your sin in your prayer time. If this happens, it can open a new door for the enemy to slip an arrow in.

Over the years, I have had moments where I just felt like I needed to go to the closet and pray and ask God if any unclean spirits had crept back into my life. As a maturing believer, you have to recognize when you are going through a rough time, and things don't seem to be as upbeat as they should be. This is when I find out if something has crept back in. You may wonder, "How could things have crept back in?" If we are going to be real with ourselves, we cannot go through this life without moments of weakness where we may gossip, hold on to frustrations with people, speak negative words over our life or our situation. Proverbs 18:20-21 reads, "A man's stomach shall be satisfied from the fruit of his mouth; From the produce of his lips he shall be filled. Death and life are in the power of the tongue, And those who love it will eat its fruit."

Even in our quest for righteousness, we can't be perfect. I wish I could write in this book that I am totally and completely free of all unclean spirits, but I cannot say that in good conscience. I can say that I do not have any sin patterns in my life, nor have I had any sin patterns since I got set free in 2001. I don't recall any conscious acts of willfully sinning for which I need to repent to God since I got set free in 2001. Yet, I do recall how I have missed the mark on many occasions with my mouth, thoughts, and even my actions. These are the things that can give way for a spirit to creep back in. The good news is that when a spirit is able to slip into our lives, it only has a foothold. It is sin that feeds demonic activity, and it is sin that creates strongholds. So, when I go to my closet for self-deliverance periodically, I am usually dealing with spirits of frustration, judgment, pride, heaviness, oppression, anxiety, worry, stress, or things such as these. They come right out when I call upon them to leave because they weren't fed enough to get their claws in me to create a real stronghold.

On-Going Self-Deliverance

This is why self-deliverance becomes crucial. No one should have to help you maintain your freedom after you have learned how easy it is to cast a demon out in the name of Jesus. I will remind you once again of Paul's instructions to believers in 2 Timothy 2:20-26, "But in a great house there are not only vessels of gold and silver, but also of wood and clay, some for honor and some for dishonor. Therefore if anyone cleanses himself from the latter, he will be a vessel for honor, sanctified and useful for the Master, prepared for every good work. Flee also youthful lusts; but pursue righteousness, faith, love, peace with those who call on the Lord out of a pure heart. But avoid foolish and ignorant disputes, knowing that they generate strife. And a servant of the Lord must not quarrel but be gentle to all, able to teach, patient, in humility correcting those who are in opposition, if God perhaps will grant them repentance, so that they may know the truth, and that they may come to their senses and escape the snare of the devil, having been taken captive by him to do his will."

This is a classic blueprint and mandate for self-deliverance. We don't want to ever be taken captive by the snares of the devil to do his will. We want to purge ourselves from any dishonor in our personal lives by casting those spirits out of us and keeping them out. Once we are saved, our personal quest is to live a life of sanctification, to be set apart and made holy. This is how we become vessels of honor that God can use. He wants us to be believing believers and use us to help others know Him, get set free, and become sanctified as well. What an honor it is to serve such a mighty God, and what an honor and privilege it is to bring glory to the name of Jesus.

Cleanse Your House

The ninth thing that you need to know about keeping your freedom is to cleanse your house from any items that are displeasing to God. This requires prayer and listening to the Holy Spirit. In 2001, when my wife and I found freedom and got filled with the Holy Spirit, we immediately felt convicted to get rid of certain things in our home. There were old CDs of rock music that we needed to throw away. There were old pictures of our younger years that were really putting our rebellion on display, such as partying. We did not need to look at those memories of rebellion toward God. One morning, the Holy Spirit told me to go up to the attic and throw away the item that was an accursed item and an abomination to Him. I went up to the attic and started digging through boxes and found our son's karate uniform from when he was five years old. The karate robe had a dragon on the back of it, and the Holy Spirit confirmed to me that the dragon was what had to go. It would bring a curse upon our family if we were to hold on to it.

Sometimes, you will have to go through your children's rooms and make sure that you are cleansing their room. There may be books with monsters that open the door for spirits of fear to torment your children at night. There may be fairies that may also need to go. You need to ask the Holy Spirit what he thinks about things like that. It may be certain video games that have grungy demonic music that is displeasing to God. There may be DVDs that have to go. And sometimes, this too is a process.

Give No Place to The Devil

About two years after I had gotten set free, I was in my home office one morning, and the Holy Spirit directed me to a "cross" sitting on my shelf that He wanted me to throw away. He prompted me to look up the style of that cross on the internet. After searching for the image, I quickly learned that it wasn't a cross at all. It was an ankh, an ancient Egyptian item that looks like a cross with a loop on top. It is not the cross that represents the cross of Calvary. The Holy Spirit told me that it was an accursed item, and it needed to be thrown away. We had received it as a gift from a friend who bought it in another country.

On another occasion, a friend brought a couple of gifts from a foreign country back home with her to give to us. The gifts were not obnoxious, nor did they look idolatrous. However, the rest of the day the Holy Spirit seemed to keep me focused on these two gifts that our friend had brought back home with her. She was amazing, so she wasn't the problem, but the gifts had curses on them. The Lord clearly showed me that these items had been prayed over, probably by a witch doctor, and had curses put on them. This is a frequent occurrence for people who live in the world of the occult.

Keeping our home free from idols and other accursed items is essential for maintaining a life and a household of freedom. Repent for anything that God reveals to you and for anything that you think you need to get rid of in your home. God's grace is sufficient, and His mercy is from everlasting to everlasting. He is faithful to forgive and restore us. And it's all because of Jesus!

Exercise Your Authority to Bless

The tenth thing you need to know about keeping your freedom is to bless your home. Whether you own your home or rent your home, you have authority over that property. It is essential that you bless your property and your home. I recommend that you purchase a small bottle of olive oil if you do not currently have any anointing oil. You and your spouse lay hands on the oil and ask God to bless the oil you will use for anointing your property. I start at one corner of my property and place oil on the fence post or on the ground where the corner of the property is. I pray for God to send the Holy Spirit to cover my property completely, and I ask God to loose His angels at every corner of my property to guard against evil. I then walk the first property line and go to the second corner and anoint that corner with oil. I do the same for every fence line and every corner of the property. After that, I anoint every door in our house with oil and pray for God's protection over our home. I encourage you to do the same. In fact, here is a bullet point guideline that I recommend to you:

- God, please bless this home with the blessing of Abraham, Isaac, and Jacob

- I renounce any and all sin that has ever occurred on this property in Jesus' name

- I repent for the sins of any person who lived on the property that defiled this land or this home

- God, please cleanse this land from all unrighteousness

- I break every ley line running through this property in the name of Jesus. (Read about ley lines)

- Ask God to: loose angels in this house to guard our home

- Ask God to: loose angels on the rooftop to war against the enemy and keep our home safe

- Ask God to: loose angels around the borders of our property to war against the enemy

- Anoint the doors with oil and proclaim the blessing of Abraham, Isaac, and Jacob

- Anoint the windows and ask God to protect every entry point from demonic entry

Don't Forget Your "Home" Away from Home

These are the basic principles involving blessing your home. Even when you travel, you should bless the place you stay in because more fights and family disputes occur in hotel rooms than in any other place you can imagine. All kinds of spirits are lurking around hotel rooms. That doesn't mean that they will be able to get inside of you, but they can cause a train wreck of chaos in the atmosphere. I've experienced and seen more family frustrations in hotels than I care to recall. You have to think about this. You might be entering a hotel room where a lot of sexual sin occurred the night before. You might have entered a hotel room where adultery had just taken place, or a drug deal had just taken place. These spirits cause frustration or lack of peace in the unseen realm. If you lay your hand upon the door frame and pray for God to bless your hotel room and plead the blood of Jesus over your hotel room, you will see a difference. Here's what my wife and I do. As we open the door and walk into our hotel room, we repent for any sin that occurred in that room before we got there, and we ask God to fill that room with the Holy Spirit and His peace. Since we adopted this protocol, our vacation times and travel times are amazingly different.

Even though there are ten specific things to keep in mind to maintain your freedom, they all really have to do with a Christian lifestyle. It is not a "to-do" list, and it is not too hard to accomplish. These are just things you need to know in order to fight the good fight of faith as a believing believer or a victorious believer. None of this exempts us from trials, tribulations, persecutions, or sufferings. These are all things that we, as believers, will have to walk through and grow through. They are part of the fight. Always remember this, it is a whole lot easier to fight the enemy from external attacks versus internal attacks. When we have to fight the enemy internally, we also have to fight him externally. Deliverance and the things that help us protect our freedom keep us from having to battle the enemy from within. That has been a game-changer for our family, and I hope it is as well for your life and your family.

Key Points

- Be continually filled with the Spirit of God.

- Learn all you can about the Holy Spirit and being filled with the Spirit.

- Embrace the power of fasting, prayer, and generosity.

- Every person has a different freedom experience. Embrace the process!

- Do not compare your freedom experience to other people's. This can set you up for disappointment.

- Be willing to walk out your deliverance with fear and trembling, no matter how long it takes.

Ask Yourself

- Are you filled with the Spirit?

- Have you been baptized in the Holy Spirit?

- What are the areas mentioned in this chapter that you need to grow in?

- How important is it to walk out your deliverance?

- Do you see a correlation between Paul's teaching on sanctification (2 Timothy 2:20-21) and self-deliverance?

For Further Study

- *Blessing Your Spirit* by Sylvia Gunter and Arthur Bark

- *The Fasting Prayer* by Franklin Hall

- *Power* by Danny McDaniel

TESTIMONY

Set Free By The Power of Jesus

I never knew how bound a "Christian" could be! I had no idea that a Spirit filled, Bible-believing christian could be so taken out by the enemy because of "a lack of knowledge."

My wife and our two boys were diagnosed with ADHD and had to take medication. I never realized that, even as a Christian, you can open doors and give the enemy access and permission to wreak havoc in your life by participating in things such as certain games, movies, etc. For example, my boys had been exposed to Pokémon, which opened the door for demonic oppression in the form of ADHD, a fractured mind. After taking my boys and my wife through freedom by renouncing and breaking the power of those demonic forces, all three were set free from ADHD and never needed any meds again! II Timothy 1:7 says, "For He has not given us a spirit of fear but of love, power, and of a sound mind." Hallelujah! Thank you, Jesus!

We also dealt with a spirit of calamity. For years, we would be at the doctor's office or ER every month because someone was sick or injured. That is not normal in most homes, but it was our normal. My wife had a car accident once a year and also had chronic bronchitis that was not looking good long term. I had dealt with lust for years and years with no apparent way to stop that behavior. Once my wife and I understood the scriptural truths laid out in Danny's book, we took action and tossed the boys' Pokémon cards. My wife and I stopped watching paranormal investigation shows, and we were all set free by the power of Jesus and have been living in freedom ever since!

— Kirk, Texas

CHAPTER TWENTY

Deliverance and Children

"Freedom is never more than one generation away
from extinction. We didn't pass it to our children in the
bloodstream. It must be fought for, protected, and handed on
for them to do the same."
—Ronald Reagan

When Diane and I first got set free, the only thing that we could think of was, "How has our past affected our children?" We instinctively knew that whatever we were carrying, our children were most likely carrying. That doesn't mean our children were exemplifying manifestations of all the spirits that we had operating in our lives up to that point, but we knew they were certainly there. Derek Prince, arguably one of the most brilliant Biblical scholars of the twentieth century and deliverance expert, used to teach that 95% of all demonic entry occurs from the womb up to the age of five. Children inherit demons from their parents because they are a part of us, and they are under our authority. Children can also be exposed and vulnerable to demonic oppression if the parents are not living a Christian lifestyle. We had not been living as Christians for the first few years of our two oldest boys' lives. When we were set free, our oldest was nine, our middle son was almost six, and our youngest was two.

The Reality of Generational Curses

I am convinced that children inherit more things generationally than they do genetically. We can call things "genetic predispositions" or "things that run in the family", but I call it "a generational curse." When we repent for the sins of the fathers and break generational curses that have come from our ancestral lines, we open up a whole new realm of blessing and opportunity for our descendants to thrive and serve God wholeheartedly. Unfortunately, there are consequences for the sins of the father, and our prayer is that we will always see God's mercy fall upon our lives and not have to deal with the physical consequences of the sins of the father.

We had fine young boys. They were loving and obedient, but we knew that they still needed to get set free from our past, not theirs. We recognized consistent patterns of frustration, fear, and anxiety. All of the other things we knew were like Jack-in-the-Box. There were a whole bunch of spirits waiting for the day that they would be wound up enough so that they could pop out of the box and unleash their assignment to steal, kill, and destroy our boys' lives. That was not going to happen on our watch as parents!

Identifying the Spiritual Kidnapper

Here is another picture to think about. If someone physically kidnapped your child, what would you do? Most people would call the police, get help, and begin an immediate search.

This might even entail social media campaigns, flyers, signs, postings, and any possible means of communicating the news of your lost child to the public. Most parents would not rest until they found their child and brought him to safety. When it comes to demonic oppression, the enemy is spiritually kidnapping our children. When children grow up with unclean spirits inside them, the enemy is hijacking their destiny and attempting to lead them into patterns and paths of failure and destruction. How important is it for parents to understand the spiritual kidnapping that could be taking place in their own homes?

Ministering freedom to our boys came about sixty to ninety days after Diane and I got set free. We were really mindful of God's direction and timing in ministering to them. We were also very candid with the older two boys that they had essentially done nothing wrong. We explained to them how we had made choices before they were born that brought evil spirits in and around our lives, and we explained to them clearly how those same spirits would try to attack them because of our mistakes and/or our sins. They were both very receptive and allowed us to minister freedom to them at nine and six years old. Our youngest son was two years old, so we spent a few nights praying over him in his sleep.

The battle for our souls never stops, but our kids were given somewhat of a head start compared to the start that Diane and I had. Our boys still had to grow in the Lord. They still had to find their true identity in Christ. They still had to face grueling temptations that face young males in our society today, accompanied by smartphones and social media that became more readily available each year as they were growing up.

I am happy that Diane and I began to give our boys a fighting chance. We would not allow the enemy to destroy our house from within. Our boys are now 29, 26, and 21 years old. They all three love Jesus, and they all three have had to overcome various trials and tribulations. As parents, we consider their trials and tribulations minor compared to what we see on a regular basis. However, trials and tribulations are very relevant to each individual person. Our boys are champions. They love God. They honor their mother and their father. They are great husbands. Our two oldest married their high school sweethearts. Our daughter-in-laws are amazing. Our oldest is also a great father. Our grandchildren sing and dance to Jesus all the time! Our youngest son is still in college, and he is a fine young Christian leader.

Child-Like Faith

What we have to remember about kids is that they have child-like faith. They usually aren't carrying around the emotional baggage that adults do. Young kids aren't running around with skepticism, doubt, unbelief, mistrust, and cynicism. They are open to their parents' leading, and, as long as the parent is leading them in the right direction, trust stays consistent. Here's a reminder of what Jesus said about our faith, "But Jesus called them to Him and said, 'Let the little children come to Me, and do not forbid them; for of such is the kingdom of God. Assuredly, I say to you, whoever does not receive the kingdom of God as a little child will by no means enter it'" (Luke 18:16-17).

Kids are a lot easier to minister to than adults because they generally have child-like faith. There are some incredible books and videos concerning deliverance for children. I cannot say all that I possibly need to say about deliverance for children in one chapter. If you are a parent, it is vital that you study some materials that are specifically written and designed to help parents know more about spiritual warfare and children. Some recommended books are included in the Resource Section at the back of this book.

What I will say is this, "If freedom is good enough for you, then it is good enough for your children." It makes no sense for a single parent or a married couple to get set free and then go home and watch their children grow up in bondage. You cannot disciple demons!

The Role of Godly Discipline

When it comes to young children, I believe that certain demonic forces can be discouraged, weakened, and driven out by safe, Godly, loving discipline. Proverbs 22:15 states, "Foolishness is bound up in the heart of a child; The rod of correction will drive it far from him."

This doesn't mean that we beat down our kids, but we did spank them when necessary in order to teach them how to obey. I believe the Bible clearly states that spanking will drive foolish behavior out of the heart of a child. That is driving foolishness out of the "core" of that child's spirit, soul, and body. Earlier in the book, we discussed the 'core' as the set and center focal point of one's physical and spiritual being. For you, spanking may be a wooden spoon from the kitchen. For others, it may be spanking with your hand, and then for others, like me, it may be a belt. Our sons all got spanked with a belt most of the time. We did have a wooden spoon that we used sometimes. None of them were abused. None of them got welts. None of them were emotionally scarred, but they all dreaded being spanked. When used wisely and properly, the belt helped drive foolishness out of the lives of our children. We also learned not to spank our children out of anger. I knew, as a dad, I had to sit down with my son and explain to him why I was going to need to discipline him. In turn, I would ask him if he understood why he was going to get disciplined. When he came to a point of understanding, which was usually quite clear, I spanked him. Afterward, I told him that I loved him, usually tried to hug him, and let him know he was loved.

The point I am trying to make for your benefit is that Godly and loving discipline is a vital part of a child breaking free from foolish behaviors, which most of us call a "rebellious nature." On the other hand, you really can't disciple demons. You must drive them out or cast them out.

Use Wisdom

In general, children, from birth to the age of one, are really easy to pray for because all you have to do is hold them and carry them around while you pray over them. Children can be a bit more challenging from the ages of one to four years old. Sometimes they need to be prayed over while they are sleeping. Children between the ages of five and ten have child-like faith and can be prayed for directly. Keep in mind that these ages and descriptions I am providing are generalizations from my experience and not clear-cut and definitive lines.

After children get closer to sixth grade and up, parents can face a whole new set of challenges. If the parent has just gone through freedom and has a child in this age bracket, it will take more prayer, time, and patience. I believe it will take some teaching and real understanding. Most children this age have been exposed to so many more things around them than the five to ten-year-old. These children have seen and heard new things that can cause them to be a little more challenging to reason regarding getting set free from demons that they might have inherited from their parents. In this era, they have most likely been around peers with smartphones and full access to social media. Peer pressure and social media influence can begin to fashion strong-willed mindsets that a young male or female in this age bracket may not want to let go of so quickly.

Live Out Your Freedom Before Your Children

If a parent has just gone through freedom and has high school-age kids, this battle can be even tougher. High school kids hearing about deliverance for the first time from their parents are generally not very excited about the topic. Middle school and high school kids want to see fruit. They want to see the dramatic change in mom and dad. They want to see righteousness, peace, and joy lived out in the household in which they live. They desire time and attention from mom and dad. They do not want a Bible to be shoved down their throats now that mom and dad have supposedly gone through some drastic change in their lives. Mom and dad, remember that you become the living Bible to them. First, you have to become the book they want to read and the book they want to pattern their lives after. This really applies to all of your kids, no matter what their ages. This is the real key to deliverance for children: parents living like Jesus and loving like Jesus.

The Importance of Right Timing

Deliverance is amazing for children, but we as parents have to really seek the Holy Spirit for wisdom, guidance, and the proper timing for each preparatory step involving leading our children to the point where we can help them get free from things they inherited or even picked up through personal sin. God is redemptive, and He is full of grace and mercy. Just seek Him first in all of these areas. Don't just follow a bunch of recommendations from a book like this. Make sure that the Holy Spirit is leading you every step of the way. If you feel like you have a hard time hearing from God, I want to tell you how simple it is to hear instruction from Him.

Here is how you hear from God. It is the free flow of thoughts that go through your mind when you fix your eyes upon Jesus and ask God a question. Therefore, quiet your spirit, and fix your eyes upon Jesus. Ask God a question about your children, and listen to what He tells you. He will guide you in all truth.

This is just an overview of the subject of deliverance for children. If you are a parent, please study this subject from experts who have had much success in this area and have the resources available for you to either go online and view, or purchase. Make sure that you check out the Resource Section in the back of this book for some recommendations.

Key Points
- The enemy wants to kidnap your children spiritually.

- Kids have child-like faith. Their walls are usually not up at a young age.

- Godly, loving discipline in the household helps kids walk in freedom.

- Be a great role model for God to your kids. They see God through you at a young age; therefore, how they see you is what often dictates their view of God.

Ask Yourself
- How does it make you feel to think of the possibility that demons are trying to spiritually hijack your children?

- Have you thought about demonic spirits that could have entered your child in the womb?

- What is your perspective of healthy, loving, Godly discipline for children?

For Further Study
- *Let Our Children Go* by Rebecca Greenwood

TESTIMONY

From Bondage to Freedom

In 2008, my belief and faith were restored by God's power as I was set free from demonic curses that had plagued me for fifty-one years. God used my best friend and spiritual mentor, Danny McDaniel, to minister to me and helped bring deliverance to my life from a very deep demonic oppression and infirmity. I experienced a kind of freedom I had never known! Not only did I find total freedom from demonic oppression, but God also healed my left ear, which was 92% deaf. It was a miracle!

Through this experience, God showed me that He is, in fact, all-powerful, all-loving, all-healing, and all-forgiving, and He will use ordinary men like Danny to minister to me and others. Now I understand, just as God used Danny to help lead me to a life of freedom, I can do the same for other men.

In the beginning, I was skeptical and confused; yet, God healed me and set me free! My freedom came through the power of the Holy Spirit and Jesus. I have learned it is through freedom that God's will for your life is revealed.

— Eric, Texas

CHAPTER TWENTY-ONE

What If There's Just One?

I understand very well that a book such as this can be challenging. After all, the devil has been working hard for over 2,000 years to discredit the ministry of Jesus. He has even masterfully created division among the Body of Christ over the issue of demons and demonic oppression. The devil doesn't want anyone to cast out a demon. He doesn't want anyone to believe that a Christian could ever have an unclean spirit inside of them. He wants people to become numb to the thought of demons actually being able to reside inside of people.

I still believe that the massive amounts of movies and video games to which we have been exposed over the years have helped the enemy deter people from believing that being oppressed by a demon could actually happen to them. From the movie *The Exorcist* to modern-day horror films, the enemy has launched a strategy to make you fearful of demons or unclean spirits. He has also successfully convinced most people that if you just avoid Satan and his demons, they will just leave you alone. One may operate under the principle of "See no evil, hear no evil, speak no evil"; however, evil does not care if one chooses to recognize its presence. Evil is coming after you whether you choose to acknowledge it or not.

So, let's examine the question, "What if there's just one demon inside of me?" Think about airport security for a moment. We go through the pain of taking our shoes off, removing our liquids, and removing our laptop devices to go through security screening at the airport. Why? Because all it takes is one bad person with one huge wrong motive to blow a plane up. You may be getting on a flight with 150 other passengers, but all it takes is one individual with bad intentions to destroy a bunch of people's lives. So, we show up at the airport grateful that there are processes in place to safeguard against the one bad person that might be plotting to bring destruction to a whole lot of people's lives.

How Much Is Too Much?

What if you just have one unclean spirit inside of you? All it takes is one bad spirit to cause disruption and chaos in one's life. One bad spirit can do so much to affect the soul and harm others around him, or her. The harm may not be physical, but it could be through words and actions that are contrary to walking like Jesus walked. One bad spirit can destroy a friendship. One bad spirit can destroy a marriage. One bad spirit can bring ineffectiveness to a parent. One bad spirit can strike our child with uncontrollable fear or anxiety. One bad spirit is too much and needs to be addressed, just as much as a bag of explosives entering the airport needs to be exposed and dealt with.

Lives depend on it. Destinies depend on it. As long as you live upon this earth or until Jesus returns, walking out your deliverance with fear and trembling will be part of life (Philippians 2:12).

Self Assessment

In the past twenty years of my life, I can safely say I have been able to grow more in the love of Jesus than the thirty-five years prior to knowing about the teachings I've discussed in this book. I have been a much better husband in the last twenty years than I was the previous ten years. I am confident that I have been a much better father in the last twenty years than in the previous ten. I have been a much better leader and communicator in the past twenty years. The comparisons could keep rolling on.

Consider what kind of Christian you want to be over the time you have left on this earth? For me, I want to be as effective as I possibly can by living free and obeying what Jesus commanded us to do, as I described to you in this book. Think about the different roles you fill in your life. What kind of spouse and parent do you want to be? What kind of leader do you want to be? What kind of neighbor or friend do you want to be? What kind of impact do you want to have on the lives of others and upon society?

The Battle Before Us

The choice is yours. The battle will always be out in front of us. Our adversary will always be launching a formidable attack upon our lives as we move forward. Hence, we need to put on the whole armor of God. However, the enemy will always try to create a battlefield in the heart, the core of your spiritual and physical being. The battle is for your soul, and the enemy wishes to penetrate your gates and defile your body and your soul.

Call to Action

My hope is that you have been encouraged enough to take the Holy scriptures at face value because they haven't changed. Jesus Christ is the same yesterday, today, and forever (Hebrews 13:8). I hope you can read the four gospel accounts with a whole new set of eyes, a set of spiritual eyes. May the Holy Spirit illuminate your eyes and your heart to perceive what He desires for you to see and understand in God's Word.

Finally, I hope that you become intolerant of the schemes of the enemy. Whether it was the illustration of rats in the attic, a Jack-in-the-Box, or one bad spirit that could blow up a plane, my prayer is that something made sense to you. I hope this helped you understand the battle that is occurring and the reality that there is an enemy trying to invade your temple gates to destroy you from the inside out. Like getting rid of the rats in the attic, we can seal the cracks and crevices so that the enemy is not a constant nuisance. As far as Jack-in-the-Box is concerned, we have the power to open up the lid and rip Jack out of that box from the root of its connection. And when it comes to one bad spirit that could blow the whole thing up, the Holy Spirit is dedicated to helping us expose the enemy through the discerning of spirits (1 Corinthians 12: 7-11).

The most important instruction of all is to read God's Word and obey His commands. In Luke 6:46, Jesus asked, "Why do you call me Lord, Lord, and do not do the things I say?" Don't ask, "What would Jesus do? Rather ask, "What did Jesus do?" If we adhere to this principle, we will love people well; we will win souls for the Lord; we will see the sick healed; and we will set captives free. In 1 John 3:5, the Bible says, "And you know that He was manifested to take away our sins, and in Him there was no sin." Then John goes on to say in verse 8, "He who sins is of the devil, for the devil has sinned from the beginning. For this purpose the Son of God was manifested, that He might destroy the works of the devil."

The Choice is Yours

Let's also ask, "What did Jesus tell me to do?" If you don't know the answer to this question yet, you must open up the New Testament of the Holy Bible and read every passage with this question in mind. The Holy Spirit will teach you all things, and the rest will be up to you!

Key Points

- One unclean spirit is all it takes to steal, kill, and destroy.

- When you rid your life of demonic attachment, you will become a different person than you were before.

- Live a life intolerant of the devil's schemes.

- The most important instruction of all is to read God's Word and obey His commands.

Ask Yourself

- What kind of Christian do you want to be for the remainder of the time you have left on this earth?

- How are you going to live differently now that you have the knowledge from this book?

- What has Jesus told you to do?

Overcoming Suicide: You Have More Authority Than You Think

This chapter was written post-production of *Freedom*, and it pertains to experiences and insights that I have had since the original manuscript was written. It will provide to you further knowledge and wisdom as to why fighting for your freedom is essential, as well as fighting for your family's freedom.

Just Visit:

www.thefreedombook.org/bonus

PREPARING FOR YOUR FREEDOM

1. Don't limit God:
There is no formula! God is sovereign, and His word prevails over any system or protocol. However, these are basic principles that will help any person prepare the "soil" of their heart for true freedom in Christ.

2. Prepare your mind and heart:
Read, listen to, and watch every good thing that you can on the subject of blessings and curses and deliverance. Gaining knowledge and revelation on these subjects helps build your faith and expectation.

Refer to recommended readings, recordings, or viewings in the Resource Section at the end of the book.

3. Personally affirm your faith in Christ:
Declaring your faith in Christ is as simple as praying: "Lord Jesus Christ, I believe You are the son of God, and the only way to God is through You. I believe that You died on the cross for my sins and rose again so that I might be forgiven and receive eternal life."

4. Humble yourself:

You must surrender. When you completely surrender to God, humble yourself, and become vulnerable, God can work with that. You might pray something like this: "Lord God, I renounce all pride, religious self-righteousness, and any dignity that does not come from You. I am nothing without You. I am weak, but You are strong. I need You to invade my life and set me free by the power of the blood of Jesus. In Jesus' name, I pray."

5. Confess any known sin:

Refer to "Prayer for Confessing Personal Sins and Sins of the Fathers" in the Resource Section at the end of this book.

6. Forgive other people:

Forgiveness is essential in obtaining freedom in Christ. If one is unwilling to forgive those who have hurt him/her, it gives unclean spirits related to bitterness and unforgiveness legal access to oppress him/her while on this earth. It is like drinking your own poison! If you want to be free, you must forgive. It is an act of your will. Reread Matthew 18:21-35.

Forgiving others is not always about having a good feeling. It is merely a conscious choice to let people go and hand each situation over to Jesus, who bled for that issue on the cross. One way of viewing it is by refusing to take back something from Jesus that He already took for you when He hung on the cross and shed His blood for that offense. To help you find freedom through forgiveness, a "Prayer For Forgiving Others" is included in the Resource Section at the end of this book.

7. Break any ties with the occult and all false religion:

Refer to "Prayer for Breaking Curses."

Ask God to reveal to you by His Holy Spirit, any objects you have in your home or in your possession that are displeasing to Him or that dishonor Him. He will show you, and you will want to throw them away!

8. Break any and all curses that may be over your life:
Refer to "Prayer for Breaking Curses" in the Resource Section at the end of the book.

9. Break any unhealthy soul ties:
Refer to "Prayer for Breaking Soul Ties" in the Resource Section at the end of the book.

10. Fasting:
It always helps immensely to fast and pray diligently prior to experiencing freedom. Committing to a 24 or 48 hour fast before a freedom encounter is recommended. It may be good to end your fast the morning of your ministry time for freedom. Eating a healthy meal or drinking a healthy shake is good for restoring your physical energy levels for the body. This is only a recommendation and not a requirement. Commit to praying and meditating on God's Word. Read Isaiah 58 out loud. Go through the Psalms and read various Psalms out loud. These are things that can help you prepare your spirit, soul, and body for your freedom encounter with God.

RESOURCE SECTION

Prayer for the Forgiveness of Personal Sins and Sins of the Fathers

Heavenly Father, in the name of Jesus, I confess my sin and my rebellion before You. At times, I have willfully chosen to rebel against You and Your Word. I have fallen short of Your standards. At other times, I have sinned against You unaware. I declare that Your standards are holy and just, and I renounce and repent of all my sin, known and unknown.

At times, I have chosen to think and act in ways contrary to Your will and Your Word. I have no excuse and no one to blame. I have sinned against You and in the name of Jesus, I now renounce and repent for the sin(s) of _____

_____

_____

_____.

In the name of Jesus, I also confess the wickedness, the sins, and the rebellion of my fathers. I now renounce their sins, their wickedness, and their rebellion and submit those to the blood of Jesus so that their effects might be nullified according to Your Word. Specifically, I renounce _____

_____

_____

_____.

Have mercy on me, God, according to Your unfailing love. I can do nothing to pay the debt of my sin; therefore, by faith, I plead the blood of Jesus over my sin. Your Word declares that when I confess my sins with Godly sorrow, you will be faithful and just to forgive me of my sin and cleanse me from all unrighteousness.

By the blood of Jesus, I ask you to blot out all my transgressions, wash away all my iniquity, and cleanse me from my sin. Your Word declares that, in Christ, sin will not have dominion over me, and I now come into agreement with Your Word.

I turn away from my sins and the sins of my fathers and receive the power of the cross. By Your grace and by the blood of Jesus, I am now dead to sin, my own sin and the sins of my fathers.

From this day forward, with Your power, I will walk in freedom, no longer submitting to sin but to the righteousness of Christ. I now submit every area of my life to the Lordship of Jesus. Father, I ask that You totally break the power of this sin in my life that I might serve Jesus wholeheartedly.

I now joyfully receive Your promise of forgiveness by faith and give You thanks. Your Word declares, in Christ, there is no condemnation. I renounce the condemnation and the accusation that the enemy would speak against me. Therefore, I declare that I am free in Christ from sin and the condemnation of sin. In Jesus' name, I declare my complete forgiveness. Amen.

Prayer for Forgiving Others

"Lord God, as an act of my will, I freely choose to forgive all who have ever harmed or wronged me. I lay down all bitterness, all resentment, and all hatred. Specifically, I forgive _____." (name each person in whom you need to forgive) "Father, in Jesus' name, I pray for (that person you forgave) _____. I pray that You bless them as they walk with you. If they are not serving You, I pray that You put people and situations in their life that will lead them to salvation. I speak blessings over their lives, in Jesus' name. Amen."

Prayer for Breaking Soul Ties

Father, in the name of Jesus, I ask Your forgiveness of the sins I willingly participated in. I also confess ungodly covenants and relationships that I established in my past, intentionally and unintentionally, contrary to Your will. I renounce those covenants and renounce all my past sinful and destructive relationships that were not submitted to You.

In the name of Jesus, I now renounce, break, and loose myself from any soul ties related to (person) _____ ___ _____. I cut that tie on my end, and I am asking You, God, to cut that soul tie on the other end, in the name of Jesus. Thank you, God." (Repeat for each person.)

In Jesus' name, I now place these relationships under the Lordship of Jesus and under His blood. As a result, I declare complete freedom in Him. Jesus, thank You for forgiving my past and setting me free. May I walk only in Your will in my relationships in all my days to come, in Jesus' name. Amen.

Prayer for Breaking Curses

Heavenly Father, I repent of all sins in my life or my ancestors' lives that have resulted in a curse. I repent of all disobedience, rebellion (witchcraft), perversion, idolatry, lust, adultery, fornication, mistreatment of others, murder, cheating, lying, judgments, and vows. I ask for your forgiveness and cleansing through the blood of the Lord Jesus Christ.

I take authority over and break any and every curse upon my life in the name of Jesus. Father God, I realize that You are a jealous God, visiting the iniquities of the fathers upon the children unto the third and fourth generation of them that hate You, as the Bible declares. I renounce, break, and loose myself and my family, from any curses of mental illness; from any curse of divorce; from any curses that lead to being "accident prone;" from the curse of death and destruction; and from any curses of sickness and disease that have been put on my family. I break the curse of heart disease, blood disease, cancer, and lung disease, in the mighty name of Jesus. I renounce, break, and loose myself and my family from all curses that have come upon us as a result of sexual sin and adultery, in the name of Jesus. I renounce all of these curses up to ten generations before me. I renounce, break, and loose myself from every word curse that has ever been spoken over me by others, including what I may have spoken over my own life, in the name of Jesus.

I renounce any oaths that my family, my ancestors, or I have made to Freemasonry, in the name of Jesus. I rebuke any and all lying and deceitful spirits of Freemasonry that may think they still have a claim on my family or me. In Jesus' name, I renounce all spirits of Freemasonry and declare that they no longer have any power over my family or me.

I repent for any involvement I have had with the spiritual practice of yoga. Even if I did it out of ignorance, not knowing the spiritual implications, I repent and renounce any curses that might have come upon me or my family as a result of my involvement.

I renounce any involvement that I have ever had with witch-craft (rebellion) and objects of the occult. I renounce, break, and loose myself from any involvement with Magic 8 Ball, Ouija board, psychic hotlines or psychics, tarot cards, palm reading, charms, superstitions, old wives tales, trances, séances, horoscope reading, or fortune-telling.

According to the Word of God, Jesus came to "fulfill the law" (Matthew 5). I understand that Jesus died on the cross to take the curse for me. According to Galatians 3:13, I have been re-deemed from "the curse of the law" because of His sacrifice. I exercise my faith in the blood of Jesus and loose myself and my descendants from any and every curse. I claim forgiveness through the blood of Jesus for the sins of the fathers.

I take back all of the ground that my family or I have ever yielded to Satan, in the name of Jesus. Whatever claims Satan had on me or my family's lives, I cancel them in the name of Jesus. The devil has no legal claim to control my life. Satan has no legal claim to my family. I choose life and not death. I choose the blessing and not the curse. Thank you, Jesus.

All of my sins have been remitted, and I loose myself from the curses that came as a result of all disobedience and rebellion to the Word of God.

The weapons of warfare are not carnal, but mighty in God for pulling down strongholds, casting down arguments and every high thing that exalts itself against the knowledge of God, bringing every thought into captivity to the obedience of Christ, and being ready to punish all disobedience when your obedience is fulfilled (2 Cor. 10:4-6). Therefore, I pull down every stronghold in my life in the name of Jesus.

314 • FREEDOM: Winning the Battle Within

I exercise my faith, and I know that confession is made unto salvation (Romans 10:10). Therefore, I confess that Abraham's blessings are mine (Galatians 3:14). I am not cursed, but blessed. I am the head and not the tail. I am above and not beneath. (Deuteronomy 28:13). I am blessed coming in and blessed going out. I am blessed, and what God has blessed cannot be cursed. I bind myself to the promises and blessings of God.

I have prayed and proclaimed all of these things on behalf of my family, my descendants and myself. I have prayed this in Jesus' name. Amen!

RECOMMENDED RESOURCES FOR FURTHER STUDY

Never forget, "Eat the meat, and spit out the bones." The Bible is the only 100% truth that we have in written form. It is important to partner with the Holy Spirit and ask God to guide you in all truth and guard your heart and mind from deception. People who are looking to mature in their walk with God have the heart to be open to new revelation of the scriptures. God has revealed some things to me that would not have come to me unless it would have been through the writings of others. One must be open to receiving from God through another person's writings. I may not agree with every word contained in the following books; however, I have gotten some great revelation from the Lord through the writings of these people. What you get from any of these authors or teachers is up to you, along with your willingness to partner with the Holy Spirit for proper illumination. Nothing compares to God's Holy Book, which we call The Holy Bible.

- *Protection From Deception* by Derek Prince

Blessings & Curses
- *Blessing & Curse* by Derek Prince
- *Breaking Curses* by Marilyn Hickey
- *Identifying and Breaking Curses* by John Eckhardt
- *Come Up Higher* by Paul and Donna Cox

YouTube videos on the topic of Breaking Curses
Search "breaking curses" with these names attached: Derek Prince, Robert Henderson, Marilyn Hickey

Freedom/Deliverance
- *Born To Be Free* by Tom Vermillion
- *Truly Free* by Robert Morris
- *Shadow Boxing* by Dr. Henry Malone

YouTube videos on the topic of Freedom and Deliverance

Search any of the authors listed above, as well as other credible ministers.

Soul Ties

- *Breaking Unhealthy Soul Ties* by Bill and Susan Banks
- There are other multiple options on Amazon under this subject.

YouTube Videos on the topic of Breaking Soul Ties

Search "breaking soul ties" along with these names: Derek Prince, Terri Savelle Foy

Jezebel Spirit

- *The Jezebel Spirit* by Francis Frangipane
- *Unmasking The Jezebel Spirit* by John Paul Jackson
- *Discerning and Defeating the Ahab Spirit* by Steve Sampson
- *Jezebel: The Witch Is Back* by Landon Schott

There are other multiple options on Amazon under this subject.

YouTube Videos on the topic of the Jezebel Spirit

Search "Jezebel Spirit" along with teacher's name such as Robert Morris, Francis Frangipane

YouTube Videos on the topic of Ley Lines

Search "What Are Ley Lines?"

For further information, look up Arthur Burke

Deliverance For Children

- *Deliverance For Children and Teens* by Bill Banks
- *Let Our Children Go* by Rebecca Greenwood

YouTube Videos on the topic of Deliverance for Children
Search "Deliverance for Children" along with teacher's name such as Derek Prince, Rebecca "Becca" Greenwood

Masonic Lodge/Shriners/Eastern Stars
* *Masonry: Beyond The Light* by William Schnoebelen
* *Deadly Deception: Freemasonry Exposed By One Of Its Top Leaders* by Jim Shaw and Tom McKenney
* *Freemasonry* by Jack Harris

YouTube Videos Search "Freemasonry Exposed"
* For more information on this topic, include Bill or William Schnoebelen in your search.

Yoga
* *The Heart of Yoga Revealed* by Judy L. White
* *Seven Reasons I No Longer Practice Yoga* by Mike Shreve

Mormonism
There are too many books on this topic to list. Amazon is flooded with books that will educate you on the long occult history and the dark arts practices of Joseph Smith. However, here's one book on the topic of Mormonism I recommend:

* *The Mormonizing of America* by Stephen Mansfield

Satanism or Satanic Ritual Abuse
* *Satanic Ritual Abuse Exposed* by Katie
* *He Came To Set The Captives Free* by Rebecca Brown, MD
* *Prepare For War* by Rebecca Brown, MD
* *Unmasking The Devil* by John Ramirez
* *Out of The Devil's Cauldron* by John Ramirez

Healing
* *A More Excellent Way* by Henry Wright
* *The Fasting Prayer* by Franklin Hall

- *Divine Healing* by Andrew Murray
- *Blessing Your Spirit* by Sylvia Gunter and Arthur Burk

Look for books and information by any of the following authors:

- John G. Lake
- Oral Roberts
- Smith Wigglesworth
- Maria Woodworth-Etter
- R.W. Schambach
- Lester Sumrall
- Francis MacNutt, PhD
- Charles and Frances Hunter
- Kenneth Hagin
- Bill Johnson
- Randy Clark
- Cal Pierce
- Kathryn Kuhlman
- Aimee Semple McPherson

Autism

- *Defying Autism* by Karen Mayer Cunningham

END NOTES

Chapter 3

1. Dr. Harold Eberle, *The Spiritual, Mystical and Supernatural*, Worldcast Ministries & Publishing, 2004.

Chapter 4

1. Malcolm Gladwell, *Outliers*, Little, Brown and Company, 2008.

Chapter 5

1. Derek Prince, *They Shall Expel Demons, What You Need To Know About Demons — Your Invisible Enemies*, Chosen Books, 1998.

Chapter 6

1. Derek Prince, *They Shall Expel Demons, What You Need To Know About Demons — Your Invisible Enemies*, Chosen Books, 1998.

2. "stronghold." Merriam-Webster.com. 2020. https://www.merriam-webster.com/dictionary/stronghold (23 November 2020).

Chapter 8

1. Robert Morris, *Truly Free, Breaking the Snares That So Easily Entangle*, W Publishing Group, an imprint of Thomas Nelson, 2015.

2. "devil" Blue Letter Bible. 2020. https://www.blueletterbible.org/lang/lexicon/lexicon.cfm?Strongs=G1228&t=NKJV (23 November 2020).

3. "demon" Blue Letter Bible. 2020. https://www.blueletter-bible.org/lang/lexicon/lexicon.cfm?Strongs=G1140&t=NK-JV (23 November 2020).

Chapter 9

1. Robert Morris, *Truly Free, Breaking the Snares That So Easily Entangle*, W Publishing Group, an imprint of Thomas Nelson, 2015.

2. Derek Prince, *They Shall Expel Demons, What You Need To Know About Demons — Your Invisible Enemies*, Chosen Books, 1998.

3. Dr. Harold Eberle, *The Spiritual, Mystical and Supernatural*, Worldcast Ministries & Publishing, 2004.

Chapter 10

1. Craig S. Keener, *Gift & Giver, The Holy Spirit for Today*, Baker Academic, A Division of Baker Book House Co., Grand Rapids, Michigan, 2001.

2. "saved" Blue Letter Bible. 2020. https://www.blueletter-bible.org/lang/lexicon/lexicon.cfm?Strongs=G4982&t=NK-JV (23 November 2020).

3. "salvation" Blue Letter Bible. 2020. https://www.blueletter-bible.org/lang/lexicon/lexicon.cfm?Strongs=G4991&t=NK-JV (23 November 2020).

4. "cast out" Blue Letter Bible. 2020. https://www.blueletter-bible.org/lang/lexicon/lexicon.cfm?Strongs=G1544&t=NK-JV (23 November 2020).

5. "I adjure" Blue Letter Bible. 2020. https://www.blueletter-bible.org/lang/lexicon/lexicon.cfm?Strongs=G1844&t=NK-JV (23 November 2020)

6. Henry W. Wright, *A More Excellent Way, Be In Health: Spiritual Roots of Disease, Pathways to Wholeness*, Whitaker House, 1999, 2005, 2009 by Be In Health, Inc.

Chapter 11

1. Derek Prince, *They Shall Expel Demons, What You Need To Know About Demons — Your Invisible Enemies*, Chosen Books, 1998.

2. "curse" Blue Letter Bible. 2020. https://www.blueletter-bible.org/lang/lexicon/lexicon.cfm?strongs=H7043&t=K-JV (23 November 2020).

3. Derek Prince, *Blessing or Curse, You Can Choose*, Chosen Books, 1990, 2000, 2006 by Derek Prince Ministries International.

4. Derek Prince, *Blessing or Curse, You Can Choose*, Chosen Books, 1990, 2000, 2006 by Derek Prince Ministries International.

Chapter 12

1. Derek Prince, *Protection From Deception*, Whitaker House, 2008.

2. Henry W. Wright, *A More Excellent Way, Be In Health: Spiritual Roots of Disease, Pathways to Wholeness*, Whitaker House, 1999, 2005, 2009 by Be In Health, Inc.

Chapter 13

1. Smith Wigglesworth, *Ever Increasing Faith*, Gospel Publishing House, 1924.

2. Frank and Ida Mae Hammond, *Pigs in the Parlor: A Practical Guide to Deliverance*, Impact Christian Books, Inc. 1973, 2010. Much of this chart's

Chapter 14

1. Craig S. Keener, *Gift & Giver, The Holy Spirit for Today*, Baker Academic, A Division of Baker Book House Co., Grand Rapids, Michigan, 2001.

Chapter 15

1. "yoga." Merriam-Webster.com. 2020. https://www.merriam-webster.com/dictionary/yoga (23 November 2020).

2. What's The Matter With Yoga? 2020. https://whatsthematterwithyoga.wordpress.com/demonization-2/ (23 November 2020).

3. Ralph P. Lester, *A Look To The East, A Ritual of the First Three Degrees of Freemasonry*, Cook Publications, 1966.

Chapter 16

1. Jack W. Hayford. 2020. https://www.azquotes.com/author/21822-Jack_W_Hayford (23 November 2020).

Chapter 19

1. Andrew Murray. 2020 https://deeperchristianquotes.com/prayer-and-fasting-andrew-murray/ (23 November 2020)

FREEDOM
Winning The Battle Within
Review

If *Freedom — Winning The Battle Within* inspired you or helped you in any way, I would love for you to help me get this book in the hands of as many people as possible. By taking a moment to recommend this book, you could very well change thousands of lives as a result of one person reading this book and taking action with it. That's what happened to me! One special person gave me a book that created the domino effect of life, after life, after life, getting changed. Be a difference-maker and influence others to learn more about freedom. The easiest way to do this is by leaving a positive review on Amazon. Just visit:

Danny's Author Page on Amazon

amazon.com/author/dannymcdaniel

Click on **Freedom – Winning The Battle Within**

Then click "Create a Review."

Thank you for purchasing this book!

I appreciate you.

" *And Jabez called on the God of Israel saying, "Oh, that You would bless me indeed, and enlarge my territory, that Your hand would be with me, and that You would keep me from evil, that I may not cause pain!" So God granted him what he requested."*
1 Chronicles 4:10